CHOOSING TO LIVE NOT TO DIE

A Story of Three Altered Lives

Kerri C. van Lanten

Inspiring Voices

Inspiring Voices books may be ordered through booksellers or by contacting:

Inspiring Voices
1663 Liberty Drive
Bloomington, IN 47403
www.inspiringvoices.com
1 (866) 697-5313

ISBN: 978-1-4624-1226-6 (sc)
ISBN: 978-1-4624-1227-3 (e)

Library of Congress Control Number: 2017919603

Print information available on the last page.

Inspiring Voices rev. date: 12/21/2018

INTRODUCTION

There are times in life when you meet someone you'd least except. Is it coincidence, or a remarkable connection, meeting someone with an incredible story to tell? It is at these times that we may open up ourselves to someone new, unknown to us that they will become part of our close, inner circle.

We individually shared what was experienced in our lives. Adding to that, Curtis filled-in and completed the story. Eventually, an idea took root to write a book.

How many times do we miss-out on lost connections, or don't understand the true meaning of our purpose? We miss the path that we are supposed to be on. Time is also a factor. No one knows how much time there is, the last time we will see someone, have the last hug, or hear the last words spoken. Don't take any of these moments for granted. These stories were brought together. Call it a dream, a vision, a gift from above—there truly is a divine connection out there, if you acknowledge it and choose to be a part of it.

Hopefully you will learn something from the following pages— something you can connect with, something you can realize. The stories will touch your heart, so that you too can heal, and a part of this book may help you in understanding why someone would have taken their own life. It was a brave effort, this chance and opportunity to share this. It was a path well-worth taken.

Kerri C. van Lanten
Jennifer J. Adams
December 14, 2016

For Jack, from Kerri
For Sadie, from Curtis
For Greg, from Jen

In loving memory of Curtis L. Statten.
Your story lives on through us.

CONTENTS

CURT

JENNIFER

INGRID

Kerri

CHAPTER 1

That Day

Life is full of meetings and partings, of hellos and goodbyes, but more often than not, endings that we'd rather soon *forget*.

That's why I wrote my story, because endings are *unlikable*, and no one wants someone to break up with them.

People have told me to forget about it. That's rude. It was a part of my life. It happened for a reason, so that I can write my thoughts out on paper, heal a little and help others, too.

I hate to go back in time. It's a chapter in my life that I've closed. I'd rather forget all about it. However, mine is the beginning story. There is no story that is more important than the other. There is no priority on this—it's just in an order of progression.

It's hard for me to talk about what happened. To this day, I still don't know *why*.

It happened one year; I can't remember the exact date now. I remember *he* called and said he was coming over. It was dark and later in the evening.

It was cold that day, but it would become a day that would lay colder on my heart. It was a day that would forever change me, and shatter any feelings of love for a long time.

I was waiting for him to come and visit me, like he usually would.

I didn't completely expect but lightly anticipated a ring for Valentine's Day. That's what I thought I might be getting when he said he would be arriving soon.

I was so thrilled he was coming over, like I always was. I remember going out to greet him. As soon as he came in, I knew something was wrong. Devon didn't seem like himself; he seemed distracted and wasn't looking at me. His gaze was down and off to the side. He seemed like he had something really awful to say.

Then it came out. I asked him how he was, since I was always happy to see him. He said he was thinking and realized that he just couldn't stay in this relationship, since probably within a year or so he would have to give me a ring and then marry me, and he couldn't do it. He even spoke in the third person.

While he was glancing off to the side, you could see him thinking as he spoke these words: "I just...can't...marry...this girl. I would have to give her a ring, and then marry her." "You don't want to move with me," he said. He continued: "You aren't the type of person to sit home, and you don't want to move away from your mother." I always knew in my heart that this was my home and somehow, I would make it here and I would survive, and I have.

He said that day, "Let's be friends." I didn't get that. How could we be friends? He was my *boy*friend.

He did say he couldn't stay, since he'd probably have to engage himself to me, maybe in a year. He had to get out of this relationship before that time frame elapsed. He had to get loose before that moment was up, before that commitment bell was ready to ring.

After that, I walked into the house, crushed. I recall that he came in with me. I kept asking him, "Why?" and I would plead on, "*what* can we do about this?" He stayed at my house for a few hours, into the early morning. I kept looking for answers. He said that he needed time to think, that he needed some space. I was crying, but attempting to keep my composure, and reminded him that I loved him, and we *can* make this work. My efforts were useless; I wasn't going to win this battle.

He finally left. He took my heart with him. I was just exasperated, and didn't know what to do at that late hour. There was no one to call.

My parents asked what happened; I told them that Devon just said he "needed some breathing space."

I went to bed, crying throughout the night. I didn't know how I was going to get through the next day, or any of the days after that.

I thought this was the guy I was going to marry before he walked away.

The next morning, I was just beside myself. I couldn't function well. I don't know if I went to school that day.

At work, I became very good friends with two people who made all the difference in my life. My boss was one of them.

After things happened to me, the lady boss was the first one I called. She was very receptive on the phone, listened to me, and really cared about the situation. I know she felt terrible about it. She took the time that day to hear me out. I was just beside myself.

She was kind, considerate, and offered her sympathy and empathy to my situation, and said I could call her anytime for help. Believe me, I did. I could not have survived that initial impact without her. She encouraged me and would say polite things to me. I looked up to her and thought of her as a confidant and my friend.

I also called a friend of mine who was home on break from college. I went to visit her after I talked to my lady friend. She made me snacks and cookies and listened to me. She tried to help me and console me the best that she could. I was just floating thru the day. I eventually had to go back home. I don't know if I went to school later that day or not.

Cassidy felt there were other people out there and no to be so hung up about it, but, a lot of people say that even though they mean well.

I told other people that he left, but I don't think that anyone really understood how I felt. It's easy for someone else to tell you how to feel, when they're not going thru it.

CHAPTER 2

Before

I thought he was the one, but he wasn't. I was just smitten. I wasn't even thinking straight. I was just glad to have my boyfriend. I was proud of it. I had someone to go to dinner with or to the movies, spend time with, and talk to.

He came to a party I was having. I was so excited about it.

I still did have my friends, and I went to see them a lot.

I remember him saying stuff like, "You're smart, and do you really want to be with a guy like me?" I thought to myself, *no problem, I'm not even thinking about that*. I never really did think about it. He was polite, nice-looking, older than me, had a job and a car. He took me out a lot. It was good.

I thought this was forever. I had no idea it was going to fall apart.

I guess I missed the signs. There were things, as in every relationship. I remember asking when we got together, if he had any attachments to anybody. I didn't want to be with anyone who had any feelings left for someone else! I was very careful of that.

I don't think he ever really opened his heart to me. It was always with someone else he liked. I don't think I could ever feel close enough to him. I tried, boy, did I try. I had a need, and for a time he fulfilled it.

In the back of my mind I could hear myself saying, *don't do this!* I knew better than to get together with someone who had or recently just had a girlfriend. These three-ring circuses usually don't work. Someone chooses between the two, and you can really never trust *that* person. For someone dating a person who got left, that person takes on a lot for helping out that person. You can't really fix someone; you can encourage, but not fix. At that time, was I really thinking about that? I was having the time of my life, so I thought.

I had lots of friends, my boyfriend, my family was nearby. If I had a break, I would often go to Grandma's and visit.

My boss that I mentioned was kind, and others that I worked with were great. I was outgoing, friendly, and just thoroughly enjoying the whole experience.

At the same time, he came first. He wanted to control the situation and have it his way. It wasn't fair. I came last, after his time with his friends, or what he needed to do or wanted.

His personal life came first; he wasn't budging on that. That was always more important than me. Somehow, in this relationship, he took it out on me to be more independent, probably so he wouldn't get hurt. And to make sure of this, he had a full life separate from me. I don't believe he was ever trying to move together forward, as if he hadn't made that decision to do so.

His friends and interests often took priority over me. I know he once said that he'd never put himself into a situation again where he was giving everything to somebody. I should've caught that clue.

My dad said that I was protective of him. I was. I didn't like anyone getting chummy with him, especially another girl. Who would? My mom's friend would say, "If you don't take care of your special person in your life, someone else will."

We went other places and we'd go to his friends' parties. I was bothered that at a party he was upset. I tried to talk to him but it was no use. I don't know if he thought someone was flirting with me or I was flirting with someone. He was protective of me. It's ironic. He thought I would run off with another guy. I was constantly trying to prove my worthiness to him, and my loyalty, too. I had no idea that it meant nothing. He thought that I was going to leave him.

One time I was out and I felt this girl was interested in him. I was upset. I don't remember what I said to her, but I wasn't happy about it.

There were a couple of guys at school that I was friends with, and they were nice guys. We'd eat lunch together. He didn't like that.

There was a party at this friend's house, and others. Another time, a friend of mine came, and one of his, too. It was a real nice night, even though she didn't like his friend that way.

Another night, people that I knew met him and his friends out. It was a good time.

One time we went out with someone else I knew. He was always trying to get us out together with his friend and one of mine.

I think he just had this thing for having people together.

I feel his family liked me at first, but then thought I shouldn't be there afterwards.

I questioned that for a very long time.

It was good while it lasted. It's when you're on that merry-go-round of love, and things are just so perfect, you feel you're never going to fall off. When you do, you just crash and burn.

Towards the end, he would go places with friends. He was pulling away.

His friends were fine; I liked them and never felt they tried to break us up. I know they liked me, too. I just didn't get it why he tried to make them more important than me.

Meanwhile, I had things all planned out. I was going to work locally with my brother. He is older than me, and got a job just a few days after he graduated from school. The owner of the company had offered me a job if I ever wanted to work there.

The thought never entered my mind that things would turn out differently.

I do admit when this happened, I knew something wasn't right. It didn't seem like he was happy.

For example, at a party at a friend's house, I knew something was up; I could feel it.

Then, I had a party at my house. It was a great night, but he didn't show up till it was almost over. It's like he didn't want to be there. He probably was thinking of jumping ship, even then.

When he bought me a piece of jewelry, it was like it was an obligation. Also, when that person slyly suggested an engagement ring for next year and he said nothing, I could really tell something was off.

Towards the end, he would complain about buying me stuff, or paying for tickets for events. He bought himself a new car; it was strange. He would say, "You never pay your own ticket." Before, he was never cheap with me. He always took me out to nice places. I was surprised after his investment of time and money that he would leave.

CHAPTER 3

Taking someone else out and other things

He also went out with another girl. He said it was a friend of his. He just announced it to me that they were going out to get a snack.

It was a friend of his, from long ago. He said they were going to talk about some personal issues.

Just like that.

I, of course, didn't like it, and I was upset about it.

He never liked it when I talked to guys at school, yet here he was, going out to get a snack with her.

"Do you want to go out with this person?" I asked.

"No," he replied.

"Then why do you have to go?"

"Because we need to talk," he said, adamantly.

I remember I had a real tough time with it.

If it was just a friend who he was going to meet and she had a problem, ok, but then leave the same flexibility for me.

That wasn't the case. I was very distraught as that time approached. I would call my friends and ask for help. They would talk about it to me the best they could, to comfort me. I had to work that night. I knew what time they were going. I was very hesitant as that time approached, as if you knew someone was going to die or their time was up. Unfortunately, unknown to me, my time was nearly up in this relationship.

I remember talking to him and asking him not to go before he left to meet her. I was asked if I was going to call my friends and tell them about this. I didn't understand.

You know how people might've changed their mind about you and now they want out? This was the same thing. He said he was going and that was it. And he was very matter-of-fact about it. This wasn't repayment for anything I had done, but I couldn't stop him. He had his mind made up.

I fretted all night. Him being out with a friend, to talk about us? Who was she to get involved in my affairs, and then know about it? Surely it was discussed. I'm certain I didn't get much sleep.

I don't remember when we talked after that, or how it went when we did speak. All I knew was that this drove a serious dent between us. I've considered that perhaps he did this on purpose, so I would leave first.

Also around this time, he bought a new car as we were breaking up. It was probably a sign of his new freedom. I obviously missed that signal.

For Christmas, my mom got him something small. He didn't like it. My mom isn't the type of lady to go overboard; had we been married it would have been a different thing.

CHAPTER 4

After

I felt I was left alone in the world.

I was just stumbling through the day. The nights were worse. And the weekends, how lonely those were. I would dread Friday and Saturday nights. Thankfully, I still had my school friends, but the loss was deep.

I remembered how I told my brother after we broke up that I was distressed, since someday he'd meet someone else or get married to someone else. He said this is true. I was affected by his matter-of-factness about that statement; I was hurt.

Talking about the situation did help. Not everybody listened, but if I found the right person to speak with, it was a good thing.

Another lady confidant and friend was also a blessing. She gave me her time. We would meet and she would help counsel me and sort thru some things. She would explain to me that my feelings were genuine and *real*. Even though this person left the relationship that did not mean that what I felt was not love. That statement made quite an impact on me then and still does to this day.

It was the middle of winter and after the holidays. One of the lady friends said that was common. I can see that lots of people's relationships crumble around, during or after the holidays.

Breakups are painful for some people, but not for all. Some people just recoup and go on to the next person. They can even be pleasant to that person. Some people don't need to see that other person, and some people need to continue to be friendly. I guess it's all in who you are, and within what parameters you're willing to live with.

Many breakups do happen around endings, like high school

graduation and college graduations, moving, changing jobs, leaving a certain location or after a three-month summer vacation.

The person already has their mind made up, and has decided it's time to go. They're not going to put any more effort into it, and that's it. They end it, and move on. It's always tough for the person left holding the bag. The other person holds the key, and won't unlock their love for you again.

Many people breakup after a lengthy relationship, perhaps even after several years. It wouldn't take me that long to figure out that I don't want to be in that situation. I wouldn't drag something out with a person for that long that I was unsure of.

Most people stay in relationships, because they don't want to be alone. It seems people keep getting into another relationship, because they don't want to sacrifice time for someone truly special that they will meet another time.

I possibly couldn't continue being friends with him. That wouldn't work for me.

I felt my dream was taken away from me by his mom and family. Who did they think they were? Who were they to make that decision? I struggled with that for a long time. All those tears couldn't bring him back to me. He was gone.

I was faithful. The bond was tight, and I wasn't about to let it break easily.

I was very loyal. I make my mind up; I make it up once and make it up right. I will be there taking great care of someone. I'm a good, kind person, a nice friend, and a great significant other.

Once I let someone in my world they're in, and I have a hard time letting go. I don't like to take people in, unless they really want to be there. I'm not here just for the moment; I've never been this way. I'm always thinking long term, and ahead of schedule.

So, I set out to get him back. If he called, I'd talk to him. Coincidentally, when he called I'd pick up the phone. It's not like he called all the time, only at times.

I was a sucker for the phone calls, and I just *had* to talk to him. They weren't very long conversations, and often he'd have them timed and knew exactly when he was going to get off. He'd always call from a payphone or from somewhere that I couldn't call him back. I didn't get that.

I felt I was up against a brick wall with him. When I would try to contact him, he would block me at every angle.

He made sure it was one-sided, of who could contact who. I couldn't understand all this. It was too much to accept.

I stated one time how long we were together. He countered with a different answer. He really had to emphasize that point. It seemed it was very important to him to do that.

I asked him after he broke up with me why he bought me jewelry. He said he wanted me to have something nice for Christmas. You don't buy such a nice gift like that for someone and then just leave them.

I wore it for a long time, until one day I lost it. I went somewhere with a friend I met, and I noticed that it fell off. We searched diligently for it, but couldn't find it.

He told me he was leaving the area, so the next time he called I told myself I'd be ready to let him know that I would leave with him if that's what he wanted. He did call again, and I told him, "I will move with you, if that's what you want. I am ready to go." I remember telling my brother and dad about it. They said, "What, you're moving with him? You wouldn't have any of us there. You'd be all alone if anything came up." I considered that, but, it was my *heart* you're talking about here.

I was all set to go. Somehow, he had already considered that I might be thinking of going and he had an answer prepared. He countered, "Oh, no. I can't possibly take you away from *your* family. You are close with your family. I'm not going to do *that*."

I was mystified. Here I was, letting him know that I would leave my home for him. And here he was, not going to give me a chance in the world to keep this thing going. Once more, I was blocked from being able to add the glue to piece it back together.

The money thing was a thorn in my side. All I wanted to do was marry a nice, local boy who also had it in his heart to stay here. I had no idea that money was such an issue to him.

It is to a lot of people. Not all jobs are going to pay you very high wages. I'd rather be comfortable and happy than have a lot of money and not have someone special to spend it with. And, if people do have money, their kids can't or don't necessarily make what their parents do, and they can become resentful. I wanted to just live happy medium, and have a house full of love, kindness and support.

Someone mentioned he was trying to get into another career; another person told me he thought about doing something else. I wasn't sure what to make of it all. He didn't seem to know where he fit in.

When he left, he also went to a gym to work out. It was local; I didn't know which one it was.

It's bad enough that he moved after he left me; and now with the once-in-a-while phone calls from unknown locations, it really made things even more confusing to me.

To add to this, he sent me a card with no return address. It was a generic card. I didn't quite get that, either. I remember telling my friends at a party about the card, since I was excited about that. They took me out for my birthday that night. My friends were polite about it, but tried not to make it more than it was, more than I really wanted it to be. That night was lots of fun. They really took care of me well that evening.

Going out to see my favorite bands was a relief. I felt good going out, but I missed him. I would feel better for a time. I knew he probably wasn't going to go out since I was there

He might have called me from that unknown number. He always had those phone calls pre-planned. He would say, "Can't talk long; I've got to go." He still was in control.

I wondered what he was doing that night; was he out with someone else?

So, here I was: young, without my boyfriend, facing this world alone.

I realize everyone at some moment is looking for someone, but I picked him. I just fell into it without thinking about it. Yes, I really cared for him, and I liked a lot of things about him. Over time I didn't realize the price I would pay. I didn't realize the effect the loss would have on me.

Sweetest Day and other days were also difficult. No more flowers showing up, no dinner, no chocolates or a cake. I was so lonely without my significant other. I tried to do my best to get thru these days.

I do remember a bright spot in all of this. We did get together one day and went to eat. I recall going to his house and being invited by him.

It was a nice time, and he was affectionate and smiling as I was leaving. I was quite content and felt lighter about the situation. When I got home I told my brother that I was feeling so much better, and I was glad—I felt such *relief*. He said, "You are happy because you just saw him." I did feel really good.

Unfortunately, time passed and then I was awash again with all of those uncomfortable emotions.

There was a time that didn't go well, when I went to pick up some items he had borrowed. I was clearly upset and said what I had to say to him. I felt I was in the right and needed to vindicate myself, especially with what happened. I said what I had to say to him and his mom and left to go back to work.

A friend who was dating a friend of his at the time told me on a bus trip about a comment he made. He totally dismissed our relationship. That was low. I was crushed that he would do that. My heart and soul were completely in it. My feelings were true, genuine and valid.

Was I stupid or something? I didn't get it.

I'll never forget that moment. That comment stirred my soul that weekend in an uncomfortable way and stayed with me for a long time after that.

My trust in people began to fall apart. *He* broke my trust in *him*.

CHAPTER 5

Getting on without him

What did the future hold for me? The unknown was scary. It was hard to be alone. My parents felt that things would change for me. I didn't know *how*.

I needed to talk to people, to express myself. Since I couldn't call him to do this, it was amazingly difficult. He had moved and shut off any communication, and I couldn't call him at all or visit. I was subject to that occasional phone call from him. This was just something I couldn't handle.

It's not something I even like today. When a friend stops calling, I have a real hard time adjusting. If they call back someday, it's not the same for me. If it happens again, that's another split. Too many splits and you can't piece it back together again.

I started questioning myself. Was I not good enough? Did you not like how I looked? My family? My personality? My friends? What was *wrong* here?

When you're young and things aren't working out, and you have nothing to go on to and nothing to look forward to, you begin to feel like you're not achieving the next level of life. If you don't have any college or trade school plans, or aren't getting married, or you don't have kids, or your own house, you can feel left out.

I was confused. I wanted him back. These questions would plague me constantly, day and night, with the ever-asking, *why*?

I would still dress nice, and would go to exercise. I did the best I could.

Going on was a challenge. Sleeping and eating were a priority, just to make it thru the day. I just couldn't seem to be pulling myself thru. It was as if someone had died. But something did die, and that was my *heart*.

I was absolutely devastated. I could hardly get anything done. I was out of sorts. I would want to get up and take care of myself, but it was so hard going on.

Every day was a struggle. I was completely done for. Just waking up in the morning was a chore; getting dressed was a bother. Going to an exercise class was tough. I could hardly get it together. Even going to school functions was a test.

I left my brother once, at a game, because I was so upset and couldn't stay. How stupid, because now he lives out-of-state and I don't see him a lot. I think to myself, *what a wasted moment in time*.

It was tough to get out of bed in the morning and nighttime was definitely a challenge. It's like you're busy in the day and not so much at night, even though I had a tremendous amount of homework to do, and I was up most nights into the early hours of the morning.

I was distressed for giving so much. I was left with nothing in the end. He was able to go on with no problems, and I was the one holding the emotional baggage, exhausted, exasperated, and cried-out.

I was in a slump I just couldn't get out of. It was simply devastating to me. I'd think about him, wanting to talk and hold him. I wanted to be back in his arms, making plans for dinner, just to spend time together.

Not being able to pick up the phone and call was debilitating to me. My open line of communication was suddenly shut off like a valve, with my emotions being squeezed inside and backed up. No more open, receiving vessel to flow to. My emotions had to stay blocked up within myself, with no one to release it to. It was unnatural to me.

In retrospect, my mom would mention, "He left, but look at all the things he did for you. He took you out, bought you lots of dinners, gifts, bought you flowers, and was nice to you." She didn't understand; he was gone. I didn't know how I'd go on, how I'd live without him. I couldn't exist without *him*.

Hurting and smashing my finger right around this time (and again on my birthday years later) was a double whammy. I couldn't believe it. My middle finger, smashed right into a safe. It pained me even more, because he wasn't there to comfort me. I couldn't call when school was tough or some mishap occurred like this particular injury.

Years later, I would smash the same hand again in my car as I was getting gas, on such a blizzardy day. It was freezing out, and it hurt terribly. What a painful reminder of what happened so many years ago.

I tried to understand what was going on, but I wasn't able to. I couldn't get it off my mind. It was always there. Was he out with someone else? Why was he ending this? I just didn't get it.

I cried a lot; I prayed for his return. I even had a dream about him; the setting was in the past. He said he couldn't stay; it's just not something he could do. I didn't understand. Just like in the present, he decided to go.

He would say it just won't work out, that we're *different*, and that I'm a *career* person. You know, I think he'd try to make me feel guilty for my schooling. Whether one uses it or not, the time to go to college or trade school is when you're young, so, what's wrong with that? (Not that you can't go later.)

He seemed to have a complex about the potential of me making more money than he did. I really don't care one way or the other.

Anyway, I wondered how long his family had planned this out. Was it long before the holidays or that week or after? What was it about me that you suddenly changed your mind?

I don't know what ended things or if the chain of events was already in place.

At his house that day, his family was quietly polite to me. I was sitting on the couch and talking to his mom. She gave me a small gift. I don't recall what I got for him that year or his folks.

It bothers me, when I see people in long relationships and then one person leaves. For example, your girlfriend or boyfriend is a different religion than you. Then all of a sudden, you have to go because now it's an issue to them. Well, you knew that when you got into the relationship. Why is that a problem now? That's how I felt then. I wasn't looking to nitpick at him—I just wanted to *love* him.

I would never drag someone into a situation like that—it's not me. I can see how you are, and I either like you or not from the beginning. And that's that. I'm here to stay.

19

I felt he was being selfish and was looking for a reason to get out. Sometimes we fall into things by routine or duty. Those are wrong reasons to stay. However, there are relationships in life that are obligatory, and that's how it is. But this wasn't an obligation to me, this is what I *wanted*.

Friends at school tried to cheer me up, but found out how difficult that was. My best friend there would give me a lot of her time, and I appreciated it. People at work were kind and made me feel very comfortable. Those two lady friends older than I were such a helpful support system. Without them, I don't know what I would've done. God always puts people in my life to sustain me when I need it.

My school kept me grounded; I was quite busy with it. There was so much work. I had too many assignments due daily to work on; it just had to get cranked-out and finished. There wasn't time to waste. Even getting out for a semester or two would have put me behind at least a year.

I had considered leaving school for that amount of time. I felt that the ability to just sit back, think and heal might have helped me in my journey to feeling better. I thought maybe in a couple of semesters I could have relaxed and tried to come to terms with things, so I could come back at a later date with a fresh start.

I didn't do so great in one of my classes; I just couldn't focus. Not that this class was any less challenging than the rest, I just couldn't get my attention on it. I tried, but I knew that it wasn't getting any better. My teacher could see I was obviously not having an easy time and inquired about that. I said that, "I had broken up from an important relationship and I just cannot get myself together." I added, "I am trying hard in here; this is the best I can do and I am sorry."

I knew at least I could graduate. I don't like it, and I'm not proud of it, but I'd like to see other people go thru such a challenging program with having to work and pay for their school, and also having responsibilities at home, and endure this stressful and traumatic breakup.

I did good for all of that.

Marriage was constantly on my mind. A friend got married, then another.

I was in both of their weddings. I remembered thinking, *I should be getting married. I should also be doing this and having my friends be in my wedding. This should be going both ways, and I should be wearing my engagement ring, too. I should also be buying my dress, getting a hall and a cake and picking out flowers, and looking for my own house.*

I was planning to work with my brother the following year after graduation, and hoped to find a small house to live in on a nice side-street. I was hoping to have my *own* home.

I wasn't jealous of these girls; I was happy for them. I love parties, the more the merrier. People out together, having a good time. I just wanted my time, too. But, just running into another relationship, I felt, wasn't the best idea.

A friend was having a no-date party. There was a mix of people there, and we all tried to make it good for everyone else. It was hard, but it was somewhere nice to go. I appreciated that she invited me. It helped me to be somewhere rather than home, due to the recent emotional upheaval in my life. I tried to be a polite guest at the party, but I'm sure I missed him and I felt really bad. It was not easy.

Sometime before that, he agreed to come see me. I went and had my hair done, and I talked to one of my friends right before he got there. I was so excited that he was coming to see me. I was going to put my best foot forward. I was dressed nice, too.

He came in; someone let me know I had a visitor. Excitedly, I went out to greet him. He didn't smile or seem as thrilled as me.

I was presenting myself as best I could; we talked a bit; I was doing some of the talking to keep the conversation flowing. It was cold that day; I know we went outside. Then, he said something like he loved me, but he couldn't do this. I said, "Why?" I don't remember much else, other than the situation was thorny. Here I was, trying to salvage this thing and piece it back together. The bonds were shattered, not on my part; I couldn't do it on my own. I believe we were shedding a tear or two. He walked to his car and left. I did too, devastated.

Exasperated, I went back home to try to recoup. I tried to eat; I tried to nap; I tried to go to bed. I spent the rest of the night miserable as usual, crying and lying there, exhausted from the day's events.

I was wondering what he might be going for next. I feel they were the type of people that weren't going to be satisfied with me as a daughter-in-law. They thought it was nice that I was going to college, but were wondering what decisions I would make after that.

I wanted to stay near my family. What was wrong with that? Was that such a bad choice? I don't think so.

I didn't realize he wanted to live by other family who had moved, to be near him. I wasn't aware that this was so important. He had schooling; he had a job. I didn't know it was a priority to move. Why did he just not get into a relationship with a girl who obviously was staying by her family? There wasn't a desire at all in my heart to leave my home. My place is here.

I questioned myself for years with his decision to leave me. I couldn't understand it. I couldn't grasp it. It lingered with me for a long time.

What was wrong with me? I mumbled this over and over. *Great, here we are. Now, I'm in the middle of my college years, two-and-one-half years in and I'm stuck. Life is on hold. This is a calamity, and the only way out is to not be here anymore,* I thought.

I can't possibly go on without him being in my life.

For a short while, I didn't want to be here anymore. I was emotionally impaired; I was damaged; I was broken. From the depths of my soul I was crushed.

I knew I didn't want to hurt myself, and I didn't really want to end my life. I thought about how my family would feel. This did not go on for a long time. I thought about how their lives would be without me. Shattered, I am sure, as it is for all families who've had a member end their own life.

CHAPTER 6

People along the way

It was tough adjusting. Some people who knew me were compassionate, but wouldn't know what to say at times. They'd use that old adage, "there's other fish in the sea." But, I'm swimming in my ocean, not yours.

I would talk to anyone who would pay attention to me about the situation or could help in any fashion. I remember phoning a local call center when this whole thing happened, since I was crushed. They were nice to talk to. Later, when I met another friend, she told me about another call center and I'd call them, too.

They were there to take note and offer outstanding advice. They heard what I needed to say and let me get it out, and I believe that this is what many people need in this situation. Those around you just need to listen to you; not tell you what to do.

My parents tried to encourage me to continue my exercise classes a couple of times a week, something I enjoyed anyway and would like to go to off-and-on. This was nice and the other ladies were fun to be with, but I don't remember how long I attended.

I continued to go to church on the weekends. I would always pray for God to send him back home. I asked for strength and help just to get thru the day. I wish now that I could see where God was moving in my life.

There was a girl at school who would help me with some reports; I couldn't have gone on without her.

No questions asked; I just got the help that I needed. My friends helped me as best as they could, as I helped others. We had to work as a team to get through.

Melody was a good friend, going thru her own possible divorce. She told me to tell him, "If this is your choice, you have to help me to get thru this." I told him this; he said he was trying to help me get thru this choice.

But again, it wasn't my decision, so it was difficult to understand.

However, for him, he was just getting out, and I don't believe it was as stressful.

A girl I knew also knew him and had also broken up with her long-term boyfriend. This individual understood what I was going thru. She related to how it felt, since he just wanted to be friends. It was hard for her to get over things, too, and told me that I had to also try to get thru it and move on.

My two cousins were additionally helpful. I went to school with one of them, and he always listened to me. He would be kind and sympathetic and told me how he went thru this and he seen other people go thru things, too. He tried to keep my spirits up.

My other cousin was also caring. I was talking to her one day, and she had me sit down and take it easy, and got me something to drink. She said she didn't realize how much I cared for him. I was telling her the story and what happened. My girl cousin let me use her phone to call him, if it was going to allow me to feel better. Whatever number I called, no one answered. At least I tried. I don't believe I was able to reach him. She didn't know much about him but said, "Wow, you must have really liked him." "Yes," I said.

There was this girl at school that I talked to, too. She was quite helpful and listened to me as well.

There was another friend of mine who listened to me a lot. We'd talk about the situation, and he'd help me. He'd spend so much time helping me out—another godsend.

He would tell me how his previous girlfriend left him, too, and how difficult it all was. I knew it was painful to him. He did marry, but it was a situation that stayed with him for quite a while. Benton tried to get me thru it. I was able to call him and talk to him whenever I needed to.

He'd make me laugh, and encourage me when I could stand up for myself.

Other people I knew at the time would try to support me the best they could.

I also ran across Devon's buddy one day. I had the chance to talk to him for quite a while. It was comforting, even though I cried so much. I told him how I felt; he said he still cared about someone else and never really quite got over her.

I revealed how much I still cared and I couldn't believe what happened. I wished he was back. I prayed for him to come back.

His friend felt that he wasn't coming back. That was hard to hear. He knew I cared and was loyal, but because of his past attachments, it wasn't enough.

I remember that day clearly. I could have stayed there all day talking to him, but he had to leave and so did I.

I talked to another friend of his that I knew. We used to hang at his house, and I felt comfortable talking to him.

One day, I called him to let him know what happened, and that he left and was also planning to leave the area.

Did he know this, I asked? He said he didn't; he wasn't aware of it. I thought he'd want to know, since his friend would be taking off.

He felt bad for me. We talked a while. He liked me as a person; I believe that's why he didn't push me off the phone.

Finally, one of us had to get off.

I know I was able to call him back if I needed to. He said I could.

One day I ran into a person who knew the both of us. This person asked me if I had seen him, after we were broken up and if we still talked, and were friends. I was surprised they would even ask me that. Not everyone is friends after, and how could you be?

After we split, various people I knew were always trying to introduce me to other people. I liked some of these folks, but I never quite made the connection with them. Nothing was wrong with them; it just wasn't there between us.

I went with a friend to get some food, and his friends seen us out. He called and made comments to me that I wasn't even waiting to go out with another guy. Why would he care, if he didn't want me?

It was hard to see other people with someone having so much fun. But, are they really having fun? You might see a couple together, but, do they have a strong bond?

It was difficult to see people together. Those days were over for me; I didn't know when I would have another relationship like that again.

A friend took me to eat, and she was attempting to help me thru this situation. She recently broke up with her boyfriend, and went with someone new. She didn't feel bad about it.

Sometime after the breakup, I ran into his friend's brother and other people that knew me. They were very nice to me, I have to say. It made the moment less awkward.

CHAPTER 7

Running into him

A friend had seen him out one day with another girl. She thought they were just friends.

He seen my parents out one day driving by him, and he waved at them. My mom said he actually kept waving, to make sure they had seen him. That was odd.

I ran into him at school one day, and then we went over to a nearby restaurant to talk. He said he'd take me home later. We ordered; he didn't say much at the restaurant. I tried to be friendly and make small talk. I might've even paid for my own food. He didn't say much.

I asked questions, and I don't remember much of the ride home. I believe he said at one point that, "It wouldn't work." It was lonely after he dropped me off at home. I was bothered that he wasn't excited to see me.

He was aggravated that we crossed paths that day, and I feel he felt obligated to talk to me.

When he moved out, he didn't give me the number because he said he wasn't allowed to. I don't think that this was true. The day after we broke up, I did call his home. His mother answered the phone. I recall that she wouldn't let me speak to him, and she assumed and stated, "It was for the best." He was sleeping, and she wasn't going to let him know that I called at that time, but she would tell him after he woke up. I might've called back, but it didn't matter. I did not hear from him that day.

I would be distressed because there was that waiting period before the next contact.

He would call me and say he's trying to help me through this, like

Melody had suggested. I think he felt he was being helpful by phoning and stating why he was calling. It was unusual. I believe I would ask when he would call again; he didn't know.

At some point, he stopped the phone calls.

One day, my friends took me out, and he was there. This was after we broke up, and I was just too glad to see him! It had been several months since our breakup, even though we talked sporadically during this time. I was so thrilled that he was there with a guy friend of his that I also knew. I know I asked my friends to hold on and wait, so that I could talk to him. He was a bit neutral, not really being forwardly excited to see me, neither being mean, but he made a comment to me. He took his friend with him, and we were able to go off to the side and talk.

I was just all too happy to see him! Here was my chance! Oh my God, here he was, right there in front of me! I could talk to him, see him, and even get a hug! I was my usual sweet, loving, kind self, all too happy to just get back to where we were at. I wanted it to continue. I needed to talk it out, and attempt to work it out. After we said "Hi!" to each other and got to conversing a little I asked, "Why?" It's always the eternal question, isn't it? "Why did we break up? Aren't we good for each other?" I inquired. I desired to get answers to my questions. I wanted to be at peace with this, and the only way to be at peace was to have him back.

He said to me, "It's better this way—it just wouldn't have worked out." Who was he to make this decision for me? I just wanted to keep talking to him. He mentioned a letter I wrote him.

I was upset that he thought I was trying to hurt him, instead of letting him know how I felt. I was so taken aback by it, that he was so offended by it. I was disgusted.

I did not know that he wouldn't like it. I was just expressing my heartfelt feelings. There was nothing in it that wasn't nice. It was done with the best of intentions. I wanted him to read the letter and really *think* about what I had written. I wanted him to come back, and see and hear what I was saying.

I dislike being cut off. I may be silent at times, depending on what was said. I believe it stems from the fact of me getting cut off from others, and then when *he* did it after our relationship, it hurt. I hated when he did that.

Amazingly, I seen him another time, and he and his group said, "Hello." I just looked at them, and turned to my friend and walked away.

One day I was out with a friend, and I was very surprised to see him there. He was with another friend, a girl. I thought he had moved. He kept repeating, "Hello!" and smiling as if nothing had ever happened. His voice was joyful, and he made sure that I heard him. It was quite strange, and I remember just standing there with my mouth open in surprise, not saying a word.

My friend didn't say anything, and she didn't know what to make of it, either. She felt bad, like she shouldn't have asked me to go with her that day. "No," I told her; it wasn't her fault. She couldn't help what happened.

It did feel odd that we crossed paths. I don't know which time was the last.

Also, a mutual friend of ours passed away. A friend told me about it. I went to the calling hours, not thinking he would be there. A nice family was talking to me. Out of nowhere he appeared behind me. He had his head turned off to the side, trying not to be noticed. He might've said, "Hi." The awkwardness of the moment was relieved by this nice family conversing with me. When we got inside, a family member who knew both of us asked, "Did you guys come together?" I know I had this look on my face that gave this person his answer. I don't know who left first after that.

CHAPTER 8

Trying to move on

I went on a vacation late that summer. It was a much-needed rest.

A friend asked me to come and visit. I left my job around that time, too. I was just very distraught at work. I was miserable, I missed him so much, and I couldn't take the stress. I had to go.

I couldn't take the strain of it anymore. He left our relationship, it fell apart, and I couldn't take the stress of the memories. And worst of all, he was lost to me now.

I went on this trip for about two weeks. I needed to unwind and get away. My friend took me everywhere, to several of the resorts, and we'd go and see some of her favorite bands. Her family would make me nice dinners, and it was all very relaxing. I needed that trip more than anything.

I remember my friend's mom felt bad for me, but felt that Devon was too influenced from his own family to make up his own mind about things. She knew it hurt, but she was kind to me and I really appreciated that.

She took me to several historical places, including where she worked at that time. She was a kindhearted, nice woman. I came back refreshed and rejuvenated for school that next year.

Being in school kept me very focused. I began to recuperate. It kept me paying attention. Getting thru school and planning to go on afterwards—it wasn't just a matter of getting thru; it *helped* me stay on track.

The demands of school and then planning to go onward kept me busy and focused. So, I decided to continue going to school. I felt if

I did not go to now, I probably wouldn't in the future. I'm sure I was partially right.

I needed something new and different. There was a strong desire in me to be a professor. I thought I was going to teach college, but life circumstances dictated otherwise. It took me a long time to decide to move on from that, and I don't regret that choice.

However, during this time I couldn't stop thinking about him, what he was doing, who he was with, why he couldn't or wouldn't or didn't want to contact me any longer. I just couldn't comprehend it.

A breakup of any relationship is a split. Ever run into someone you used to know really well? And, you don't know what to say to them? Now, it's just an empty exchange of words. No longer is the closeness, the bonding. It's over; it's done. Things are discontinued.

It's like you go thru a trial separation when someone you love leaves you. However, instead of a trial separation, it's permanent.

It's like that in a lot of things in life. Things were said at home, with extended family and friends, or people at work that you liked. Words can't be retrieved; neither can feelings. These are the discontinuities on the line, the 'open holes' in life that can't be filled. You can't fix what was said; you can't repair what was broken. You can't bring the relationship back to its prior status.

I personally have a tough time going back to people after we've had a break. I've taken a few people back, but it's been seldom. It doesn't always work out. Some go back to their old habits, which often includes not necessarily being kind, good or polite to you.

There is that final moment of loss, that final destination that you get to, that you know what's done is done, and there isn't any turning back.

You just have to let it go and be done with it and move on, and be open to what could be.

I didn't keep anything from our relationship. I didn't keep anything after we broke up. I don't like reminders of people who've moved on.

I got rid of all the pictures, sweaters, gifts, and any mementos. Those flowers he gave me just had to go, and I couldn't keep them anymore. I met a friend in school who told me to get rid of them. I did and felt better about it. They were dried-up, just like my heart. It did take a couple of years to do this.

I didn't journal at the time, but listened to a lot of music and wrote some poems.

At this time, most of the friendships that I made had ended. Many people had moved and taken jobs elsewhere. It's tough to keep things up once that happens. Other people stayed, but things changed. Most of my friends had graduated the previous year, and I was left with only a couple of them.

It's often like that when endings occur. Even if it's not with a significant other, it seems a lot of 'friendships' disperse when high school or college graduation takes place, or a job is finished. Perhaps there isn't enough bulk to the relationship for it to continue beyond that point. What brought two or more people together in a commonality or interest wasn't sufficient to make it long-lasting.

Unfortunately, I got injured a few years after we broke up. This was also hard. I was injured through no fault of my own.

My doctor helped me out a lot—he was always there to listen and support me. He didn't know about the bad breakup of my relationship, and how it was still affecting me, a few years later when I met him. He did help me thru that car accident.

When I choose to continue to go to school, I was just going through the motions. I borrowed a lot of money and made a commitment to be there. I was attending classes and doing ok in my course work. I thought I would make a lot of new friends, but that didn't happen.

At the other school, it was different. Sometimes it wasn't as exciting as I hoped it would be. Things weren't going how I'd have liked them to. There weren't a lot of people to talk to. I also questioned where my life was going, and when I would get out and where I would work. Would I ever get married? Who would I meet? These questions carried with me in my mind. I'm sure other young people have had the same thoughts, especially when you're in an in-between time, trying to get yourself established in life with a family, home and job.

I did meet people, but I broke off a few relationships with some guy friends that wanted to be pursued more on their end. You can't keep something up when one person is in love and you're not. I met some very nice guys, and some that weren't respectful. If someone was interested in ways that I wasn't, that ended, too.

However, there were some really nice, mature people I met, and we didn't keep in touch. They were good people.

Jill, a good friend that I've known since high school, would write me lots of letters when I was in school. She helped keep me going at times, especially when I would feel lonely if a situation with a guy I was interested in didn't work out. God gives us what we need to see things through, or get through a tough time.

I wasn't just going to get involved with anybody there. It's not that I didn't meet people, but most of the other students had lives of their own. They weren't there to make new friends.

In my heart, there was a commitment to finish school. That ended up taking a while with getting delayed by a class and the car accidents.

At times, I had my school or some sort of job and I would feel, well, *I can do this on my own*, but I don't want to. I'd feel really lonely and empty inside.

Funny, how things went like that, that I had this great time for a few years, then it all stopped again.

Sometimes, God gives me the good with the bad, so I am appreciative of things when they are working out fine.

At the end of year two, I just wanted to come back to the comforts of home.

CHAPTER 9

Jack

He was my friend, teacher, and mentor.

We met on a late August day in the fall. He was such an interesting man. I'll never forget the first day of class.

He had us all turn our chairs together toward each other, in groups. He taught the class that way that day and on other occasions, but for those of us having him for the first time, it was different.

After the class lecture, he had us all turn out chairs back. Then he asked, "What did you just do?" We "shifted."

He taught his classes this way. He taught us to think and to question.

Beyond the classroom, he was my friend and mentor. I feel he knew I was meant to be there, before I knew it.

Jack was a minister, who also was a teacher.

He decided to go teach because he felt God had called him and being in a public area allowed him to meet people that he needed to reach.

Thru this, he captured the attention of those who wanted to learn more about God.

Jack told me the other person left to make room for someone else. He modeled to me what he thought a good Christian man was. He told me this and said he would continue being there for me and modeling to me that he wasn't going to "cut and run" as he would phrase it. He felt if he could represent this, then I would start believing there was someone else out there for me.

Since he was an only child with no family, he thought of several of us as his kids. Many of us called him, "Dad," because he was a father to many. He's in my heart to this day. Sometimes I get quiet, close my eyes, and try to think of him.

Every time I open up a Bible, I smile to myself, for he was the one that taught me the different chapters and to learn the verses and their "addresses," as he would call them.

He felt that people have their focus on themselves, not God, and that's what messes everything up. We live in a time of what we can do for ourselves, not what we can do for each other.

He lived his life for others, and believed it was an honor to serve God. He felt he was a messenger, and got "out of the way" when the Holy Spirit needed to touch others.

He brought me with him to his biblical studies class. I also went to church with him when it was possible. He taught me a lot.

As time passed, I remember in particular one sunny, fall day that I was visiting him. He was sitting on his front porch swing, looking outwards; he was so glad to see me.

We'd discuss school and other topics. I loved talking to him. We had great conversations about life, God, biblical things, school, and work. He was happy that I married my husband.

There were other times we'd speak on the phone for lengthy amounts of time.

He respected me, and he would persuade me to look and question, with an open mind and heart.

He shared with me what he knew and what he had figured out.

On Fridays, I was invited to come to a Bible session/discussion. Other folks who he worked with also attended. It was nice, and I was honored to be there. He was such an inspiration to me. I think of him often.

He wanted me to learn the verses, and understand how to find things and understand certain words and meanings. He truly modeled for me what a good, caring man was, and things to look for in somebody.

Sometimes, my brother would come to see me and we'd all go get coffee.

My brother even came to class with me one day.

He thought he was a neat guy.

"It's all about the *coffee*," he'd say. He'd talk about people getting together and having coffee, and talking about God.

In sticky situations, he would remind me of Romans 8:28, a verse to help you through challenging times. We can't see what He is doing, but we need to understand that He is allowing circumstances for a greater good.

He'd always be there, for an added dose of support.

Students would often be in-and-out of his office, talking, looking for help. He'd stay up as long as he could, to assist them, sometimes up until four a.m. if needed.

He lost a student long ago, who had killed themselves. He was crushed. He'd often mention this person, and felt he just needed someone to listen to him.

I believe he had spent time with this person, but didn't know how serious their situation was. He never got over that.

I watched a video that was taped by Jack of a get–together honoring this person. (This video was the one sent to me the week I learned about the several kids in Mentor, Ohio that had passed on and I received it the day after I was going to give up on sharing my story.) The students were just in awe. They couldn't believe that their friend took his own life. They never knew anyone that did this before.

He always talked of how self-centered people are. When you're thinking of yourself and your ego is in the way, then God isn't at the center. The other person is not your focus. You have to get your needs met, of course, and if you're hurting someone else, oh well. That's how it is.

He taught me not to look for someone like that, to instead look for someone who was strong, and loved God. I believe he was in my life for several reasons, and he helped me to wait for my husband. In addition, he taught me how God works, moving people and situations in-and-out of our lives.

He was very connected to things, and always knew when I was calling.

Discernment was also a gift of his. He'd question things, look at things; try to understand what paradigm people were in.

He didn't want to see me with a man who was going to cut and run.

He taught me to read the Bible. I didn't even know where to start. He gave me a paperback Bible, one that he had taken off the cover and rewrapped. He taught me about *agape*, and that's where he started healing me.

I was still very broken inside from that relationship. He showed me the difference between the different types of love, and explained how someone not of agape love will leave.

He also told me that, "Love is the desire and will to seek the highest good and best interests of the other person." He said he heard it on the radio from Pastor Tony Evans. I never thought of things that way prior to that; I never met anyone like him before. He was looking out for me.

In other relationships, he explained, one only stays when one's own interests are being kept up. There are shared commonalities, or mutual traits. However, when something uncomfortable happens or the other person loses concern for the other, so begins the demise of the relationship.

That is precisely, he explained, what happened to me.

That person was not interested in my greater good, and was not concerned about staying.

"If your greater good was the most important thing to them, they'd still be there," he'd say.

He added, "That is why you have to find someone that does have your best interests at the center of their heart. That is the *key*. That person won't back off at a fight or at an argument, and won't cut and run on you."

He felt that person left, to make room for another. I didn't look at things that way, either, but it made sense.

Jack would say, "Be careful what you do, because you shouldn't take from someone what rightfully belongs to their future spouse. People don't realize how much it does hurt their spouse.

He also said, "Love is the desire and willingness to look out for the greater good and best interests of the other person." He always looked out for me, as if I was his own. People who look out for each other don't cut and run.

Light bulbs were going on, and it made me feel better. I knew he was right, and God was showing me what I needed to learn from him.

37

We'd meet to talk, after our mentorship was beginning. It started out as hanging out after class. There were always lots of students wanting to learn more and more from him. I wasn't the only one.

He always was there to listen to all of my stuff. He and I were close, like family. He thought of me as his daughter. It's not like we didn't argue, or get mad at each other once in a while and didn't speak for a time.

He had also suffered from colon cancer at one point of his life. That's when God touched him the most.

If something happened at school, he's come find me and talk to me about it, whether it was about some situation that didn't work out, a friend issue or something up at school. He was an arm I leaned on.

As he was getting ill, I'd go to see him as much as I could. He must have known his life was nearing the end. He had a host of ills, including a bad heart and diabetes. He needed a lot of care, and had a mobile chair.

I'd go up to his home to visit him.

I remember his last birthday party. I bought him some chocolates, and he passed it around for everybody. I'm glad we didn't miss his party.

There were lots of nice people he knew from school, and it was so nice to be there with him.

He was proud of me for finally finishing school. He never gave up on me.

I knew I'd never see him again.

When he went on a long trip, he entrusted me to stop at the house if I wanted, and to check on things. He even left me with the code to the alarm.

Luckily, they found a renter, Deanna, who would take care of these things. She also became my friend.

I called one day to come up to the house, since I had his permission to borrow his papers or other books.

Deanna and I took immediately to each other, and talked like long-lost friends. We felt as if we knew each other forever.

We would talk about so much, and she was so interesting. We had so much personal information to share, and had similar life experiences.

One day we decided to meet. I brought her some coffee. My husband came with me. It was wonderful. We had such a great connection. It was amazing. No one wanted to go home. We would continue our phone friendship and visit.

She never met Jack. Her relationship with him was by telephone, me by knowing him. My relationship went thru to him leaving; she had begun her friendship with him at that point.

He never talked to me about him passing on; he would talk to her about it. She would tell me that he told her he knew it was near the end. She had lost a daughter in a terrible accident; death was too close to her, being a first-hand experience.

She grew fond of Jack. She felt it was just meant to be that way for me, that he didn't share these things with me. He didn't want me to hurt, she felt.

Meanwhile, Jack was getting weaker and weaker. He had a leg amputated.

I regret that I didn't visit him there, when that's all he asked of me. It lay heavy on my heart that I couldn't go see him. With looking for work, it was hard for me to just go and see him like that. It was a missed opportunity, for sure. It would have been great to go and visit him.

One day, he died. His wife called me to tell me what happened. He was my friend and mentor; I was crushed to lose him.

I stayed in touch with his wife, and she wanted me to have all of his books and notes. This took several trips to retrieve all of these items. My car was so packed each time I went up there. It meant a lot to me that she wanted me to have those items. I still go thru them. Each time I do, I run across a good book or note I missed from before.

CHAPTER **10**

Staying True

After my relationship broke up, it was bad enough that he left; I wasn't going to get myself involved in all kinds of mixed-up situations.

I would be friends for a while with different people.

I did go to a few church groups. There wasn't anyone there my age or interest, so I stopped going. I remember telling this one married couple how I wanted to really meet someone and also get married.

I met my husband at a friend's party. We really liked each other. He'd come out with us at times. His dad got sick after that, and we lost touch for a few years. He was at our mutual friends' wedding; I said, "Hello." We didn't get the chance to talk too much that evening.

We got separated for a few years—that time was difficult. I was going to school and working, and in a transition time. I wanted to get married, and I didn't know when that was going to happen.

For a few years, I worked at a local store. It was where I met my husband again.

On one of the last days I was there, possibly on the last work day, near the end of my shift, my husband came in. It was so good to see him. I knew this time to give him my address, phone numbers, and, a big, special hug. We walked each other out to our cars and promised to call each other.

Since that time, we called each other over a course of six months, and worked together. I also ran into him at church one day. I knew that was a blessing.

Over the next few months, we started dating and got engaged. I was thrilled! It was not a question of whether he was good for me or compatible; this was God putting two people together who needed to be together, and whose hearts were in the right place. That's *why* it works.

My husband always wanted to spend time with me, too. I thought that was odd. I'd always have to fight for time before; with him I didn't. He always says how I was so surprised that he wanted to spend time with me.

He is a prayerful man. The prize for me was the most wonderful guy in the world.

My husband comes from a strong faith-filled family. He is a very forgiving man, but he does make good judgment calls. He has done things in a very traditional fashion.

What I'm saying is that I've been in this fantastic marriage for many years. We have a great love and commitment for each other.

Just like the wedding and the house. They were *enduring* plans. I would never date anyone if I couldn't see it thru and make it last. I date you; I want it to continue. Dating, according to my father, was "a prelude to marriage, not to hang around someone for a few years and that's it."

You diminish the marriage relationship when you get involved with a lot of people. I wanted to wait for that special relationship and I did. During this time of waiting I worked a lot and had lots of friends. I wasn't ready to have someone else, and I wasn't the kind of person to just go out with anybody. I am a serious, commitment-minded person.

God was really there for me, too. I believe he created the situation of me continuing with school so that my mind would be so occupied. And, he put all kinds of people into my path to help soothe and heal the wounds.

You have to be able to release things in your life, so God can open up new doors. I believe that's why you run into someone or think about them, to forgive them and release it. That's what God wants.

You need to be happy with yourself. If people aren't worth putting the time into them, then don't do it. If you feel someone wants to be your friend or partner, give them time. Sometimes a person's past hurts don't allow them to jump into a relationship with their full heart. People are scared.

If someone can't love you or like you for whom you are, then forget it. We're here to bring each other up, not down. Everyone else can find someone else to hang with if they don't like you. You shouldn't be rude to people, or have others take advantage of you. That's not care or love. True concern doesn't ask someone to do the wrong things.

Kids make bad decisions. If that person is pressuring you, they're wrong. It's a slim chance that relationship will lead to marriage. Most relationships from that time don't last, since usually one person eventually wants out. Many young people don't understand that.

I believe a lot of people, especially young people, think only for the moment. They are impractical, and make bad judgments based upon their *feelings*. They get into all kinds of mishaps, often with lifelong consequences. Keep your convictions strong. You don't have to get caught up in others' lies.

A friend of mine, Patrick, comments that a lot of people in high school think their relationship is going to last forever, and it doesn't.

When someone falls in love and they lose that person, they will be searching for that reconnection for the rest of their lives. More often than not, they get caught up in liaison after liaison, attempting to re-bond with what was lost. This is most difficult for a tenderhearted person.

I haven't seen too many young relationships work out long term. It's something that will break because of immaturity. Some do get married, and that's great. Other relationships fail because that person wants to see "what else is out there."

CHAPTER 11

Trust

Trust is important to me. If you are not trustworthy, you are *not* worth my time. Trust is being there for me; it's not blabbing out our private conversations with other people. Trust, to me, is personal respect and mutual understanding. Trust is not letting me down and not taking advantage of me.

Not everybody makes the cut.

There was a lady who really broke my trust. She got nasty with me towards the end. It often goes like that. She said a few things that weren't very nice. Other people did that, too. I wouldn't take any of them back now.

A close pal asked the other day, "Do you trust people?" Not as much now; I've been too disenchanted. People are disappointing. It's experiences like that and others from which we begin to cut ourselves off emotionally from people, and withhold bonding with others. We've been so hurt that we don't know if we can rely on anyone.

People leave and disappoint us. If we knew what they were thinking, we could alleviate some of our distress. But we don't know their thoughts, so we really can't be prepared when someone does leave.

These situations make me immediately want to end a relationship when it happens now, be it a friend or a business situation. It's saying, "Well, I'm done here." I've done it to people when they've gotten me mad enough. I get to a point; that's it. They're surprised when I do that, since I'm usually a nice person. But that doesn't mean you have the right to unfairly get upset with me or treat me disrespectfully.

My friend Mary said, "There are people out there who love to break your peace. They are people who could be related to you, or someone who you meet on the street. They emotionally disrupt you." I feel this is because they're having a bad day or just can't seem to settle themselves, and they want to take it out on you. When you notice this happening, try to walk away from the situation and take a break. Limit this person if you can, and don't let them interrupt your day.

People will try to take your emotional energy from you. Don't let them drain you. We all only have so much to take us through the day. We are especially drained when a relationship breaks up, be it with a friendship or significant other. We are embarrassed about the situation. But you have to remember, that is someone else's shortcomings that ended the relationship, not necessarily yours.

I dislike it when people interfere in something that they have no right to. I have seen relationships severed or destroyed by this. Someone might not see where God is moving. You don't know who God is touching or trying to take you or another person. People then get separated, move or die. We feel it's often too late to attempt to reconcile or make amends. Often it is.

I personally try to reconcile at every chance I get. I try to forgive those who have hurt me, or attempt to understand *why* I had to go thru a certain situation. I believe if you make amends on your part, God can open doors for you in other areas.

I ran into people who didn't treat me well or misunderstood me. I was upset at some of them. God worked on me with my feelings as I forgave them one by one (at different times). Since that, he has opened up so many other areas in my life.

I have even learned to let go of things that were said. The past has to be done with to make room for the present, no matter how long that takes.

I did have the opportunity this past year to reconnect with people who didn't treat me so nicely in the past, and I did not pursue those past relationships.

I did, fortunately, run into a friend who lost my contact information a few years ago, and was able to reconnect with this person. She gave me her information and asked me to call her. I did, and it's great to have her back. It doesn't always work out like that.

Recently, I ran into a friend of mine who I hadn't seen in years. It happened by accident. I was sitting somewhere and a person came in to say she was here visiting, and where she would be. I went and said, "Hi!" to her; it didn't turn out like I wanted it to. I believe it was a door to close. These things happen to me. They probably happen to all of us; many of us don't even pay attention to it.

I might've missed reconnecting with this friend, but there I seen someone from years back that didn't know that my other friend killed himself. This person needed to know that, since his brother was best friends with this person, had moved away from the area, and needed this information delivered to him.

I also saw an old friend. It was awkward. She was very happy to see me but I was neutral. I wished her well but did not go into details about my life or hers. I kept it simple. A few weeks before that, another old friend told an acquaintance of mine to let me know she wanted to hear from me. I did contact her years ago, but she asked me why I was calling her. I have tabled both of these issues for now.

I am particular about taking old friends back. I told a few people that this happened recently. Both shared that it also happened to them, and thought I handled myself well. "You never know who you'll run into and when, or who they might know, for that matter," I adamantly stated. However, one of them added that, "If these friends of yours would have done you right, what a good relationship you still would've had with them today."

The point is, sometimes we have to realize that God wants to put someone back into our lives that we need to resolve issues with. I feel it's His way of opening and closing doors.

When we offer forgiveness for others, God opens up new opportunities.

Which people or situations in your past or in the present are holding you back from moving on to good things?

Lately, a good friend of mine and I were talking about boundaries. Many of us get caught up in things that don't have good limits. Often young people and young adults do this. As I've stated, people love to see how far they can take you. If they can talk you into doing something that you know is wrong, they've won for that moment. It's up to *you* to be able to walk away before things get out of control, and do something that you regret. Most of those people, if any, will not even be in your life five to ten years from that point. Don't do stuff you'd regret later.

Not all relationships are godly. By this I mean, why go out with someone just to go out? People get caught into a cycle of endless relationships because they can't be alone. You don't know where someone is at and their beliefs. It can be a game to them to get you to submit to their wrongdoing. Don't let your insecurity get the best of you.

If you are having a bad feeling about something, it's probably best not to get involved with the situation. It's a warning not to be a part of it.

I've heard Pastor James MacDonald talk about deception. "Not only is deception lies, but it also is not telling someone the whole story. Not saying anything is also bad. It destroys godly and good relationships." There have been people who were deceitful to me, from when I was younger to present times. I really look out for that now. Not everyone is honest or has integrity, or wants to be truthful. Not everyone has your best intentions at heart.

I'm not against being friends and staying friendly with people. Go out and get coffee with someone new. Take it casual. Some folks do meet their spouse early in life and others have to wait longer.

Don't fill all that time with liaison after liaison. Don't diminish that future relationship with your beloved. A person told me I made a good decision when I married my husband, and that I chose wisely.

Life is hard enough, with its challenges and pitfalls, so why bring so many more people into it that really don't need to even be there? Wait for that one special person. You'll be glad you did.

Think of yourself as being given a love bank account of one thousand credits. You start giving yourself away when you're young, that being a physical relationship or not. And as time progresses, those relationships can change. The more relationships you get into, the more credits you're giving out. You share yourself emotionally, mentally and physically with several people. What are you left with when you finally meet the person you want to marry? Do you want your bank account to be at zero or in the negative?

These are personal things you are sharing with other people. Why do you want to bring several people home to meet your family? Get to know you? Learn your secrets? These are things I don't think young people consider, or even older people who are emotionally immature for that matter.

I made this analogy to relationships when I heard a person talking on Moody Radio. They were speaking about a "memory bank" that a widow was glad she had, since her husband died. Thoughts of every nice time they had went into this bank. She had these memories she could recall when he would be gone.

I also was listening to a younger woman on the radio who talked about how things were when she was in high school. She dated several people—she pushed the limits. She realized she was sharing intimacies with many people and so decided to stop this. God was in her heart showing her that she was giving out too much to all these guys.

Either she or another caller suggested for guys and girls to write love letters to their future spouse. What a great idea! What love letters would you write to your future spouse? What would you like to have in your memory bank when you're older? Memories of your spouse, or memories of multiple people that shouldn't have even been there? And, over a lifetime, where do you want those love credits to go? I choose my husband. I want him to read my letters.

Don't let folks talk you into things. Don't let yourself be talked into doing something that's wrong because "everybody else is doing it." They just want to use you. Just because "everybody else is doing it" doesn't mean they're right. So many people feel bad later in life about what they've done with other people when they finally meet the person they want to marry.

Don't disrespect people and don't take advantage of them or let people take advantage of you! That's wrong either way.

CHAPTER 12

Faith and getting thru

It took a long time for me to be comfortable with myself, who I am as a person.

That doesn't mean that things won't change, that you won't be able to find your niche. I've been thru a lot of things—job losses, family losses, and friend losses.

If you have faith and follow what you're supposed to do, God will be with you and show you what you need to do. I'm not saying it will be easy. Did you know that He is obligated to help you if you follow Him? I heard a pastor recently say this.

Trust me, it does work that way. But, often He has to wait on us to finish our tasks that He has given us before He can move in our lives and work certain situations out.

My faith in God carried me thru tough situations. At times life was hard, but God was always there. I wish I trusted Him more, that things would work out in the end.

He has always sustained us. My bills have gotten paid. I know that if I'd immediately had lots of money, I wouldn't need God. When you have money, you feel you've done it on your own and you don't need Him.

I have a very strong faith, even though, believe me, it does get tested at times.

Often, we have tasks to do. They might not have anything to do directly with our job or schooling. It has to do with the setup of who God places in your path. Indirectly, He allows you to bump into people. My friend, Jane, told me, "Be aware of what you say and how you say it, and to present yourself to other people with godly speech and action, since you might be the only person they come in contact with that really knows Him."

People have free will and have choices set before them to make. Since he had made a choice, rather unfair about me, God used those experiences to help others and to help you.

I don't believe that everything in this world is "meant to be." It is a fallen world, where people make devastating choices. These decisions end up affecting themselves and those around them. People don't make prayerful or thoughtful choices; they make decisions based on the moment or frivolous advice from friends. Also, people that we trust to be there in our time of need don't stay with us. It is difficult when a friend, family member or significant other leaves.

God gives us all gifts, special gifts to help each other. Did you know if you don't use your gifts and respect Him, that He will take them away and give them to someone else? Use your gifts wisely.

Also, we all need good counsel, as Pastor James MacDonald would say. "Counsel, is good listening, not the secular version of counseling. It is the ability to listen to someone and then offer wise advice."

A lot of people don't possess any wisdom. And, they interrupt you often with their sage advice. You can't waste your time talking to those types, whether they're degreed or not.

There were times I didn't know if I was still going to have a house, or if there was going to be money to buy food. I didn't know if my husband was still going to have a job. Little by little, God provided for us. Our moms took care of the house payment and any food we needed, and we had just enough coming in to pay the other bills. My husband was able to keep his job. See how God works? He works thru other people, like with my mom, and the money I brought in helped pay the utilities. It wasn't easy, and for a long time we didn't know how we'd get by.

He has guided me throughout this entire process. I had a dream about writing a story, people have come into my life that told me to get started, and others showed up when they were needed most for encouragement. If one of my big supporters chose to move on, another was sent in their place.

Through it all, I wouldn't have changed a thing. If I had a regular job, I wouldn't have been able to get this story done.

I do pray a lot, and I pray often. I requested help as I was writing. I sought support, fresh ideas, and I asked God for guidance to remind me of anything that needed added to it, and where I should look to make corrections. My eyes were brought to paragraphs that required amending. I asked for sustainment that I would stay on task regardless of how busy things were at home. I further asked for people support whenever necessary and the strength to continue and finish this project.

I would work on my breaks at my job, or I would have to give up time with my family or stay up late. At lunch, I'd eat and then get right back to where I left off.

Any extra breaks at work were a blessing.

Right before the holidays, I was talking to a very nice lady, Shawna, who was intuitive enough to speak to me about my writing. She added that I needed to make the time to get it done. I have to make the time to finish.

I ran into Shawna after that, and she would ask me about my project. Sometimes we would be interrupted, but I was glad she gave me her number if I needed any additional support.

Furthermore, Jane added I just need to end this and finish it, and save anything else for another story. She was even willing to open up her home to me and make a space so I can come there and work. (Maybe next time!) She also got me a job at a company she used to work at, and it immensely helped me to pay my bills.

Towards the end of the holiday season, I was praying and asked God to help me out as to what is the holdup. I told Him that I was very tired physically, and that is part of the problem. I felt He understood what I was expressing to Him. I also told Him that I have so many responsibilities, and that is also contributing to this work not getting finished.

I was home from work early one day, and my intake coordinator called again. I told her I keep editing and adding to the project, and I was still trying to put it in chronological order. She told me I could still hand it in as it was. That took a lot of stress off of me, because I thought I had to hand it in completed. It was a gift from above.

Then a support person from the publisher called and introduced herself. Both of these people called as I happened to be home from work.

It is because of all the support I have that I was able to finish.

Now I will have a little more time each day to tend to myself, rather than rushing thru the day and fitting in time to do the work. The time could be replaced with some time exercising, taking a walk or calling a friend. This would help relax me, and I would still have time for my family. And I do have immediate plans for other stories.

CHAPTER 13

For the young people

School. It can be a challenging place for young people. You can be discluded from the group, and left out. And everyone thinks they're not somebody if they don't have a significant other.

Kids spend too much time worrying about their looks and how they fit in. People can be mean and inconsiderate. And, that ends up having somebody not feel good about themselves.

Students tell other students not to hang around certain kids. That adds to a false sense of superiority. They might even not include someone at lunch.

Friends might be here and there. They also come and go.

It's not easy being the kid who's not sporty or in any of the popular activities. No one wants to be left out.

A girl might interrupt a conversation that a girl is having with someone else, and completely ruin someone's chance to talk to someone they might be interested in.

I think if a guy is interested in a girl who his friends don't consider an "in-crowd" person, he won't pursue the relationship.

Some students like to embarrass other kids or talk about someone behind their back. This does nothing but contribute more to their already low self-esteem.

Gossip doesn't help, either. Goes to show you, you need to keep your mouth shut, even about the smallest of things.

It's a tough playing field. It can be unfair and hurt. It's not easy. It's hard not being part of the in-crowd. You are a more mature person if you don't have the need to gossip about people, make fun of them or talk behind their back.

Being ignored isn't fun.

Some kids have to work a lot, or have a lot of home responsibilities that others don't have.

Kids are sensitive and caught-up with wanting people to like them. If they're not into sports or dancing, you are not part of the team. No one wants to be on the sidelines and not being involved in things.

And people don't think. If they're dating someone, they might just breakup and go with someone else. Nothing hurts more than that sting.

And, there's always peer pressure. Someone breaking up with someone because they won't do what they want to do isn't right.

Everyone is looking for someone just like everyone does at that age, but it doesn't necessarily happen.

Friends also can leave. I don't know why people try to talk to you later and act like nothing happened.

I'm seeing through adult eyes what a child goes though. I'm seeing though grown-up lenses how stupid and immature it all really was. Kids are adolescent. I know you can talk to them somewhat, and they can talk and have a conversation with you, but you have to keep in mind that they are limited in their life as a young adult and can't think as a mature person, so how can they treat you as a grown-up, when they aren't even one?

My friend Nichole states on how it is in high school: "It's the twenty-four/seven part of it. You're with these people half of your life. It's your second home, even if you don't get along with these people. They're your 'other' family."

She adds, "I don't think people are trying to get along with everybody. They don't even try. It's a tough place to be. I've run into some of these people after school; some have changed, some have not."

Sometimes I meet people, and they're still stuck in high school. I just don't get that. They don't even look remotely like they once did. Get over it. It might have been good for you then, but wasn't that way for everyone. Young people have the right to their feelings.

I have noticed that many people who choose helping fields had a good time in school. They usually weren't the ones that didn't have a fun time. At school, a lady came in to talk to the kids to be more respectful to each other. I commented to her, "School's tough, isn't it?" I was surprised that she recalled a person in her school that had a hard time and related that story to me. It seems that people in the helping fields didn't necessarily go thru the experiences themselves when helping others. I'd rather someone come into my class that's actually *been* there.

It ticks me off when people say stupid things like, "No one can take advantage of you unless you let them." That's an untrue comment. People take advantage of other people all the time. As a friend and I have mentioned, what's a kid to do when a few kids or a group of children goes after you and you can't defend yourself? You're just a kid. You can't walk away; they'll just follow you. You're not an adult that can just get up and leave. I don't believe there is enough done to help young people. One person standing in a crowd of many, nasty kids isn't going to be able to take them all on. You are only a helpless child, not an adult in authority who can correct the kids.

A lot of us just go with the flow of friends around us at the time. The only thing that keeps us together is the commonality, like being in school or in a club. After that time is up, many of these relationships disperse.

Young people make dumb decisions, and one of my teachers told me not to get caught up with what other kids were doing. This person said they could see that I was uncomfortable about that issue. I am glad they took that chance and confirmed what was right.

Thank God for high school graduation, and for things moving on. There is life in the next level for all people, if you're willing to go there.

CHAPTER 14

Now

Today, I don't let others' stupid behavior or insecurities ruin my day or get me down. I'm still going to get the work finished that needs to be done.

This is about being an adult. You're not subject to the rules of the game. You can eat lunch with anybody you want; you can eat lunch all by yourself. There's no one to bother you. It's funny, how graduation changes all that. You can get dressed up, get your hair done, and go out to dinner.

People just want to rant and rave and throw their useless opinions at you, and be argumentative. They just want to cause problems, or control you. You don't know what agenda someone has. Don't get caught up in it all. Sometimes you have to leave someone if they won't quit—I myself have had to do this on occasion.

Also, people will try to displace their anger or unsettledness upon you. Walk away! Excuse yourself! Don't allow someone to unfairly use you as a dumping ground, or swear at you. I am not going to sit somewhere and let someone unload on me. I'm not here for that.

When two people are sharing, that is different. They are helping to heal each other, to get thru something—*that* is beneficial.

Before, in dealing with others, I felt so obligated that I would set off to places they wanted to go to, and up to some time ago, I was letting my life be overrun with unnecessary obligations. Therefore, I let a lot of people out of my life. Now, my life is very much prioritized for me and with what God wants me to do, not what other people want. No one is going to get in the way of that.

I would also watch what I would say, not to offend others. But other people don't do the same, do they? Maybe you were brought up in a nice family, taught respect and manners. You don't talk nasty to people or make fun of them.

The older I get, I do let my opinion out, in a cordial way. I do have the right to my views.

To be nice, I would give a few minutes of my time if I ran across an acquaintance, friend, or family member. However, if this person is being rude or questioning me for information, I cut them off. I have even had to walk away from people in this situation. You don't owe anybody anything about yourself.

I am much more aware now of people taking advantage of me. I am stronger, and don't rely so much on other people. I am getting over these things now. I relax more and take care of myself. That does not mean I am selfish; I just know when to stop with myself and others.

New people are on a thirty-year plan. I'm not going to give you all of my time. I will space out our time together, in order to keep things at a slow pace. If you choose to leave, so be it. Perhaps it's to open new doors for me. I'm not going to enter into any friendships wholeheartedly again. It will take years for someone to earn my trust, the trust I previously gave out too easily. And, if you leave, I will not spend a lot of time reminiscing about our friendship. You left; it's done.

This year I've even had to take time out to grieve over the loss of friendships and family members, whether they've decided to move on or if they've passed away. I've even taken time out to grieve the loss of a beloved pet. With the passings of people or a pet, you need to realize that it probably was a result of a physical ailment and this happened thru no fault of your own. Among people, their feelings about you can change at the drop of a hat.

I had a real good friend who wanted to see me often. We would meet at a local eatery, and at one point I didn't call her when a family member was sick and my time was occupied. It wasn't for an extended time that I didn't speak to her. She was worried that I didn't like her anymore and thought our friendship was over. She sent me a letter about this situation. I immediately called her and we talked and all was well again.

However, as time went on, she married and had children. I never judged her for being married or not. When she started having kids, I noticed our contact became less and less.

Still, I was very supportive when she needed me, but I noticed that she only hung around her friends who had kids or were going to have kids—I was discluded from the group. I tried to reconnect our friendship but I could see where it was going. We talked occasionally but things changed.

This is why it's imperative to clear out your emotions. You're carrying these emotions and energies with you when a relationship disperses. It's ok to grieve over these losses. I've had to do this and I do feel better. With the people that moved on, so be it. I am then able to be more available for the things I need to do.

I've decided I'm going to allow myself time at least a couple of times of year to have this "clearing time" if anything new presents itself.

Not everyone is going to find good friends when they're younger. Mine showed up later, and they're still showing up. They are a fine bunch.

I don't stop enjoying life and I never will.

I am very happy for how things turned out in my life. My husband is the love of my life. He is very good to me. God brought him to me, since I did ask Him to find someone for me.

God did provide for me a very kind, loving, man, raised in a good home with good guidance, and who makes good value judgments. He helps me all the time and supports me, including any mistakes I've made, from before and now knowing him.

Being married to him has made my life better and fuller.

He never complained about money. I remember when we got together he asked, "What expenses do you have?" I answered that I have a car loan and a student loan. He said, "I'll take care of it." He had no qualms about splitting wedding costs or anything else I needed. He immediately put me as a user on his credit card, and gave me access to his bank account. Money was not an issue to him.

The past can't keep going on. I do believe God uses our past to make a difference in the present. He uses our mistakes to grow from them and move on. And, He uses our experiences to help others, like this story.

I know now as an adult that I can choose how I spend my time, and what I'm going to do in that moment. I spend it wisely with family and friends, who are all a part of my family. I meet new people often who want to be my friend, or want to help me out. I don't waste the effort with people who don't have my best interests at heart. I have more important things to do.

Like guitar lessons. I started them in my last year of high school, and was too busy working to save money for college. I had to pay my own way. I didn't have room in my schedule to practice.

Now I take lessons from a local musician who has become my friend. We even sing together on occasion when he is playing out. I have acquired other musician friends who enjoy my guitar playing and singing. It's a part of me that I enjoy very much. The point is, don't let someone's comments to you intrude on your enjoyment of something. Don't let their misunderstanding of things going on in your life take away from your joy and peace. Not everyone else will understand our current or past situations—they haven't experienced what you have experienced.

Today, I'm proud of who I am. Not in an arrogant sense, but what's been accomplished. I'm married to a wonderful man; I have great friends and family members. I'm writing this story and others.

I look back on things now, and I know if I didn't look to others for help I wouldn't have made it thru.

I'm also glad I stayed local. I mentioned this to a person at work. She said she married a local person and stayed in the area and never regretted not leaving. This is her home, and she likes being by her parents and other family.

CHAPTER **15**

My story

At times, I would remember things as I would be working on my story. I would make notes to get back to that topic at another time. Since I had ideas marked down, I could then sit and put pen to paper, and not have to worry about what I would have to write about next. I would just have to contemplate on that topic. Therefore, it wasn't as difficult to figure out what to write, but there was a lot of busywork.

I got a lot done on my breaks at work.

There have been times when my writings were set aside, for months at a time. I would lose people or others were sick and I had to take time off. I knew I was running against the clock. A time that I took off at least five months really put me behind.

There were times I didn't want to work on my story; I'd be too tired or swamped with duties at home. However, I've met too many people who considered taking their own life, or had people I knew and liked very much end their life. I want people to stop and consider *what* they're doing.

You put a lot of mental thought into a story like this. This isn't a cookbook, or a how-to book. The thoughts are draining and so are the stories. It's a release for me to get it out.

It takes discipline to do this; it's work. You have to set aside your life, a few hours each day to get this done. You have to be consistent.

I hope others contemplate what I have written, to be more alert to what's going on inside them and recover.

God places me where I need to be. I knew I wanted to go with a faith-based publisher. I didn't have to go far. One day I got an email from *Guideposts*, about *Inspiring Voices* publishing. I just went with it; I knew it was the right thing to do. I somehow got on their email list.

So many times, I gave up on my writing. It was a lot of work. Maybe I had a personal issue going on at the time and I was upset about it. I would be sick or a family member would be ill. We lost multiple people. I wouldn't have work or my husband would be laid-off. We didn't know if he was going to have a job. I was greatly concerned about my finances.

Often, I would be discouraged, felt alone and didn't want to put the time into it anymore. God would wake me up, by placing someone into my life who would remind me of the importance of the work, and how it would help people to cope. He would bring a friend back in, I would get a phone call, or I would run into someone at a store who would brighten my day. One day, I ran into a lady minister that gave me a big hug and told me, "It's already done," in response to me saying how I've spent six years already on the project and I need to finish it. On other occasions, I would meet people who would tell me their own personal stories of trying to commit suicide.

This story is out there especially for the young people and anybody else who is hurting. I know your heart is tender, and filled with loss. You might have constant pain, memories, and may have been misguided. Perhaps you gave in to someone and you realize you made a big mistake.

I hope this story has helped you, to lighten your load, or let you help share your burden, and not feel so alone. This is for you.

I almost gave up my story a few years ago. I was tired and drained from it. Then, in the same week, I received a package from Jack's wife about the student that he lost, and I learned about a student that lost their life in Mentor, Ohio. Both had committed suicide. I was so taken aback by the package and the news that I had to get back to it immediately.

Jane told me she feels this book will help people to cope. It shows how I endured many trials and didn't do anything to hurt myself and others. My husband had been laid-off; I have lost jobs; we have lost people. And throughout it all, we found positive ways to deal with things. We would talk about the situation and express ourselves. We would pray continuously.

She was also kind enough to tell me that I could come to her house and work on the book. She said that she and her husband would set up a spot in their house for me to work on it.

I would tell some people about the book; some responses were positive, and some weren't.

When speaking to people about this, I'd receive feedback from some folks who just thought they had the right to put their two cents in.

This one lady told me to not write it, and not to finish it. Who did she think she was?

And another said to change the book just for younger people. How could I really change my story?

This is my book, and this is the way it is written.

I told Lila, an acquaintance, recently how I lost a friend and I took off over two months to recoup. She was shocked that I went back to writing, and said she wouldn't be able to do it. She admired me.

I said, "Sometimes it's hard with him not being here."

She said, "He's always looking down on you and over your shoulder."

She was proud of me and gave me a big hug, and told me to go and finish, so she could get a copy!

I felt so good and relieved after that, and it inspired me further, since the next day I ran into that lady that was trying to talk me out of the book.

She didn't succeed.

I told my friend Nick about that story, and he said not to tell people, or if I do, I'm going to have to be prepared for their dumb responses. He's right! I guess I'm friendly and like to share—a mistake at times.

My friend, Cassandra, had called periodically to help me, to keep me on track, and to keep me going.

Cassandra's friend Gavin said, "This book is about love and loss." It's true. Above all the explanations of suicide, cancer, and loss of people and broken relationships, what else could the simplest explanation be? If you've really lived your life, you have experienced at least one of these things, some more than others.

I believe God allowed this to happen, so that this book would be written.

It's hard to grasp sometimes why things happen and how they do, but I do understand now. If I wasn't strong enough to endure my trials, I wouldn't be here.

Timing is everything, and it's crucial to get the work done when it needs done.

This is the third time I've had to go on with a project with losing someone important. When my father died, I had to go back to finish school. Jack died when I was starting a new job. Another friend died as I was trying to finish this book. Go figure.

This is the story that I have lived. I am brave enough to let people know about it, to help them.

CHAPTER 16

Suicide

Choices. It's all about choices. What we eat, what time we get up, what we do, who we talk to, what we say. Some decisions are more important than others, like who we marry.

But there are other decisions that have lifelong effects. We don't realize it at the time, but there are decisions that we make that do affect others. It is in those choices that we either reclaim ourselves or let it all go.

Suicide is one of those choices. It is something we don't have to do; it is something that is final.

It will be the choice to end your life, and affects everyone around you. It will leave everyone around you at a complete loss.

I don't feel that everyone who commits suicide thinks about it for a long time. For some, it was probably a lengthy amount of time; for others, it was a split-second decision. I wish people would find another, healthier way to deal with their feelings. I hope this book helps others to relieve some of their thoughts and pain. I desire that they can emote rationally, and work on getting out their feelings and be able not to make this final, disparaging decision.

I still hurt when I hear someone has killed themselves. I met a young lady at school who lost her friend, and other folks who have lost family or friends. My friend Susan just lost someone without knowing the reason why. I called her a few times regarding that, and I'm sure each time it happens it's a painful reminder that just doesn't go away.

Years ago, a young person who lived near me went in their garage, shut the door and put the keys in the ignition. You know what happened after that. What a waste of a life.

I was very taken aback when I heard about a young boy in Mentor, Ohio, that killed himself because some kids told him to. I was appalled at the situation.

And then when the young lady from Croatia killed herself, I was wondering, "What is going on there?" I was saddened when I learned that a total of four students from Mentor, Ohio, had killed themselves. No one has the right to be hurting young people's feelings like that.

It wasn't for a long time that I considered not being here anymore.

I was so crushed by the situation, that I couldn't get it together enough to get thru it. I couldn't let it go.

It wasn't something I wanted people around me to go through.

I was hurting so bad inside, but I wasn't going to put them through that.

Talking to Anna, I said, "I can't believe I felt this way at that time." She said, "Something gets broken, and *you* were broken, *kaputt*."

I couldn't believe that her grandfather had killed himself. He didn't want to go to war. Her grandmother never remarried.

I believe I experienced this for a short time, because of all the people I would meet later, and what an impact it would make on my life.

I needed to experience that, in order to be able to write this book.

I don't feel you've done an evil deed, or that you're going to hell. I don't feel God is cruel or wants you to end your life. I believe He wants you to look for the positives in life, and if you're having a hard time with something right now, it will pass. God will provide the tools you need to get thru a situation if you would just let Him.

I would've missed out on so much—new friends, people, relationships, jobs, good experiences, reading books, writing, playing guitar, and just enjoying life.

I don't blame people for wanting to kill themselves; they feel so damaged or betrayed. But, they can make a better choice.

Some people want to kill themselves because things went too far, and now they have deep regrets. I've seen what that can do to a person. If you've made a mistake, ask God for forgiveness, and move on. Don't wipe yourself out over it. Saying sorry to the people you've hurt helps, too. Teach your kids to do better. Be an inspiration to them.

I also would have missed out on great friends and family relationships, different jobs, learning experiences, and writing this book. I would have missed out on *my* life, just because someone else chose to make a decision to leave my life and move on. So be it.

I would've missed out on a great aunt and uncle. I would've missed out on family events and parties and great neighbors and playing guitar and just hanging with my dog.

I just would've missed out on all of it, my husband and Jack, and all my other family and friends who God has placed in my life.

Obviously, when you're ready to kill yourself, you can't get focused on anything else. You can't get past the pain. The reality of what you're doing isn't sinking in. That hole in your heart just can't seem to be filled.

I don't think people set out to kill themselves. It just goes that way.

You get yourself in a situation, or it finds you, or it happens by default. It becomes so overwhelming, that you can't stop thinking about it, and it just consumes you. It upsets you so much, that you can't focus and regroup.

Someone isn't being rational or clear. This is a wounded person wanting to unload themselves, not someone who is being balanced with their thoughts.

You get to a point, and you can't think of anything else or anyone else, other than being able to end the situation that you are in.

The topic is so much in the news, that I believe young people feel that it's an option available to them. It's another way they can end their pain. But, it's permanent.

How I feel now—I wouldn't think of not being here. I would've missed out on family and friends, and new experiences. I would've missed out on touching people's hearts through this book.

Loss means different things to different people. Loss could be your house, job, dignity, education, prestige, your soul. Loss could be your wife, husband, mother, father, sister, brother, cousin, child, other relative, or friend. Loss could be someone you wanted to marry.

I don't wish to see someone who lost their job kill themselves.

I know how hurtful suicide is for other people. They will miss you terribly, and you don't know how much you will wound them. It's such a waste. I know things hurt, and you are in pain.

Do not judge others if they are cheerless, but try to encourage them. Lift them up. Perhaps you have not experienced a tragic breakup or loss. It is not for you to judge them or me.

If you have experienced this, realize that the person might have had shortcomings and did not appreciate your value. Maybe they had a problem and tried to blame things on you.

If people had their hearts in the right places, most relationships would be stronger and better.

I was talking to someone I know, and they told me that they feel that young people who commit suicide don't think about the future. She said, "They feel that there is nothing else out there, that there isn't any future. There isn't anything left to live for. They can't see past the here and now, what *is*."

I concur. If you did feel that there was something else to live for, you wouldn't consider doing it. "There is a brighter tomorrow," this person observed. "You can do something different tomorrow. This too shall pass."

Another friend of mine committed suicide recently. My family knew him, and my mom attempted to call him. She called me, and I phoned him. No answer, and the number wasn't working. I phoned her back. She decided to go to his house, since he told us where he lived.

She went there, and a neighbor let her know that he shot himself; she wasn't sure why. My mom was very taken aback by the situation. She wondered if things would have been different if she had gotten the chance to talk to him before he did this.

I felt awful when I heard about it; I was numb. I really couldn't speak for a while. I told some friends about it; they listened. I don't believe there was a financial or relationship issue, but I can't be certain.

Strange, before I found out about the situation, I had a thought about my other friend who ended his life a few years earlier. I was thinking of his family and children left behind. When I lost my friend a few years back, I was devastated. This person knew my book was coming out and wanted to read it. It was completely shocking to me, the finality of it all.

I attended his funeral. I had seen him and his wife on New Year's Eve the winter before he did this. I told him about my book, and he said he wished God would take him. I was shocked, but felt it wasn't my place to interfere with their relationship.

I just never got past it that I talked to him about suicide.

His funeral was packed, having come from such a large family, and of course a lot of people came. I'm still crushed about it.

A friend had five family members do this. He said, "You do this book, and help people out. If it saves just one life, it's priceless."

Another friend, Angelo, says, "I've known several people who have done this—I've lost so many people this way. It hurts me as a friend, and I feel bad that I couldn't help them. If they could've talked to me, it could have deterred it. Maybe they wouldn't have done what they did. You still care about them and love them."

Angelo adds, "It's up to them to make the final choice. I wish they would make the right choice and not even consider it. I feel that most people can't handle the emotional or mental pain that they're in."

He further states, "Maybe something in this book will trigger somebody not to do it. Perhaps they will read thirty pages of this and it will change their mind."

I hope you're right, Angelo. I do believe people will read it, and find something that they can relate to. And, I hope they make the right choice, to go on with their life, and not end it.

CHAPTER 17

Losing Dad and others

I heard long ago that divorce is second only in trauma next to losing a family member. That hit me like a brick. My family didn't experience divorce firsthand; I did not have to share my life with two families or watch my mom or dad date and/or get remarried to someone else who had kids or have additional children with their new spouse. I didn't have to personally endure that.

On the other hand, I had to learn of my dad falling flat on his face and dying from a massive heart attack. I had to go to the hospital and identify him. It was a trying today.

I always had a feeling not to go too far from my family. I was right about that. My father died not too far from our family home, a few years after my husband and I got married. I also lost my grandmother and my dog before this. I lost half of my immediate family in a few years, and it was devastating. He probably wouldn't have been there for me thru it all.

My husband and I were eating at a local restaurant, and my mom called, screaming. She said that my dad could be dead. We left the restaurant, and picked up my good friend, Nick. Another friend talked to me on the phone as my husband drove the car.

Driving to the first friend's house, I wanted to scream. I could almost hear my father say, "Don't do that! Liam could wreck the car!" They were silent screams—I was speechless.

We met my mom at the hospital. I couldn't believe it that he was lying there, lifeless. She asked me to call my aunts; I did. They each cried on the phone. Some of my relatives came to the hospital. It was unreal.

We spent some time with him. Then, my relatives left, and my mom, husband and I had to leave.

We were all numb for a while; we didn't know how to respond. People meant well, but didn't understand our loss. Emotionally, it was a tough place to be.

Lots of people came to the calling hours, and sent flowers. Many people sent food.

My cousin who was only around thirty-five, died from cancer about a week before my dad's passing. It was tough to see the family so soon again at the same funeral home.

I remember calling my husband's aunt often. She helped talk me thru a lot of the pain.

It always seems like yesterday when there's such a tragic loss.

I notice that some families can talk about the loss; others cannot. We talk about my dad often: things he would've said or done, the way he could fix things around the house, or how strong he was.

He also was an excellent cook and baker—I now have his "pie duty" at Thanksgiving. On his birthday, we do remember him.

Holidays are a difficult time. We do the best we can, but we celebrate quietly. On Father's Day, I do something nice for my husband, but we also visit with our moms. We don't make a big spectacle about things.

Other families don't mention the person, how they acted or what role they played. They don't give it any thought. Or, they don't want to upset anyone sitting at the table.

"Embrace it," I say. Let the feelings out and let them flow. They need to be released. When people say to you, "Get over it," let them "get over it." I'd like to see how they handle it when something tragic happens to them or they have to endure multiple losses simultaneously.

A few years before my dad died, my husband and I both lost many relatives. It was a difficult time.

My grandmother had two strokes. I took care of my grandma before our wedding. I stayed there with her and helped her. Unfortunately, she had other strokes and died.

We've lost animals, too. A dog I had for years died a year after losing Grandma. It was a deep loss. He was just getting older and weaker and things were shutting down, and he had an abscessed tooth. My dad decided to put him down. I was real upset, since he was my dog and loved me the most. However, it had to be done and we all had no choice.

We decided to do this, and spent the last day with him. Then we took him to the vet's and had to have him put to sleep. It was tear-jerking. The next day, my husband, Mom and I went shopping. It was really tough. It took a long time to get over things. It was difficult losing Grandma, one of my dogs, then Dad within a few years of each other.

I lost my other beautiful dog in recent years. I don't think I'll be getting anymore animals. He had a growth on his gums, and each time it was removed it grew back too aggressively. He was starting to have other problems, and he couldn't move too much. It just happened so fast. I had him at the vet's a few times the last week of his life. He was even at the emergency vet's two evenings before he passed, since his gums were bleeding so much.

We were to take him to a veterinary hospital. He was to meet with two surgeons; one to look at his mouth and the other to try to figure out if he was having any stomach issues. My husband called to tell me that our brother-in-law's funeral mass was scheduled for that Monday, and we had to cancel the vet appointment. It was a Friday, and I had to do that. I was glad that they were able to reschedule us so soon. I called my husband back to let him know that I was able to change it.

Unknown to me, he passed as I was at work. I was so sad when I found him. It was such a difficult weekend. I really haven't been able to get another animal since.

Fortunately, we were always able to talk to my doctor about losing my dad, other people, even my dogs. This person was always there for help. He is a great friend to turn to.

Someone else who meant a lot to me was this wonderful older lady friend who I knew for many years.

She invited me to some really nice dinners. She was so nice and took to me immediately, and would always talk to me.

We stayed close after I left, and she came to my wedding.

We'd also had a few New Year's Eve dinners at her house. They were so nice. Her friend Dahlia would come, and we'd all make something. She cooked so well.

Unfortunately, she got sick with breast cancer, and had undergone treatments. I visited her when I could. I knew I was losing my friend; she meant so much to me.

We would sit and talk and have coffee or tea, and snacks. Sometimes I would bring food and other times she would have something there. She was always glad that I came. I would make a special treat if I could. I would make the most of the time, not knowing how long she would be here for. I guess I was right.

It's a shame—a year later she died. She had a heart attack in the car as someone was taking her to the doctor's. They ended up going to the emergency room, and then she had a stroke. She deteriorated over a couple of month and never recovered, even though she was sent to a rehabilitation hospital.

I was crushed to hear this the weekend before Christmas, and I had to attend the services the day before Christmas Eve. She was like a mom to me, and I was like a daughter.

It was tough, going to her funeral. I even had to go to the doctor's that morning since I was coming down with something. My doctor's brother, also a physician, took care of me that day. I told him what happened. He said, "She's in heaven, and someone like that who was so busy would not have wanted to be here like that. They wouldn't have been able to get around, and she couldn't work anymore."

I told him I felt bad, because I didn't get to see her before she died. He told me not to beat myself up over it; he was right.

I was having a party near the time she had her heart attack and she didn't show up. I knew something was terribly wrong. A month went by, and I didn't hear from her. I even called her house a couple of times. Surprisingly, a mutual friend called me, Brian, and told me she had a heart attack the day before my party. She also had a stroke and was in the hospital with an infection. I immediately called the hospital, but they asked me not to come up because she was in isolation and was contagious. I respected this and decided to wait. I was highly concerned, since each week that went by I couldn't go. They didn't want me bringing anything in to her.

She then went to a rehabilitation hospital, and we were trying to get there. Every weekend when we tried to go, something came up. Then,

I didn't hear from my friend Brian or her daughter-in-law, so I called each of them.

Ginny got back to me first; she said that she wasn't doing well, that she was very sick and in a hospice center. There was nothing more they could do for her. I told her we were coming up the next day; she was glad to hear that and was going to meet me there.

I called Brian back as I found out more information, since he was near to her. He didn't get my message that she had moved to the hospice center until after he went to the rehabilitation center and found out she wasn't there anymore. It was too late to try to make it to the hospice center after that.

The next day, as we were getting ready to leave in the morning, her daughter-in-law called me and told me she had died. I was crushed. I immediately called my friend, and told him what had happened. He had called that day. I told him to call his mom.

That weekend, I just didn't know what to do with myself. It was Christmastime, and I just didn't feel like doing anything about it. I was just muddling through stuff.

I told Ginny she could call us if she needed anything, especially any help with the funeral, and if she needed my husband to be a reader. She asked him to be a pallbearer, and also to do the readings.

Going to the funeral was tough. The calling hours weren't easy. I got to see her son that lived with her, and other family members, and Dahlia. It was hard to let her go.

At the funeral, the priest said he knew how people there felt. He had just lost his mother recently, and a sister died long ago on Christmas Eve.

There was a dinner afterwards. I'm glad so many people attended. My friend and his mom were grateful that I would call them to let them know what was going on.

Strange as it was, as we were gathered together for the dinner afterwards, people in the restaurant at other tables were happily getting together, we were just trying to get thru the afternoon.

It was a quiet evening for us, even though we had to go shopping. I got my trees decorated before this, so I didn't have to do that when I got home.

The next day on Christmas Eve, I had to cook for my family, and get ready for two family dinners to attend on Christmas Day. It was tough. After, on Saturday, there was too much time to think about it.

Friends called on Monday; I was grateful for that. Still, a part of me is sad that she died near Christmas. I remembered how we would always get together at this time, and go eat at each other's houses. There was one year I made a delicious brunch. It was really nice.

The hardest thing about this is that I can't call her if I need her. I am losing people in town since another lady friend moved, and now this friend died, and her one son moved in with another son. It's not the same that she is not in town anymore. This will be the first Christmas we won't be connecting.

Most recently, I ran into the sister of my lady friend who died. It was so nice to see her, since my friend passed and her son who lived with her is with other family, and is no longer in town. We both asked how each other was.

Actually, in a period of forty-eight hours, I ran into or talked to five people that I have been trying to get in touch with for months. It's amazing how things work out like that. And, she was the most current one.

We continued to ask about each other's family, and she asked me about work. I invited her to get coffee sometime.

I told her about the book that I'm writing. She then told me about her cousin's wife who killed herself. This person was in their seventies and thought they had cancer. It wasn't true, and she was going to visit her cousin today who is close to ninety-years-old, and lonely. She said it was shocking when it happened in their family.

I am hurt that my dad died, that my dog died, and that I lost my grandmother. We can't bring them back, but we can speak about good memories with them, and that adds to our lives.

I also worked with a lovely person named Gina. Gina had breast cancer when I met her. We were always trying to go out, and never had the chance to go. One day, she called me and said she'd like to pick me up and take me to eat. We went to a hometown breakfast place, and we ordered food. She wanted me to have a full meal, leaving nothing out. Even though it was the only time we went out, it seemed like we always knew each other. She told me I was like a daughter to her. She thought a lot about me.

That moment was like one of those perfect moments in time. It's like when you've only known someone a short time, but they've left such an impression on your heart. She talked about God and what it would be like on the other side. Gina felt we are still connected to those we really care about. She was a religious person, and she seemed confident that we would still be connected.

After that, she had gone thru a lot of treatments, and I talked to her on the phone. She had stopped at my house that December. I didn't realize it at that time, but she had stopped because she wouldn't be able to come by anymore. I was busy at the time with something, but I did invite her in. She said she had to go.

In January, I called her house and left a message to call me, so we could go out again. Her husband had called back, letting me know she passed on.

I didn't know what to say. I felt bad, but I didn't know. He said I could call again at any time.

I wanted to write about her in this book, because for that short time she touched my life. We don't know what lies ahead, and when the last time will be that we will see someone again.

In the past few years, I lost family and friends, my dog, and I knew a lot of people who lost their sons and other family members. It impacted me greatly, and still does. You cannot be around death and take it lightly. I pray for their families when I think of them.

Things aren't as grievous for other people. Lots of people don't get it, since they haven't been through much. They've never lost a job, a significant other or a close family member tragically, or all three.

I worked with a nice person at the beginning of Thanksgiving week, and she shared with me how she had to travel out-of-state last year since her mother died, and when she came back home, her father-in-law died. It was a very trying autumn. I reminded her of my book and shared how I lost a lot of people this year and knew many people who have lost family members. She said it was good to be able to talk to someone who understood.

CHAPTER 18

People and Relationships

People have problems in their relationships because the relationships become *real*. People are so focused on the divorce rate; what about all the other relationships that don't make it? That number must be huge. We shouldn't be so focused on the divorce rate; any relationship that means anything to anybody that ends is a loss.

It takes at least two years to heal for relationships that have really meant a lot to you, or hurt you. It's painful to let go of someone you really love. For some, it takes longer to heal.

An acquaintance from long ago mentioned the two-year time span, and I feel this is really true.

However, it can be quite painful for someone to have to remember the loss about someone that they deeply loved.

When people leave they get something stuck in their head. Yes, people do leave for other people, too, but they do leave for selfish reasons. The reasons could be: "You won't sleep with me, you won't move with me, I don't like your job, you aren't educated enough for me," etc. The list is endless. If some guy or girl passes you over, try not to take it so personally. Maybe they needed to go. In a godly, loving relationship, you wouldn't have to worry about stuff like that.

For example, a guy is dating a girl just so he can try to use her or a girl is dating a guy just so she can say she has someone. This is wrong on both accounts. Both are being selfish. Or, you have a friend you only call when you need something. This is the same thing.

Sixteen, seventeen and those teen years to the twenties or even thirties can be a challenging time. You don't know where you fit in, and you are attempting to get a hold of your life. You want things to go a certain way, and they don't. The world we live in can be an unsettling place, and it's tough to find your niche. Some people meet early and some people meet later.

There was a friend in college that was breaking up with her boyfriend, and she was interested in other guys. I remember her saying they had nothing in common, and he had to work to pay for school. She was a nice girl from a good family. I don't believe much was going on there, but I was surprised that she would even think of leaving him. I feel a commitment is a commitment; people just fall out of love.

It's heartbreaking; it happens a lot when people are young. She would say, "I love him; I'm just not in love with him." I never quite got that, but that's how a lot of people are—it's an *excuse.*

Distance and loss of time can also be disastrous to a relationship. Sometimes two people who have the best intentions can't seem to last once things part.

Being young seems to be a big factor in a breakup. I believe that one person would like to stay; the other person is changing too much to keep the relationship going. It can't last because one person doesn't *want* it to.

People who are heartsick repeat the pain in their hearts countless times from that last meeting, stuck in their memory. It's tough when you're stuck in repeat mode.

"We are all looking for love, regardless of how old or young we are," a nice neighbor once told me.

That's true. You know, people will spend years going to college, but they don't want to invest time into waiting for a great relationship. They miss the signs and cues of God putting someone or something special into their path. They hurry into something and have deep regrets later about choices that they made.

It doesn't help that people intentionally or unintentionally attempt to break up your relationship. That is hurtful. They don't know what is going on, and make an assumption. Funny, I've watched it work both ways—I've seen people misjudge a very good person and break up a good friendship, I've seen it done out of jealousy and spite, and I've seen people not open up their mouth when bad things are occurring, and let it go. It's amazing what harm people can cause.

I've heard comments about people changing, and that's why they leave. You usually hear that from someone who hasn't experienced that themselves, of someone leaving them. They were usually the one that left and are making an excuse for their actions. They typically weren't the one that was left behind. I'm sure that their statement would be different if someone left *them*. Not everyone is going to stay. It's hard to see it coming.

I notice that when people are young, they leave, too, for the dumbest of reasons, especially when they're growing out of a relationship. I never wanted to do that to anybody. They'll make up any excuse— "We aren't good for each other anymore; you're different than me; I don't like your family." Or, they say, "Your family doesn't like me; your family is different; our religions aren't the same," and so forth.

Well, you knew that when you were dating! So why are you changing your mind now?!

It's because, for the simple fact, they just want *out*.

You're always looking for that person—even temporarily. But even if you try so hard to replace them, you can't, because the hurt is always there, yanking out those memories.

Young love is such a touchy thing. People feel it will last forever; little do people know it won't. There's always someone out there left "holding the bag," being left alone. I feel bad for young people; they are so tender; all they have is what's in front of them. There is a whole world waiting for them.

High school and college graduations seem to be the time of a lot of breakups, because things are changing and life is moving on, and who the person thought they wanted to be with isn't that person. I am sad for people when they are left behind.

It's painful when that happens, when the person you want to see is gone. They disappeared from your life and you won't ever see them again.

That's another comment I'm not too crazy about, that you're only "in someone's life for a season." If you can't say something nice to someone or listen to them, then don't say anything at all.

I felt I was always too nice to people, so they took advantage of that friendliness. I would always be polite, so as not to upset the balance of things. I'm really trying to cut back on that now. People think strength comes from verbally pushing your opinions on someone without caring if that hurts someone or not. Not so. It is important to be meek. This means to have your strength under control. You should have your opinions, but be aware of your audience.

Since I'm older, I've really cut down on the type of people who are only there for the moment. Don't expect me to go out of the way for you.

There are people that I know who only want to do what they want to do on their schedule. You're simply being selfish, and I will limit you.

Also, if you're attempting to siphon off my time when I'm married and have lots of obligations and responsibilities, I will either stop the friendship or limit you, too.

I'm tired of that.

A few years ago, I let go of several people/situations/club offers, because I don't really have the room in my schedule for everything. Too many people will take up your time with unimportant stuff, if you let them. They see you as not being busy, and truthfully, I've got enough stuff to do and have to limit my time with people.

At one point, I gave too much to friends. Now, my husband and family come first, and some time goes to my closest friends. But, that's it.

If you can't handle it, then move on.

I'm not a selfish person, it's just I got to a point that I had to take care of myself. Too many people were in my life that just moved on, and I got tired of it, of putting time in, and then it was over.

I want people who are going to stay now.

I put myself out here for so many people and cared so much, and where are these people now?

When I don't have the time, married or single, and I treated you like family, and then you go your own way later.

I put up a boundary with people who I notice may do this.

For example, single friends or couples want my time, yet disappear after they find someone else they like or get married or their situation changes. I'm drained by that. Don't bother me, when you're just here for the moment, and then you're gone.

A power struggle in a relationship has its own rules. The man or woman is always trying to one-up the other person.

That's why I think godly relationships where people pray and honor each other work, and these do not.

It's about the money or your ego, or your pride or lack of it, no self-control, or insecurities.

You can't just be free to be you, or let the other person be free, either. You have to always be in control.

Even in the last few years, people have ended friendships with me, and just left and never called back.

Another friend I always thought highly of from years back was in town, and didn't treat me like she once did. Also, I ran into a couple who adamantly and excitedly invited me to their house years ago. Now, we were all like strangers.

On the other hand, I dislike it when people, who have left for whatever reason, see you out and want to have a conversation with you like nothing ever happened. I've always been puzzled by this. I think it's because they want to make themselves feel better. Please don't sit there and talk to me like you're my best friend. You were wrong, and/ or you left. Don't devalue me further by talking to me like we are best pals. We aren't.

We are not responsible for others' behaviors; we can only control our own actions. Of course, it hurts when people come and go, but that may happen so you can have more time for the most important people in your life. We can't take everybody along with us.

You know, often we're surrounded by people who don't understand or appreciate who we are as people. They don't welcome our differences. If your 'friends' or significant others are asking you to do something wrong or put you in an uncomfortable situation, they're not really your ally.

You can't be giving your heart to everyone—people need to earn it. Everyone isn't worth giving your heart to. Many young people don't have long-term perspective. They don't take the time to *see* how their actions today affect their future.

People do grow up a bit, but I think their core remains the same. They are not faithful people. How can you expect them to be any different? They don't transform unless they want to, and sometimes it's not for you they want to change.

Sometimes things aren't working out, and it's ok to let people go, but it's a difference between that and not staying in it for the long haul. People leave because of immaturity, selfishness, and being judgmental. They don't like this or that, and come up with dumb reasons for letting you go. Don't buy into that, or take that seriously. Maybe you don't want to go. Perhaps you wouldn't do something that was wrong or didn't want to get physical with someone. It's no reason to let go. But, people will do this.

There are some signs that people will jump ship. They buy a new car, buy a new wardrobe, start to work out, change their look or style, or complain about you. They make plans without you. I would look out for these signs, because it might not work out for you. Be careful. They want to alter themselves or their appearance for someone else, and that could have long-lasting or devastating effects on you.

People have power-struggle issues. They just want to be in control, power play, and won't do what you want to do, but you have to do what they want on their schedule/terms. It's not fair.

I'm wiser to that now. I limit people who always think they're going to call the shots. I play fair, but you're not going to take advantage of me. I'm older now. Before, people were unfair to me and took advantage of me. I'm stronger now, and much more aware of things. If you continuously think you're going to run the show, I'll either limit you or leave you altogether. You're not going to treat me that way. I'll always remember if someone went the distance for me or really took care of me or helped me at some point in time, but that does not allow you to take advantage of me or affect my emotional well-being.

I've had many relationships with people who have been close to my heart who have decided to leave, and I'm glad I've been able to move on. Once I can get someone emotionally out of my system, I don't think about them and I don't have a desire to reconnect, even though they may want to years later.

I don't rely on other people so much. I rely on myself. That doesn't mean I'm an island; it just means you're not going to be nasty, mean, or inconsiderate to me, and you're not going to run things in my life. I don't need the power strugglers taking up my energy and time. And, I have the right to an opinion and the right to be heard. You don't have to agree with me, but you can *listen.*

In serious relationships, power struggles are also unfair, but, they are there and they do exist.

For example, if you don't sleep with me I'll leave, or if you don't do as I say I'll leave. It's always something with these types of people, so, let them leave.

In a relationship, at first, you're trying to be nice and maybe you end up doing more for the other since you like them so much. But, you have to take care of yourself, too. If someone really likes you and cares for you, they'll go the distance.

I'm currently using a zero-thru-ten scale of rating new people. I really don't know you, so I'm starting you at ground zero. It's going to take you quite a long time to even get a higher rating on the chart. People get too excited about meeting someone new, and they immediately move someone off of the chart, and then get so disappointed when things don't work out. Take my advice, and don't even go there.

I'm an in-between person. I will be dismal for a while, but I will hope and pray and try to move on.

I feel that a lot of marriages don't work because people are acting like they're dating. If they've gone thru a lot of relationships, then their marriage is just another date that they can leave at any time.

That's why they can just disappear. Or, they're self-centered, and just want to move on.

There's an old saying, "If you love something, set it free. If it comes back to you, it was meant to be; if it doesn't, it never was."

That's a biblical saying, meaning if someone's lost to the world, then they don't love God then let them go. If they love God, they will be back to Him. Do not apply this "set them free" part to your situation. People are selfish and make choices.

It drove me nuts when people would say that, because they think they're doing you a favor and making you feel better, but they're not. I'm not one for old clichés.

It hurts when people leave; it hurts when you get that last phone call, letter, text message or email. The message is clear: I'm done; leave me alone.

You try to let a few days pass; maybe someone's upset or busy. You give them some space. But, they may or not be upset, and they just want out. It hurts terribly. You know that they've been leaving. If we knew what people thought, we could change things, but we can't.

Don't devalue who you are and don't let someone take away something from yourself while you're waiting for the right person or people to come along.

I'm tired of that, how people blame the other person when things break up. Look at yourself once in a while, before you start whining about someone else.

Marriage is special, and for sharing that special bond together with the one you're married to.

Some people say change is good, but not always. Change is not always pleasant. It's not enjoyable when someone you love leaves you, moves away or you lose a job. It's not fun when you're not sure that you're going to meet someone else. These are the hard parts of life.

I am a modest person, and I don't like distasteful stuff. It surprises me sometimes how open people can be with me. You attract to yourself how you present yourself to the outside world.

Do you really want to be involved with everybody?

If someone left, that doesn't mean you should go and date several people. Wait for that special someone. God will bring them to you.

Don't young people realize that they're going to marry one day, and how you're going to explain things to someone nice that you'd meet? I'd be tough. I feel that's why so many marriages break up, since it's just another date.

My mother-in-law often speaks of how things have changed so much over the last several decades. She states, "There was an understood rule of how a young lady or young man would act. You wouldn't be out doing the things young people do today. You would wait for marriage."

Don't step into the fire and ruin your life with make bad choices— look at how things will affect you or your family long-term. I am a forgiving person, especially for people who have felt bad about things they've done in the past. People tell me lots of things. Their deepest confessions stay safe with me, whether we're still friends or we've parted company. Everybody needs someone to unload on. I can't say that things I've told other people are safe; I know they're not. People are foolish.

You have to remember who you are talking to when you have a problem. Not everyone is going to be receptive; not everyone is going to be a good listener; not everyone is going to understand. People may have not been through your particular situation, or might not view your matter like you do. They may put themselves in your shoes momentarily, only to tell you what to do and what they think, and how they would handle it.

Don't search for people like that. Talk to people who are kind and compassionate and can help you. You have emotions that are worth expressing. Acknowledge that within yourself. Stop wasting time explaining your story to people who don't really care. You are hurting. Your feelings are real. Seek out folks who will listen to you. Ask them to come into your life—they will.

I say what I mean, and I mean what I say. I *feel* what I say. I can't help myself. I express myself thru words, and I am a communicator. I need to talk things out to people; I need a receptive audience. I need kind people in my life who will listen to me. There are a few, and they are priceless.

I like wholesome people and quality relationships. I like people who make good, healthy decisions, and watch carefully what words are coming out of their mouths. I enjoy being in the company of others who are kind and will listen to you, and someone you can have a fine conversation with. I like people of faith who aren't judgmental of others, but who do stand by what is right.

Wholesomeness is something that is missing from our lives today. Young people aren't taught to have and keep good values, and how destructive their lives can become from making one or two wrong decisions. They unfortunately live their lives with deep regret.

I have come across many young people who have lost their way due to making a wrong decision, and no matter what they do or say they can't correct it. They can't seem to get back onto the freeway of good choices. They're often exiting off onto dangerous paths. Some choices are erasable and others are not. Some affect you for a lifetime, often with deep disappointment.

If you're not with the right person, then maybe you should wait.

I feel bad for people who are in these young relationships, and then they change. One person wants out for this or that reason. It's very sad. Then the other person wants to stay in it.

People are selfish. They leave for whatever reason.

All people handle things in their own way. I think it's important to try to look at the positives, to learn from a situation, move on and not dwell, but sometimes you can't help that.

If you're a God-centered person, don't give up that someone else might be out there for you.

God will take care of you, if you let Him, and will show you, guide you, and protect you. You will gain understanding and appreciate the people that He sent to you.

You will get thru it all. Trust me, and trust Him.

CHAPTER **19**

Other folks who lost friends and family

Throughout writing this book, I would meet other folks who knew someone who committed suicide or they thought of it themselves. Also, I met others who have lost important people in their lives. Here are their stories.

Lucie is a good friend I met at school. She shared with me one day that a family member had killed themselves over a young relationship on New Year's Eve. She and her husband were crushed. Lucie also knew a parent of her kids' friends who did the same thing. Each time I have run into her again, she tells me of someone else she's known who has done this.

"Why don't people reach out?" she questioned. "Why do they feel there's no one at all?"

I explained to her that you get to a point, and you just feel like there truly is no one at all to listen to you. People just don't feel like you do, and they don't understand.

I couldn't believe that my friend Nick lost two relatives recently to suicide, his nephew and a cousin. I ran across him at a local festival, and he asked me if I was still writing my book. I answered that I was. He was glad, and then told me about these relatives. He said I could add them to my book.

My friend Cassandra said, "A friend of mine died. It's not natural; it's not cancer; it's not a heart attack; it's not pre-ordained. You've chosen it. And if you choose this, you can choose the other way. They don't think of the ones they leave behind. They only think of their own problems; they can't see anything else. I'm mad that my friend died."

Also, "You have to have the willpower to fight. Somewhere along the line, they lose that. I've had a nervous breakdown. I know what people go thru. People need you. That's what I told myself, before checking out. You can't give up on yourself because you think that other people don't find you important. You have to stick around and see everything thru, because it *will* get better. I try not to judge people who are having issues because I haven't walked in their shoes."

And, "These are people who want to change themselves, because they think other people want them to change. That's not the case. They are selfish. Be yourself. My friend Julie's son committed suicide on their anniversary day. She's never been the same since. I also had a friend who committed suicide in high school. He never left a note. No one knows why he did this. I still think about him from time to time. The devil tries to ruin things with people, but you have to trust God to get you thru it."

Cassandra continued: "I recently lost a friend that had cancer. Did he want to die? No. This wasn't his choice; he was sick. I'd really like to talk to the people who've considered this, because I don't think they're thinking clearly. You can make a difference; you can do better. You are worth being here."

Sophie adds, "All those young people out there, they're not thinking about what they're doing. You can find another boyfriend or girlfriend to talk to." And, "I've lost a lot of people, too, but I still go on to the next day. It hurts, but you need to pull yourself thru. You need to find something to do that is healthy for you, like being outside or exercising. You need to get your mind off of it."

Sophie was kind to me when I lost someone I knew, a lovely young lady named Sara. She was a preschool teacher and a person with a heartwarming personality and a beautiful smile and kind to everyone she knew and worked with. She was tragically hit by a semi-truck going to visit her aunt one evening. It was a life cut too short. I met her parents and other family at her memorial service. She had a very close relationship with her parents and other family. I remember one of her uncle's speaking about her; he couldn't understand, like any of us, why God would bring her home.

I still think about Sara. She didn't ask for her life to be cut short.

I talked to Taylor, who was the DJ at the family gathering after the service. I told him about my book, and how I knew Sara. He told me about an elderly man he met at a restaurant. He would talk with this person when he would see him. Taylor found out some time later that this man had killed himself. He felt awful when he heard the news about him. Taylor wished he could have spent some time talking to him, if he knew he was going to end his life.

A few years ago, a friend of ours lost his two-month old baby grandson. My heart just broke when I attended the calling hours and funeral. Such a beautiful baby boy. I still pray for the parents and grandparents and other family. I pray that God helps heal their obviously broken hearts.

Tim Jones was telling me about losing his mom and dad. His mom died first, and his dad died on Thanksgiving Day. He started the 'ten-second club.' This is a special club reserved for those of us who have lost a significant person or family member in our lives. Tim says, "I remind my friends, what would you say to someone you loved that was dying if that's all you had was ten seconds left to talk to them? I know what I'd say."

Macey was telling me about her son Travis, who was dying from kidney and heart failure. For five years, he was in the hospital many times for long periods of time. She said, "He told me he knew he was going to die young. People say it gets easier, but it doesn't. I cry about it every day. Travis would say to me, 'Mom, you can't die before me. We're always together, forever.'"

Also, "I miss kissing him goodnight on his forehead. Sometimes I feel I didn't do enough, but my kids tell me I did everything I could do. I did the best I could do at the time. Let your kids know how much you love them."

Macey adds, "Just getting up and helping take care of everybody else helps me get thru the day. Everybody can handle things differently." When I asked her what she thought about suicide, she said, "Who knows how we would act if we went thru the same thing? It hurts them more than us. It's sad for the family. They're the ones that have to go on without their loved one."

Another person I know, Victoria, told me about her brother who committed suicide after another brother died. He was so distraught about the situation and could not take being here anymore. It has affected their family greatly.

She said she was angry at such a horrible loss in her family. There was no indication and no clear signs that he would react this way. Although he was depressed, nobody thought he would've taken it that far. They were shocked that he took his own life. She says, "The situation leaves such a huge hole in your family that it's so difficult to be around the family that is left."

She says it was hard to be happy at Christmastime, and it was hard even looking at each other. She adds, "We felt guilty to see everyone's pain. We tried to be strong for each other. You just go thru the motions, and you are not fully living because you are in such a sad state. It was such an instantaneous thing when my second brother passed."

Victoria' advice is for people to go get help from whomever you trust the most or go somewhere to get help, and to pray about it. She tells me, "I prayed and yelled to God to help me. Someone actually assisted me in getting help. It was someone that I least expected." And, "We were all suffering for so long. Don't suffer alone or in silence. I felt like a million pieces glued back together. It's good to talk about it; it's good to get it out." She feels that her brothers are people who were once alive instead of a silent part of her memory.

Our friend Jeremiah said he was sheltered because he lost three people in one month: an uncle, who got hit by a car, a friend's boyfriend who committed suicide, and another person. It changed him.

Jonelle was another person I met. She lost a child at thirteen in her sleep, who had a liver transplant at age one. She felt that people need to listen to each other. No loss is greater than another. "Don't compare losses. Some people never get hit with any losses. "Yes, some people haven't experienced trauma, or there are different levels of it."

Natalie has been waiting for me to finish this. She's lost her brother to suicide, and then a few months later her son was diagnosed with brain cancer. She told me that she was so mad with her brother, that he had a choice to live and didn't. The son had no choice. He died a few months after that tragic situation.

She still had a lot of anger from losing her brother; I don't blame her.

Dave Smith had known of a young man who had killed himself. He didn't really understand why. He said it's tough on the family to this day. It happened long ago, and it still is a hurtful reminder to the family.

Claudette, a lady I met, lost her dad to suicide. He made her a lunch for school, and she left. She found out that day that he had killed himself—she didn't know why. It has been a lifelong question, left painfully unanswered.

A longtime friend, Connor, had a friend who killed herself. It was shocking and he still questions, "Why?" "I think it's important for people to talk about it, and get it out," he said. He added, "I don't know why people do that. I like to listen to people, and I would have helped her if she needed it."

Connor adds, "You need to emotionally take care of yourself. You need to get up, get yourself dressed, shave, and eat. I've been depressed myself, and a friend let me know I looked terrible. I was depressed over a girl who left me. I knew I had to do something."

And, "I've lost my mom from cancer. I know what it feels like to lose."

He says, "You have to take baby steps-shower, go for a walk. You also need a 'toolbox' to get thru. I'd like to take someone out for a burger if they feel this way, talk to them, and let them know they're not alone."

Landon told me about his daughter and unborn grandchild that were killed in a car accident. Landon's wife was in the hospital at that time, and he wasn't sure if his wife was going to make it. Another daughter was following in another car. The first daughter was killed. Landon just didn't know what to do with himself. "I couldn't believe it; I could have lost all three of them in one day." His wife survived. At another time, he had to tell her what happened.

"I just wanted to kill myself. If there wasn't a pastor there at the chapel, I would have. I have been carrying around this pain for a long time."

Landon and I talked, and he said it really helped to talk about the situation; he felt a release.

Abby lost her husband Paul to cancer. It happened suddenly one night, when she was working. Her friend told her to go home. She was glad she went. The message that she got was that he wasn't doing well and had to go to the hospital. He needed to be put on a ventilator and didn't want to be on one; she didn't know this. He deteriorated and had passed on.

"It is so difficult being alone," she states. "It's so different being without him. I know he's with us; I just wish he was still here. We knew each other from when we were very young." Also, her daughter added, "You just never know when it's the last time you will see someone. Make every moment count."

It's something we all need to do.

CHAPTER **20**

Deciding to Live/Dreams

It is up to you to decide how you're going to live. When I lost jobs, when my schooling got delayed, when I had to take other jobs not in my field, I didn't give up. When things were tough, I pushed myself harder.

I wrote this book because I would like people to heal. I wish for them to go on with their lives. I don't desire for young people to get so caught up in the stupidity and ignorance of others around them. I don't want them to feel that things won't change.

When God pulls people out of my life, or when things happen, yes, naturally, I do get flustered and frustrated, but I'm not going to give up. God is going to help me, and you, too! Just believe that.

If you're having a hard time, know that things will change for you. You can graduate and go on to something else. You are a person worth living your life for!

If you lose your job, that doesn't mean you won't find another one, even if you have to start over.

If someone left, you can't say you won't meet someone else. If you are failing school, that doesn't mean you can't try again.

I want people who were in a long-term or short-term relationship to understand that there are those of us out there who can relate to what you're going thru, and would like to see you pull thru this. I know that you can. I don't desire to see you leave your family behind. I don't want to read about you on the internet, see you on TV or get a phone call about you. I *do* care. That's why this book is here.

I want you to get your feelings out. I want you to talk to people you trust. Letters are great: they are physical pieces that you can read, and reread. They can be heartfelt, and mean so much. They are something you can hold and touch: a reminder of the situation, and a way to heal. This is one way to cope with your situation.

The situation will pass. You will have another chance to do things. You can find another to love if they left you. You can find other friends, another job. You can pray and ask God for help to get you through your situation.

Time is one thing that can heal a wound. It takes the passing of time to occur in order to let bad feelings settle and to lessen the pain of a loss. I even feel that it's good to table an issue for a while if you're not ready to talk about something.

Perseverance is so important. To get thru something difficult shows character. It shows determination that you didn't want to give up. Don't resign yourself; don't relinquish your grip on surviving whatever it is that is thrown at you.

If you went thru something difficult or if you made bad choices, then perhaps there's someone you can help. If you are a private person, you could volunteer one-on-one or talk to people anonymously at a call center. If you're more open, you could let others know about your story.

Don't give up on yourself or your dreams. We all have day jobs and responsibilities that somewhat prohibit us from doing what we really want to accomplish. That is life. Most of us have to work to make ends meet. You just have to make time for what's important. If there's something lying on your heart that you know is essential to get done, then you have to see it thru.

Perspective is a good thing. Put things in a new point of view; give something a new outlook. Years later, I realized how everything worked out. I married a great person, and enjoy the company of wonderful friends. I've healed up a lot of things in my life, and I've been able to move on.

I finished two degrees, wrote my first book, and I am looking forward to writing more.

Now, that it is getting finished, things are falling into place for me. I'm just moving on with this book.

For me, some things have taken time to be worked out, and a lot has been resolved in the last five years. Everything in my life has led up to this. I have my husband now, and I wouldn't change that for the world.

I know everything has been leading up to this point.

God has given me tasks to do, and I can't help what work He has or hasn't allowed. My life's work is to help others.

I want you to be inspired by this book. I want you to make the choice to stay, not to take your life. I hope I've been able to give you some reasons to live.

Anna said, "This book will help older people, especially with the economy and depression. There's so much hurt out there. Live day by day. The sun is still coming up. You have to think about that. I talk to my husband, and I tell him if we lose things, we'll still have each other. There *are* things to live for. This helps other people, not to do the same mistake. Step back, and take time out."

This book has been ten years of writing and editing. Lost friends, family members, pets and jobs. These collective issues brought about changes in me.

All these things combined were heartrending, but I never once thought of unloading myself. I kept my eye on the prize—finishing the book and getting it out there.

Throughout it all, I kept the faith and endured. As a friend said, "To save the life of just one person would be well worth it."

As Victoria says, "It might take a day, a year, or five to ten years to get thru it. No matter how long it takes you to get thru it, stick in there. Not everything is always good. You have to get thru the good and the bad. You will miss the good things in life."

I endear you, the reader, to consider your options. You *can* make better choices.

Curt

CHAPTER 1

My fault

We blame it on *ourselves*.

We feel that it is *our* fault. Although I know better, I feel it is *my* fault.

"It's not you; it's *me*," she said. She was there for me to love, honor and cherish. Judy broke *her* promise.

At that moment I lost *everything*, so I thought.

She was young when I met her. When I saw her, I told myself, *I'm going to marry her.* A few years later, I did.

I remember talking to her when we were young. We would talk from time to time in the living room. I loved talking to her, but there was no privacy, with all my family in the house.

I bought her a beautiful piece of jewelry as a gift of my devotion for my sweetheart. She always wore it.

I loved her, and I never thought things would turn out the way they did.

CHAPTER 2

The early years

I was born in Channistown. There were several of us kids. Later, we moved to Rogers.

I was closest with Lynn until he died, and then later, Joe. I felt I had a good childhood. We were poor, but we didn't realize it. Everybody else was, too. Me and two of my brothers slept in the same bed. In the summer, the three of us boys each had a room.

I was shy in high school around girls, except for the ones I grew up with. I liked girls' smiles and faces. Nothing worked out with any of them. I met Judy after I graduated. High school was a lonely place for me, other than for my buddies. I went to ball games by myself.

I wasn't a big sports player. I was the type of guy who would chop wood and have contests with myself, to see if I could do it better the next day. I'd ride my bike, or help my mom with the other kids. I had certain chores I had to do, but it wasn't anything too much. My mother taught me to iron, sew, darn socks, sew buttons on, fix holes, etc.

When I was growing up, I learned a strong work ethic. It was all about your work. It was who you were. Like spreading manure, or fixing something. You'd shake hands on it. Other days, Mom would say, "Boys, go to Grandma's and help her can!" I would be helping out, measuring in the big metal funnel, and cranking the musher. We would can plums, pears, peaches and apples and corn. She'd also can beef and chicken. What work that would be! But they'd make it fun, not work.

Sometimes, I think of picking up some of my family and heading to Grandma and Grandpa's, and parking my bike and playing there for a day.

I started getting interested in building things when I was younger. I learned to use a hammer and saw some wood, and I went from there.

We were best friends, Tim, Lynn and I, and Uncle Johnny, like *The Three Musketeers,* plus one. Until I moved to Rogers, we all hung out together in the farmers' fields, swam in their ponds, fished in them, rode bicycles, and went sled riding. We played in the woods, picked blueberries, and played in the creek and rocks. We had a great time, the four of us.

I was a wiry young kid. We wrestled and got into fist fights and rumble-tumbled, and protected our own. My two brothers and I, and my uncle Johnny had our group: one for all, and all for one. Brothers should do this—protect each other. We fought since grade school, especially in high school. We fought each other, and also other people.

Johnny was like our brother; we took him bowling, to a movie, and played Putt-putt. We took care of one another. It started breaking up when Johnny was in high school.

I helped my dad until I graduated from high school. I also worked at another company part-time, until I got another job full-time.

Samuel, my friend and Judy's neighbor, had moved, and his aunt said that there were lots of jobs in another area.

We were to get married in Treetop. In Johnsonville, we had already got the licenses. The waiting period was only a few days there.

Her family could've paid for a nice wedding, but they never offered. We didn't even consider it. I was really surprised when I drove back to my house, and my whole family was dressed and ready to go. I asked where they were going, and they answered, "Where you are going." Then all of us went to Judy's house to pick her up. She must have known that we were coming, because she wasn't surprised. Her sister was there, too. We were scheduled to get married in the evening. I had never been there before, and I was really excited, and nervous.

It never occurred to me that my family would want to come. It was a short ceremony, and everyone stood in the church. Lynn was in the service, and couldn't be at the wedding. When we got done, Dad had signs hanging on my car and crepe paper. We were looking for a place to eat, and we went to a hotel. The next day, we went back to get her clothes and other stuff, said hello to her parents, and left.

Jim Teeter hired me the day I went in to apply for the job. "Be here on Monday," he said. Judy found the apartment. We lived there for a year before we moved to Schroeder St. We stayed there until I bought this house. We lived on a forty-hour paycheck, and saved all the overtime.

CHAPTER 3

My accidents

I unfortunately had several injuries, and I almost got killed one time.

Someone must have put me in the ambulance. I was drifting in-and-out of consciousness. I suddenly blurted out, "Take me to Dr. Tannis at Seasons Hospital." He took care of me as a family doctor. I remember the ambulance door opening up and putting me in the emergency room. They took my jacket off, which was extremely painful. They cut my pants and shirt off, too. Later on, I found out my shoes were still in the car. My feet came right out of my shoes. I remember going down to the x-ray room. It was extremely difficult. There were cuts on my hands, face, head, arms and legs. I was all bandaged up. I could walk with help, but I couldn't put my arms around the machine to take chest x-rays. I then had to throw up. After that, we went back to the emergency room.

They found out that I had a collapsed lung and broken ribs. They put a chest tube in me and put me in intensive care. That's when I remember seeing Judy. I couldn't lift anything.

Next thing I remember, it was morning. Dr. Tannis walked in, and picked up my chart. He looked at me and said, "What are you doing here?" I started to explain to him that I was in a car accident. It was around four or six a.m. Most people would have severed the arteries. He looked at me and said, "God has a plan for you. I don't know what it is, but he has a plan for you." I've often thought about it through the years. I needed to be around to raise my kids, and now to write this story.

He started to tell me that it was going to take a long time to heal up. I was going to need an additional surgery.

When I went back for another operation, I found out that when I was there before, they did not know if I would even make it to the next shift. I had met the man who saved my life, but I don't remember his name. I often said that that would be the person I would go to for the rest of my life if he started a practice here, but he left the area.

There was a father/son combo that helped me the day of the accident. No one got their names. That's all I heard about my angels.

I was moved to the floor from intensive care. I stayed there a while. Lots of people came out to see me: Judy, the girls, my brothers, sister, friends, and co-workers. The hospital staff was great to me. One of my nurses was a co-worker's daughter. Their support helped me out. Lou, a friend, ran to visit me.

I was in shock from this whole thing happening to me. You don't anticipate it, getting into a bad accident. I hit a tree hard. I had to get through it for my kids.

In regards to the house, I always wondered who lived there, because I had seen people move in-and-out of there a couple of times.

When I would drive by it, I would salute it, even though someone would be in the car with me. About ten years ago it was removed. Perhaps the tree saved the people in the next house, if they were home. The tree eventually died.

Some of the things that I went through, God *had* to be there. I couldn't believe all this happened to me. I did get injured one more time in an accident, but, thank goodness, it wasn't as bad as this one.

CHAPTER 4

Home

Dinner was a daily ritual. If it wasn't at home, it was at my work. Most nights when I worked late, Judy would bring me a cooked dinner. She would pack up the kids, and come out and see me. I was so nice. It was such a great break in my day.

One day, I got to meet Sadie. Sharon, Cheri, and Judy came out as usual with dinner, and Sharon had this adorable Sheltie on a leash. I thought, "What the heck is this?" It was such a surprise to me. We had talked about getting a dog, but I never really pursued it, because I wasn't a house dog kind of guy.

You could see that the kids were having fun and they enjoyed her. I was hesitant. I asked, "Do you have bowls for her? Does she have a place to stay?" Judy already had it all figured out.

They left, and I came home. There she was in her box. They got Sadie because a neighbor's daughter got one and she was telling Judy about it, so they went out and got her. I lost.

I set the ground rules—no bathroom, no bedroom, no furniture. That lasted long. She would stare out the window, standing up on the chair, looking out of it. She would stop when I would come in.

She was friendly to anybody, but, she didn't like the other men coming in. She liked our family, especially the girls, but later after the divorce, she started to bond with me, and it was like that till the day she died. It was a great having her, and for me, in retrospect, probably one of the best decisions that were made *for* me.

Thank God for Sadie. She was brown and white and adorable, and a faithful and loyal friend to the end.

Dinner at home was something I always looked forward to when I didn't have to work late. On Fridays or Saturdays, I would sometimes take them out, and on Sundays we'd have a big dinner. Occasionally, on Saturdays we'd go to my in-laws for dinner.

For anniversaries and dates, I made it a point to remember Judy. I always took her to dinner. We'd get a sitter, get dressed up, and go to her favorite restaurant. We'd still have a family party and cake; but, that night was ours to celebrate.

For vacations, it was always fun, but we went where she wanted to go. We were a family, and that's how we did it.

If she needed something new, I would get it for her. She always got the best that she wanted. She still cleaned and cooked; but I missed the signs that something was wrong. I would miss the little subtleties; nothing was straightforward.

She asked me if she could go take dancing lessons in the afternoon, and I said, "Ok." Next thing you know, she was gone three times a week.

About that time, she got a job. During the time I was home from my accident and my surgery, we did spend good quality time together. She made me food, snacks, comforted me, and really took care of me.

CHAPTER 5

"I don't know how I feel about you anymore."

We were on the interstate coming back from Sally and Don's, my in-law's house. I was driving down the road at sixty-five mph, the weather was good, and I sensed that *something* was wrong, but I didn't have the guts to ask. Coming out of Mistyville, after a couple of weeks of wondering, I asked, "Honey, what was the matter?" and she said, "I don't know how I feel about you anymore." At that moment, she wrecked my world, and I almost wrecked the car. From that point to exiting off the freeway, I don't remember having any conversation at all between there and here. It was just complete silence.

I came home and checked on the girls as they were supposed to be, around ten p.m. We went to another room to talk, and sat there, and I had her explain to me what was wrong, and that's when she asked me for a disillusionment, no reason why. I had to find out my own way. She didn't know how she felt about me anymore, and that she didn't think she loved me any longer at that point.

She sat there for a while, even as I cried a lot, and tried to comfort me. Then we cleaned up, and went to bed. She went to bed first, and I went a little bit later, next to her. Judy let me give her a kiss on the cheek, and I told her that I loved her. She just rolled over and went to sleep.

Next day, I sent her flowers. Her friend Yvette was here and I don't know what Judy told her. I stayed awake all night, cried, wondering why this is happening. I would get up all night, smoke, drink coffee, and cry, maybe have a drink or two. When it was time to go to work, I got up and left, and gave her a kiss on the cheek like I always did. She didn't get up.

I went up 165, not being aware of things, of course, still wondering why this was occurring. I went down Seed Lane, left on Nottingham, to Russell, which would take me over to Janson's. I went to work, and I tried to do my things, whatever was necessary. Joseph, a co-worker, was watching me, and said, "What are you doing?! I've never seen you cut lumber like that before!" I looked at it and had seen what I was doing, and it was amateur compared to what I usually had done. At that time, at ten a.m., I told Joseph what my problems were, and thus started a long list of conversations in our lives.

After we talked a while, and he'd get my head together, he'd build me up, encourage me, and I was able to go work for a while, then he'd come back, and do it again. *He* was my angel. It's how I made it through the day. It was a tough day of my life. I'd rather hit that darn tree on 165, than go thru *that* day again. I don't remember how long I was at work.

I was completely beside myself, and befuddled. My thoughts all day were on us and the kids. How could I live my life without her? I just muddled thru the day. I didn't ruin the wood, but I would have caused myself a lot of extra work.

We always had coffee breaks and lunch, but I lived on coffee and smoked. I didn't eat that day, and for several weeks afterward. I went from a thirty-six inch to a thirty-inch waist. Cigarettes and coffee were my staples in life. I lost about forty-five to fifty pounds.

There was also a business contact named Matt Madden who helped me out. He was a salesman and a material supplier. I knew him for years and later we became close. He was really involved in his church. He was a really super-nice guy, joking around, and very friendly. Matt knew how I was at times, and tried to get me out of it.

He knew how to get me out of my moods and helped me get my feelings into perspective and build me up. How can you get by without people like this in your life? Even if it was for five minutes, it would brighten my day. While we were ordering parts, he would ask how I was, the kids, Judy, and if I'd seen her. We'd talk about it. He'd quote scripture, and remind me even though I wanted Judy back, God may not want that for me. Matt also said that life isn't always the way you want it, sometimes you have to put the past behind you, and go ahead towards tomorrow. My problem is that I want to put yesterday behind me, and I want Judy in my tomorrow.

I came home like normal, either retracing my route or taking Bridge St. back to 165. I didn't know what would transpire and be waiting for me when I got home. Driving through Morris and Zinnia, my mind was so puzzled, and I had no clarity of anything. I had no real thoughts; everything was so confused. How can I fix this? She was *my* world; what would I do without my *world*?

We went out to dinner with Beth one time, and I had taken the girls to a restaurant. I ordered a chicken dinner, and I brought the whole thing home. She remarked to Judy, "You're killing him; look how thin he is." I just couldn't eat, knowing what was going on.

It was dark coming home. I didn't remember the weather; I was driving normally to get to my address to the unexpected. I turned right on my street, to my blue house, *our* blue house. I was anxious, not knowing what to look forward to. I pulled in the drive. I parked my car, and pulled in my spot.

I came in the house, with the flowers sitting on the table, from Salen's. Judy was in the kitchen, carrying on like nothing ever happened. She said that Lee was here, and she told her that she and I were having a problem. That's all that was said about the flowers.

I went up to her to hug her and kiss her, and she pushed me away. She said, "Don't bother me." This was a change to how she used to act, when I would come up behind her, hug her and give her a kiss when she would be cooking, and she would kiss me back. We weren't afraid to show affection around our girls, but then that day it all came to a crashing halt.

We ate dinner like we usually did, and we acted like normal in front of the girls. I didn't eat very much. The girls didn't suspect anything, and we had our meal as usual.

Things were normal, but when the girls got to bed, I'd try to talk to her. Sometimes she would push me off or we'd talk a little bit. I couldn't get anywhere with it, and I couldn't find out what it was. I couldn't resolve the problem. I was her miracle man, and I couldn't make sense of it.

We went to bed, and she slept on her side, and I laid on mine. I still felt whole, but a *fractured* whole. I was starting to tear apart and I wanted to stop it, and she wasn't helping me any by not telling me what was wrong, so how could I answer it? What was the real problem? This repeated in my head. I was locked into myself; I couldn't even begin to see how my girls were going to act.

On Cheri's birthday that year, four days after Judy had asked me for a divorce, I had to go thru torture to be at her birthday party; I had to make myself smile. Judy's parents were there, along with Beth, Will, Andrea and the kids. I don't think that Sally and Don knew at the time, or any of the family. It was tough as she blew out the candles on her cake, opening presents for the last time from both of us. Judy had made her favorite, chocolate. That day was misery, as was *every* day after that.

The same thing went on for the next three weeks. I kept doing my investigating, to find out the predicament. All the days were about the same. We went through our daily rituals; she had a meal for us; Sharon or Cheri would come home and tell us about something funny that day. I'd smile; Judy would smile; no one knew the difference.

As I mentioned, Judy worked part-time at the nearby store one to two days per month. She also went dancing at the time with her girlfriend Yvette, to fill up some time in the day while I was off at work, and some evenings.

Her friend had an outfit to wear, so Judy needed an outfit, of course. I don't think that she set out to meet someone else at the dance place; it just happened.

That place took her out of my life.

I had to work a lot. I only wanted to give her the best that I could. I wasn't one to keep up with the Joneses. I wanted to be happy, make the kids happy, and well-dressed. That made *her* happy.

I got married young; I didn't change my mind. I knew what I wanted from day one: a house, the kids. *Nothing* was unplanned. I enjoyed my work; I wouldn't be anything else. I was happy with myself; I was perfectly content with the four of us: the *four* of us, in this little house; the four of us, as a family. *Why* did things have to change?

If you really wanted to make it work, you would. The excuse doesn't matter: another man or money. The excuse it just that, an excuse.

Judy went dancing a few nights a week. Sometimes I would go with her. At his time, I didn't know what the dilemma was, or what was putting us at an impasse.

When I was doing my investigating, Joseph would go and ask her questions, and then I started confiding in Beth, Judy's sister. She would ask her, "What is the matter?" The both of them came to me with clues, but provided me with a path to figure out my answers; they didn't tell me directly. I don't think they wanted me to think of them as the bearer of bad news.

They would tell me that she had a dance partner who I knew. He was having a situation at home, and he and Judy were getting too chummy. They worded it so that I would figure out that this was my problem with another man who was in the picture.

Ironically, I knew *who* this guy was. We were at a party. He was with his wife, and we met her. I never noticed at the time, but later on, when I talked to her on the telephone, she mentioned that they had separated after that. She noticed the way they danced at the party. She got conveniently sick, I believe from noticing how close they danced together. We dropped her off and he brought us back to the house. It was just a normal night after that. We slow danced with each other's wives.

His name was Bob, but I didn't call him that. He was not an honorable man in my book. I was brought up to be honorable, honest, fair, and old-fashioned. He took my life and my wife away. If he only had the guts to call me up and say, "Curt, you have a problem with your wife," I would have done the same for him. It was just the way I was raised, the way that I feel. An admirable man would do the right thing, and he did a dishonorable thing.

At that point, Judy asked me to sit down and for us to have a talk. We walked in, and *he* was already sitting there. I didn't shake his hand; I didn't think it was worth it. She wanted a peaceful disillusionment, not a divorce.

We had talked about how she wanted the house and the girls, and she wanted me to leave. I never considered leaving, and once I found out that there was another man at our conversation, I let the surprise out. I had completely different thoughts than what she thought I had.

I wanted the girls *and* the house. She could take her car, and she could also take her personal things and leave.

Once I told her that, her chin dropped, because she expected *me* to give her everything *she* wanted, instead of me wanting to stay. I think she was equally surprised that I desired to raise my two daughters, for what man wants to raise two girls, except at the loss of his wife? It was unheard of back then.

I know everyone said, "Boy, you are *different*, taking it all!" If a man has to raise teenagers, he'll take his son, as opposed to his daughter. A man can relate to his son more than his daughter.

But, not me. I related fully with my girls. I was both Mom and Dad to them. I bought them their clothes with their help, and still kept the house in order and put meals on the table. I was proud that I could do this, and it kept me going. If it wasn't for them, I would be dead years ago, and I often thought of doing that.

He told her how much he loved her, over coffee. He was sorry how the situation went. It was coming from a very low man.

He asked me to go around the corner and talk. We did, just to calm me down. He asked if we wanted to go outside. I said that it didn't help the situation. I knew at that time, there wasn't a lot that I was going to do, except keep fighting the battle.

We went back in, finished up there, picked up the girls and went home. Judy didn't really say much at the table. She did offer me the house, and she wanted the girls. She *always* wanted the girls.

I told Bob and Judy that they weren't going to get the girls and they weren't good enough to raise them. I know I overprotected her, and at that moment I had some awful feelings, but I know I would have never hurt her.

At that point, we went home, and I had my usual coffee and cigarettes, with now drinks added to the mix, and little sleep. I was exasperated, and I was my usual self, bewildered and lost.

Shortly after, Judy was still living at the house. We were in the process of discussing where the girls were going to live. I, of course, wanted the girls to stay here. Judy was trying to get Sharon to come live with her, but I always wanted to keep the girls together, not separate, and in the same school with their old friends, so their lives wouldn't be disrupted any more than it had to be.

One Sunday, when my niece Stacey was here, Judy called all three girls in the kitchen, even though I told her, "No," periodically, and she told the girls that we were getting a divorce. She told them she wanted them to go with her. I was standing in the kitchen. Their expressions were shocked, especially for Cheri, being more mature.

The girls made a decision that they would come with me. Whether in anger or haste, they told Judy as she was standing in the kitchen that they were coming with me. Cheri said it first, and then Sharon spoke up and said that she was going to stay with her sister. Judy was visibly upset, but she didn't cry. She even danced that night with Yvette, and met Bob there.

Judy asked Cheri if she would go live with me or her, and Cheri said, "I want to stay with Dad." Then she turned to Sharon, and said, "Sharon, don't you want to come live with me?" and Sharon said, "I want to stay with my sister." Judy's chin dropped, and she asked her, "Are you sure you don't want to come live with me?" Sharon refused; Stacey just stood there in awe.

Cheri looked at me in hatred, thinking it was my decision, and I told her it wasn't my fault and I want Mommy to stay. Sharon never said much else after that. Then they went dancing, and it was the beginning of the wall that built between them. Since the girls decided to stay with me, whoever got the girls got the house, per our agreement. Although, one time, Judy did say, she gets the girls and I get the house.

After I explained my side of the story, Cheri was ok with me. I told her I didn't want the divorce, and I wanted to work it out, but her mother didn't want to.

I was at the house by myself, drinking and smoking, but I never drank enough that I couldn't handle it. Actually, I drank one-fifth of vodka every night, and it never phased me. I couldn't believe it that it came to this; how it came to this. Why? Her excuses were that we grew apart, she married too young, and added that I worked too much.

After that, she would start sleeping with Cheri, until she moved out. I kept talking to her in-between, sending her flowers, acting like a date. I tried everything people would tell me, hoping I would spark something, but I didn't even have a chance. She already had her mind made up.

Around that time, we were at a show and the group sang "You Don't Bring Me Flowers," and I looked at Judy and said, "I understand what that means now."

We went out to dinner after that show, and came home like nothing ever happened.

I would talk to Joseph, and then to Matt on Tuesdays, and he was trying to keep my head together, as well. Matt would pray with me at work. Joseph would try to keep me going at my job.

Cheri had a suspicion that this is happening because of Bob. He and Judy got an apartment, and she would pack while I was at work.

This went on for a couple of weeks, until the last day she was here. It was a Saturday, and I didn't realize that it was going to be the final day. It was early evening, and she brought her suitcases out. They were packed. She told the girls she was leaving, and loaded up her car; Sharon told her she didn't want her to leave. Cheri went to her room. I asked her not to leave. "Please don't do this," I begged. She pulled out the driveway and left. We all three watched her leave and cried. Cheri was swearing and crying, and Sharon just cried and went to her bedroom.

The day after she left, she took the good dishes, the silverware, her good pots and pans, her cedar chest, and took everything off her dresser: perfumes, mirrors, her jewelry box, and clothes, just everything. That cedar chest was a gift before we got married; the good dishes were a wedding present. It was like walking into an empty house, with her being, spirit and presence just gone. It was the end of our family as we knew it. It has never been the same since, the three of us losing *our* Judy.

That night, I changed the locks, and bought brand-new door locks. I had extra keys made, one for Sharon and one for Cheri. I wasn't going to have Judy come back with Bob and go thru my house and take whatever they wanted. I don't think she ever came back, so I didn't hear any complaints about her not being able to get in.

I kept trying to get her back, since she wasn't married yet to Bob. After she was married to him, I still would try, since Beth would tell me that she wasn't happy.

In-between, I tried to get Judy to go to the pastor to meet with him, for counseling. I learned to let my daughters get the tension out, that's why I didn't correct Cheri. Then Cheri didn't use the word "Mom" anymore.

The pastor didn't know how to get Judy back. Without her there, we couldn't get this together. He just wanted me to keep me together for my kids. My head was lost, and I was trying to keep it together, since their heads were lost, too.

When she was gone, I felt like death. There's no other way to put it. Nothing mattered. I had my girls, and they chose *me* to raise them. I had my responsibility to them to take care of them, and I did, for all those years.

CHAPTER 6

Suicide

I never drank until the kids went to bed. I no longer had a stomach, and my heart went out the door with her. She still has it, though, but not as much as she used to.

After that day, I started seriously thinking of suicide. I'd think about suicide here and there and seriously when I would go and attempt it. Sometime that week, after the kids went to school, I got the bottle of prescription sleeping pills from Dr. Lintel, a skin doctor from Piperton. I had a full bottle, the pills being no bigger than a bebe. There were sixty to ninety pills in a bottle. I took the lid off, and I was in the bathroom. I had a glass of water, and I was ready to put the pills in my mouth. I wanted to get rid of the pain.

Sadie, my guardian angel, who was never allowed in the bathroom or my bedroom, ran in and pounced on me, knocking the pills out of the bottle. They flew all over the bathroom floor, some in the commode, tub, and sink. Then she backed up right to the edge of the bathroom door, with her head cocked and her tail wagging, looking at me like, "What do you think you are doing?" She brought me to my senses. I started thinking, how would my girls react to this, how would my parents act when they already lost one son, how would Tim act when he already lost one brother, and how would my other siblings act, and what about my friends? That's the way the routine went every time. After Sadie woke me up, I thought of Cheri coming home, and finding me dead.

The next day was the same thing: the kids went to school, and I went to the closet and got my gun. I took the cylinder and took all the bullets out, all but one. I took the gun back to my bedroom. I eventually gave the gun to Judy, and she gave it to my grandson. They don't know what that gun was used for.

I was standing up and looking out through the window, across the bed. I was thinking that I got to stop the pain. I put the gun to my head, pulled the hammer back. There was no pressure on the trigger, and here comes Sadie pouncing at me *again*, knocking me off balance. It knocked me out of my trance, and she ran back to the bedroom doorway, with her head cocked and tail wagging, looking at me like, "What do you think you're doing?" The same thing was happening all over again, and I thought of my girls. We're lucky the gun didn't go off.

When I was about to kill myself, I wouldn't think of Judy. I would go thru the list first, and Judy wasn't even on it. I don't know why, probably because she was the reason I was in pain in the first place.

She and Bob had no idea what I was doing. I didn't care. I just wanted my baby doll back. If the cost to being without her would be to end my life, then so be it.

I was nuts for quite a while. It took everything out of me to get to work; it took everything out of me to deal with what I had to handle. I had to contend with taking care of my girls. I would go to work and talk to Joseph, and I wouldn't tell him what I did, but that I was thinking of killing myself. He just listened to me and tried to get my head on straight. I knew I could trust him.

When Matt would come in, I would have a discussion with him and he would do the same. I would get depressed again, and start all over. Take the gun out, do the same things. Sadie would come in and knock the gun out of my hand as usual, and knock me to my senses.

When you get in that state, there's nothing to pull you out. When you get to that point, you get into a trance. You don't know what brings you out of it.

The fourth time, I went downstairs and I went into the bathroom and shut the door. Sadie couldn't get at me. I spun the cylinder, put the gun to my temple, and pulled the trigger. I heard a click but it made me so mad that it didn't go off and take me out of my trance. While I played Russian roulette with my .22 that day, I found a blank. I was disappointed. I would *never* leave it unloaded again.

I had to face life all over once more. It brought me to thoughts of my girls, my parents, and my brothers, my sister, and my friends.

Next time, I loaded the gun all over. No more Russian roulette. I wasn't going to miss *this* time. I went to the bedroom, not thinking of Sadie, and she did it to me again. Darn dog, but my little angel she was.

Another suicide attempt was one night while I was at Beth's place. It was the last time. I had Judy's car. I actually had seen her that night, when we transferred cars at our houses so she could take the kids out. After she took my car, I went to Beth's apartment because I had plans to help her with some boxes. It snowed real heavy that night—wet snow, four to five inches of it; her parking lot was behind her house.

As I tried to come up out of the driveway, I got stuck in the middle of the hill. God was telling me, "Enough is *enough!*" It took me half of an hour to shovel snow to get out of the hill in the parking lot.

I was going to take the car on the freeway, open it up and let go of the steering wheel. It was an automatic wreck job.

It was just one of those things. There wasn't really a particular reason why I did that that night, other than I still wanted the pain to go away. I was still suffering from depression. I'm glad that God stopped me that night. If it wasn't for the snow, I definitely would have been dead. In my selfish trance I didn't even think that I could have killed someone else on the interstate (A friend brought that up). That was the end of that night.

On Easter, the day before we were scheduled to sign the divorce papers, the kids got lots of compliments for taking her out to dinner. I had mixed feelings at the dinner—it was my last shot, while I tried to get her back.

I'll never forget that last Easter—our *last* meal together before the big "D". I bought Judy a beautiful corsage. The girls and I accompanied her to dinner that day; we were *so* excited. After church, she came over and we drove to Gina's Place. I was so proud. It was such a wet, rainy day, but I'll *never* forget it.

I was taking her to our last official meal as a complete family. I had on a nice suit; the girls were in nice dresses. Judy looked lovely; I gave her the corsage. It was Easter, and I was *determined*. I dropped her and the girls off at the door.

We were there at Gina's Place for quite a while. I just wanted it to go on *forever*. I didn't remember if I ate anything at that time. I probably ordered a small steak, and had a few bites of it. Ironically, the family was together as we were for the last time, and we would be officially and legally torn apart within twenty-four hours. We dropped her off after that, with her corsage and all.

The day I got divorced—I really didn't know what to expect. In the courtroom, it was just me and her, and the judge. I felt like I was in a hole, and I couldn't get out of it. He asked her if she wanted a divorce, and she said, "Yes." Then he asked me, and I said, "Well no, but how am I going to make her love me if she don't want to?" He went through the terms, and we signed the paper. We went outside the courtroom, and he had her wait while we went over and did a quick-claim deed for the house.

After being in the courtroom, I didn't know how I would feel. I had taken the gun along, and had taken it apart, and put the body of the gun in the glove box and the cylinder in the console. After I left the courtroom, I went to my car. It was around noon, and it was a sunny day, fairly warm. I took the body of the gun out of the glove box, and the cylinder out of the console, and put the gun together. It was fully loaded. I pulled the hammer back, and I started to think as I sat there and looked at the gun. I had tears in my eyes, and then they were running down my face until I couldn't see anymore. I put the gun to my temple, and just thought of my girls at that point. I don't know whatever got me out of my trance. Someone could've blown their horn, or people were talking. Whatever it was, it just brought me out of my daze. I tore up the gun and put it away. I started to realize that if I would have shot myself, then Judy would have gotten what she wanted. She would have married Bob sooner, got the girls and the house. The girls would have hated me for me putting them in that situation for the rest of their lives.

I then came home. I wasn't here too long, and I started to cry and hit the front door with my fist and heard the door crack. A little bit later on, Beth came to see how I was, and then Joseph came. Beth stayed with me for a while; Joseph eventually had to get back to work.

Later on that day, I went to Beth's. She was another angel to me. I talked to Kathy later on that evening, too. I had a lot of angels back then. Joseph came over that night as well. He was always worried about me.

Joseph wanted to make sure I was ok, till the kids came home. When Cheri and Sharon came home, I was still lost. I don't remember much about that evening. It was kind of a blur. After the kids went to bed, I sat up drinking coffee and smoking, and drinking. It was a short night; I didn't sleep that much. Next morning, it was the same routine, dropping the girls off to school. I went to work, sat down and talked to Joseph and Camren until I got motivated to go and do something. I'd concentrate on my job until I would get it done. I was trying to dig myself out of a big hole; that's what it was. I didn't know how to do it. I'd sit there and wonder, "What can I do to get her back?" I still think of it.

I had told Beth a week later about my experience after the courtroom that day, and also about my suicide notes. My final letters went like this: each time I tried to kill myself I put a lot of thought into my notes. I destroyed all the others. They were short, apologizing to the kids, and saying, "Don't hate me." I just couldn't live without Judy anymore—the pain was just too much.

She told me to destroy them. I didn't want to. I found them recently, and I haven't looked at them in years. I was shocked to have even seen them.

A friend mentioned to me that after her father died, she read somewhere that there is now a *split*. There are things that happen that are so traumatic, and there is the life before and the life after that point in time. She asked me if that's how I feel, and I said, "Yes." The people and things are the same, it's just *different*.

We *exist* at those splits in time. My friend says, "You're going thru life in a straight line. Then the first fracture comes, the first break. Then another fracture and you split again. Then another fracture and you split yet *again*. You're *never* the same again after all those splits."

Sometimes you feel you are, but you know that you're *not*.

I had already been in several major accidents, I lost my brother, and the love of my life had left. I was attempting suicide several times. How many more splits *could* I take?

When I told Beth, she was absolutely flabbergasted. She was surprised that I would take it that far. I gave the gun to Joseph. He suspected but didn't know what I had done. I trusted him with my gun. A couple of years later, I asked for it back.

Beth didn't suggest that I should go see anybody. She knew I was already lost. I never even told Matt. I thought about death a lot, but never specifically pointed it out.

CHAPTER 7

Our 'open' divorce

I don't know why I married her. Here I was, finding myself alone to raise two kids. It was hard. I worked a lot. I had to help Cheri to cook dinner every night, and assist her with the chores. Sometimes both Sharon and Cheri would make hamburgers and French fries, or hash browns and a cooked meat.

My typical day was getting to work by nine, and working ten to twelve hours a day. I'd mow the lawn, do laundry, and clean things. I was *both* mom and dad. That was hard. It's like when a parent dies, you have to be both for your kids. I had to set the rules at home for discipline and dating. I know my girls leaned on me more than they should've had to, but, that's just how it was.

I even played the role of party planner. For every function or holiday, I had to set things up, like Cheri's confirmation, or Mother's Day. I had to invite Judy to a given function, and risk her saying, "No." When she would do that, it would just break mine and the girls' hearts.

It was a strange relationship, our *open* divorce. Some people have an open marriage, but we had an open divorce, in the visiting sense. I always tried to include Judy in everything going on in *our* house, which now belonged to Cheri, Sharon and me. It was a strange setup, and the whole thing seemed rather unnatural to me. Their mother wasn't there to help with the daily issues and chores. She wasn't there for them to enjoy a good home-cooked meal, or to make home-baked cookies. The smell of fresh pancakes or waffles in the morning on the weekends was now non-existent. Now *I* had to do it all, with Cheri's help.

The girls felt that she divorced them, too, because she wasn't here to raise them. A mother should be here rearing them day-by-day, not when she wanted them, not when she felt it was convenient. She couldn't be somewhere else, or with someone else, and bringing them up at the same time, they felt.

Sharon used to pray at night, that Judy would come back. I would too, many times at night or in the day, with tears running down my cheeks when I was driving.

I was the dad and I raised the kids. How many people do you know like this? It's usually the mom that raises the kids. The mom always gets them. In this case, Cheri told her mother that she was staying with me, and Sharon said she was going with her sister. Judy was appalled. She thought for sure that the girls wanted to be with her—they *didn't*.

Anytime something happened, I was there for her, since not only I still loved her, but I took the opportunity to always win her back.

In my family, divorce was looked upon by my parents as not a good thing, but they pitied people who got a divorce. When my uncle (my dad's brother) got divorced, they said nothing. If they seen my aunt out, they'd talk to her.

When I got divorced, it broke their hearts. When Candy, my sister, got divorced, they were glad. It was such a shock to everyone when we got divorced, because we really clicked. We never really argued. Trivial stuff was really stupid to me. I didn't think it was worth arguing about. Yes, Judy did get mad at me here and there, and I got her mad here and there, so I would go downstairs and do some woodworking, and go outside and work on my cars.

The only thing I would have done differently is that I wouldn't let her go dancing so much. She was dancing in the morning, a few days a week, plus Sunday night. At dancing, she got in with a crowd that had a lot of divorcees. She would always talk about how, "This one's getting divorced, that person's getting divorced," and would even say, "this guy is leaving his wife for this woman, and she's leaving her husband for him." After six months of dancing she asked me for the divorce. It was an immoral place.

She always felt that I didn't make enough for her. Judy also said I spent too much time at work, with the girls, or working at home. There was always something she would say. There was only one working here at the house, not two. She was planning on going to school. We then had Cheri, so she didn't go. She never told me that later she wanted to go to school. If she had, I would have done everything to make sure that she could go: finding money for school, helping to watch the kids.

But later on, after we were divorced, she would call me and tell me that I'm her *miracle* man. If she didn't know that before, I don't know what to say. She told Beth that she understood why I worked, and why I did put in extra hours there.

My parents never judged Judy, but my brothers did. Even Bob said, "I don't think that Judy is ever coming back. But all she talks about is you and your family." I can't believe he said that to me.

Judy told her mother that we're just friends. Sally was concerned at any time in-between other guys, that Judy was leading me on. Sally actually called me one day and asked me about it. I didn't want to hurt anybody, so I just shrugged it off. I feel that she *was* leading me on, and I was hoping that I was a gambler, and I would hit my lucky number and get the prize. Lady Luck was *never* with me.

All of our friends disappeared because they didn't know how to handle it—they *all* stopped going out with us; they stopped coming around. Once in the mall, our best friends just let Judy have it. Judy didn't know why they were so mean to her.

To me, the divorce was worse than if she had died. I had to love her from a distance. If she had died it would be final, final that I knew she wouldn't be coming back. Instead, I had this continuous, lingering hope that she would come back to me. One time she was at the house before we got divorced. She remarked to me, "What would happen if I wanted to come back?" I said, "All you have to do is throw your dancing shoes away and stop seeing Bob." I was a forgiving man, and I just wanted to have her back in our home and in my heart, where she belonged. And to the kids, that's where they wanted her to be. Their whole world was wrapped around their mom and dad and their friends.

At the bank and in church, a friend really changed. She noticed me at both places. She would partially acknowledge me. Gone were the days of meeting at a school function or visiting these friends at their homes for cards. I really missed the evenings of coffee and talking. We were all now *strangers.*

The same year I got divorced, Lou, my brother-in-law, came to visit. He stayed for a while and got a job about twenty miles away. He lived here from around three or six months. It was his try to get back together. I knew it wouldn't work.

For a few years, Lou and I helped each other out. He was a comedian with a hole in his heart, too. Unfortunately, we had something in common that year. We would talk and visit, and offered a shoulder to lean on each other.

There were times when Judy would stop over to see her "special person." There were many times I would want to tell her to "get lost," but I just couldn't. Judy would come here to get the car washed, fixed, or visit with the kids. I was glad to do it; I just wanted to see her. But we wouldn't have time to talk, because the girls were here.

I often wanted to hold her hand, and I cared but I did not dare. I desired to, but I knew she wouldn't want to hold my hand. Sometimes we would sit at the table, and I could hold her hand, and it was wonderful.

I did enjoy her being here. I was hoping that just being me, and being nice to her, that she would come back.

Even though we were divorced, I would take her out to dinner with me and the kids, trying to get her back into the family. We even went "X"-mas shopping together, and we wrapped "X"-mas presents together. We had "X"-mas for her here before we went to see my mom and dad. We didn't want to face our first "X"-mas without her. She even helped cook.

Judy was jealous of Cheri. She was jealous that I would buy nice clothes for Cheri and nice dresses for her to go out in. She would actually borrow dresses and sweaters from her, and even borrowed a coat one night to go out with Charlie, another guy.

One time, Cheri and Judy got into a screaming match. Cheri asked her why we got divorced. Judy said that I was kind and good-hearted, a good father, and a good provider. "But," Judy said, "I don't love him, and he forgets about my inner feelings."

No one had seen Judy's comment coming. We were perplexed then, as much we were now. Lou even commented to me one time, "You need *idiot* lessons." I did; I just couldn't make myself that way.

She would come here and wash her car and even eat dinner while

Bob was at work before their wedding. One time I got so mad at her because she just started blaming things at me, and I just said, "If you feel this way, you need to get out of here."

Beth didn't like what her sister was doing. She would tell me damaging things that Judy was doing, in order to allow me to let it go. I believe she felt that if I got mad enough at her, I could do that. It just hurt. It really wasn't my business what she was doing, since she was no longer married to me.

Beth said, "There are rotten guys out there, not like Curt."

To prove this point, on our anniversary I sent her several beautiful long-stem roses and wrote on the card, "Remember today." On the next day, she showed up and took the rest of her clothes to her new home. I was just spent after that.

One time, Judy called me and told me she got married. Joseph came here that day. It was coming down. Joseph, Kathy and Beth knew it. They all knew it. She paid for the honeymoon on *my* credit card. How ironic, that I paid for another man's honeymoon with my wife. We were out that weekend, so I didn't know for sure when it was. Ironically, I put my wedding ring in the safety deposit box just the day before because I knew I wouldn't be wearing it anymore. I wore the other wedding band for a while, the one I wore to work. A few people would make comments about it, and I would tell people, "I am still married; I'm still married in my heart." Three days later, I asked for the credit card back.

I didn't get Judy anything for her birthday that year, because she had hurt me. If she would've not gotten married, I would have bought her something, maybe a real nice sweater.

I was always getting gifts. I never forgot an event. I pride myself on that. Every birthday, anniversary, Christmas, Sweetest Day, and Mother's Day, and Easter, I never forgot. I could tell you my kids' birthdays if you'd ask me.

My birthday was at my home that year, with Don and Sally, and Beth.

We went to Sally and Don's for Thanksgiving. I was very sad, and I didn't want the girls to know it. It was strange for me to be at Sally and Don's, cutting the turkey, with something important missing. I was invited to Sally and Don's, but Judy wasn't. Sally would harp at Judy for not being at home and raising the girls.

That Thanksgiving was pure misery. Like normal, I didn't eat very much.

I was very thin. It was very lonely for me, that Judy wasn't there. It was so different without her at my side.

The holidays just really did me in. That night, after coming home from Sally and Don's, I was just sitting there on the couch with Sharon. I was glad the day was over. There was a commercial about dish soap, and how your hands look after. I said to Sharon, "My hands look like a ninety-year-old person's," and joked about it. As I walked away, I said, "Yes, ninety-year-old hands, eighty-year-old skin, a back of an eighty-year-old, a mind of a thirty-eight-year-old broken man, and a heart that is broken and dead." That is how I felt. To myself, I said, "I am no good to anyone but my girls. When it is over (raising them), I got to go. Death is my best answer."

She had called that morning at ten to see if she could stop over, and of course I said, "Yes." I was so glad to see her. You just don't know how I feel inside when she comes and she wants to talk.

I went into the garage to get a hammer. I came in to get coffee, and Sharon said she left ten minutes ago. I was so disappointed.

I couldn't believe she left.

In the afternoon we got ready to go to Sally and Don's. Driving over there, back on the interstate, I was thinking that I didn't like the position that I was in, and it was *another* holiday without her. I wasn't surprised that Sally and Don invited me for dinner, since I considered them parents and they considered me a son.

The whole thing was strange since she wasn't *there*. A part of my family was gone. It's like someone dying. Every day is a new experience. Some are the same, and some are new.

We stayed at Sally and Don's quite a while, and then made the journey back. That part of the highway and those memories and what she said there to me were always in my head for a long time on that stretch of road. I might have been talking to the girls, but those memories were still with me. Part of me was gone. It was a really strange day. I would relive that day often, for years. Her words just stuck and were imbedded in my head.

Just like usual, we went home, and I put my girls to bed. I was smoking and drinking, and I didn't get much sleep that night, or the night before. Now it was over, and tomorrow was another day. I wrote in my diary, and tried to get some sleep.

I couldn't handle the situation, that's why I drank and smoked so much. I smoked one to two cigarettes a day before we got married, a half pack when we were married, then at least one pack a day or more after everything happened. I didn't quit till over twenty years later. Like I mentioned, at one point I drank a fifth of vodka a night.

It was just too much stress on me, the situation that occurred. That's why alcohol didn't even bother me. My doctor felt I was so far out there, and that's why the alcohol never really affected me. He was a skin doctor, but he was my friend. He thought my skin would be erupting by now. I wouldn't blame my skin problems directly on the divorce, because I don't know for sure if that's what really caused it. It had an effect on me indirectly, maybe. It's like the suicide attempts. I couldn't handle the situation; I couldn't handle the stress of it all.

You do forget your problems if you get drunk enough. Lots of guys do that for a couple of hours, to get that release. I just never got that drunk, since I was so stressed. I must say, I did write better when I did drink.

I would fall into the pit, many times for years.

In addition, when I would be driving on Rt. 165 to go home, I would 'hit' that tree all over again. This went on for years as well.

Joseph was the only one that knew I thought about suicide, until I told Beth. It was just the way that Joseph would say things, to make sure that I was "here in the morning to learn something else off of." Later that year, I told Beth. She told me not to keep the notes, but I did. I did write notes every time I tried to kill myself; I would then destroy them. I would keep them for a couple of days. Sometimes I kept the same note for at least three suicide attempts.

In all, there were three sets of letters. Most of the time, I would get up in the morning and take the girls to school. I'd come back on days I'd decide to do it. It wasn't a planned thing. I'd make a decision in my mind that I needed to leave them something. Then I'd sit down and write. All three sets of letters were pretty similar. If I had an unsuccessful suicide attempt, in my mind at that time, I'd put the letters back in my upper dresser drawer underneath the socks, not in any particular corner. I was hoping that Cheri and Sharon would *never* find them.

The letters went like this:

> To my Dearest Judy,
>
> This is a hell of a way out. But I have no other choice. For living without you, and the thought of another holding you and kissing you just tears my mind and heart apart.
>
> I hope you never find out or feel the pain you have caused me and the girls. But I give you this book I wrote about what was happening to me. So you can get an idea how I feel and felt about things. You say you don't love me anymore. But I really think you don't know what love is.
>
> Love is a concern, a care, a tenderness and a regard for others. It doesn't focus on personal difference, self-fulfillment, and self-importance. I guess I have lost a little of my love. But my pain has gone on too long. And my heart no longer can take it.
>
> I figured if I was out of the way altogether, I would make your life a lot easier. Besides, I only build up all these things for you and the girls anyway.
>
> I really never thought much for myself. Just for you and the girls.
>
> You just never understood it, I guess. I always figured you did understand. But you didn't. Just take care of my girls for me.
>
> Do what you want with your life. It is all yours anyway, now. I just hope Bob rots in hell. For what he has done to our family. And for what he has done to his family.

Inside my wedding ring you wrote "till death do us part."

Well, it is death we part.

The one man that loves you truly.

Curt

To Cheri and Sharon:

To the best daughters anyone could hope for. Remember I told you to remember that whatever happened, I love you very much. Just remember it. Help your mother as much as you can.

She does love you, too. But don't love me anymore. And I can't take that.

Tell Dad and Mom I love them. And that I am sorry it ended this way. And I was proud to be a son of such wonderful people. Tell your Uncle Tim and Joe and Barry, thanks for being my brothers. Tell Candy thanks for being my sister. A pretty special girl.

Tell Sally and Don and Beth and Will thanks. And I am sorry it ended this way.

Tell Joseph thanks for all his help. It was just a little bigger than I was. He kept me from going lower than I figured I could go.

Cheri, just grow up to be the beautiful girl I always dreamed you would be. Be kind and considerate of others. Be patient with Sharon and your mother. Always respect yourself. Do the best and be the best you can. Never quit like I did. Keep going to church.

Sharon, just grow up to be the beautiful girl I always dreamed you would be. Be kind and considerate of others. Be patient with Cheri and your mother. Always respect yourself. Do the best and be the best you can. Never quit like I did. Keep going to church.

In life I was very proud of both of you girls, and proud to have your mother at my side. In death I still want to be proud of both of you girls. Tell Stacey I was proud of her, too.

And be proud of who you are and all of your accomplishments in life. I am really proud of you girls.

Don't blame this on your mother. I was the one that decided it this way, not her. But please don't hate me for this. I hope one day you will forgive me.

Your Loving Father

I am really sorry girls, I really am.

Once I got out of my trance, I'd put them back in the drawer. Somewhere deep down I knew I'd need them again, for there was another time coming. The two sets I kept for weeks; the last set I kept for years. I even thought I forgot about the last set.

Until I got into that state again, I'd pull them out, and set them into position, to where they'd be seen. I would go thru the same routine. Take the kids to school; come home, decide to do this once more, get in that mood, pull the gun out, pull the letters out, load the gun, and put the gun together. After that day of Russian roulette, I always kept the cylinder loaded. I wasn't going to *miss*.

Coffee was my staple. I'd have coffee all the time. I'd have my cup; do my routine. I'd come back out, having gotten out of the trance, take everything apart, put it back on the closet shelf, put the letters back, and get my coat and hat on, put Sadie in the basement (where she stayed all day), and go out.

I never thought of doing it while I was dropping Sharon and Cheri off; but it would happen when I got home. Something would always trigger it. This would all happen within a couple of hours.

I was in total misery; I didn't care if I made it to the next step. I'd leave my house, and I didn't care. I knew I had a job, and with the girls, I knew I had to keep on going. I knew I had to figure out how to get her *back*.

My job also kept me going. All the work that needed to be done kept my attention. My whole being was there; I had to bury myself in that job. It's a very detail-oriented job, and it really helped keep me focused. Each job was different.

I worked in an environment that allowed for conversation and closeness among fellow employees. Important bonds were able to take place because of that, like with Joseph, my apprentice. I worked very hard, and you could talk as you were working. Throughout the day, I could talk my situations out. There was a constant coffee break: I'd be smoking and drinking that fine beverage all day.

Joseph never threatened to take me to the hospital, neither did Beth. Joseph probably told me to go see someone. I went to see my pastor, but I don't remember for sure what he said.

Driving down my road to 165, things were on my mind of what had happened. I'd get up 165, near Loland, and there the tree would be. I'd never salute the tree in the morning, only at night, because I'd make it thru the day.

On those days of attempted suicide, I would ask the tree, "Why didn't you just finish the job?" I would always look for the tree, even on the days when I wasn't thinking of killing myself. Then I'd pass Loland, onto Fairway Lane.

Occasionally, I'd think of the father/son combo who'd been there that near-fatal day.

Driving on Fairway Lane to Sunset Drive, over to Tanner Rd, I felt like I was drained. I'd go in, open my toolbox, get another cup of coffee, figure out what I had to do for that day, and try to get myself motivated to do it. I'd go to our manager, he'd give me the assignment, and I'd get to work. I became focused, because I always wanted to do a good job—I had a reputation to hold up.

Not saying a word about what happened, Joseph didn't know, only suspected. He could tell when I was in a certain mood, even though he'd never say anything, and hang around me extra, keeping a watchful eye on me.

I'd go thru the day doing my business, thankful for my job at the end of the day. Every once in a while, I'd drive down Fairway Lane to Jansen St.

Over Willow, down 165, I was passing Loland. I'd salute the tree every day, but on the days that I survived another suicide attempt, I'd say, "We survived another day."

One day, I'd seen there weren't any leaves on the tree. It died. It was an oak tree, at least two feet thick, and thirty feet high. I took over a two-foot vertical section of bark off from the impact.

The days I'd wanted to shoot myself, I'd go about my daily routine, talk to the girls about what we were having for dinner, what they made, or if they needed any homework help.

I ignored what happened those days; I just let it go. First time was a shocker; second time was alarming, third time, it was like, "Oh, well, just another time." "I got used to it; it was just habit.

I always wondered why she left me. She would often say, it's not me, it's her. "It's not your fault, it's mine," she would say. I would ask God for her to come back, and tell me what to do. Sometimes I would holler at Him, and ask, "Why, what can I do? How come you're not helping me? Why don't you send her back? What did *I* do wrong?"

I always went to church. When Judy left, I went more. I'd really listen to the sermons, and they seemed to be saying, "Curt, this is *you*." In addition, Matt Madden would be quoting scripture, and helping me out that way.

Here I was. I was out of my mind for her. I still am.

At that time, I wasn't glad that I didn't succeed. Like chords in a song, we progress thru, like moving thru the rounds of people that I wouldn't want to leave behind: my girls, Mom, Dad, Tim, my younger siblings, my friends, and Judy last. I had to then live another miserable day. Immediately after, I felt stupid. What was I *thinking*? When the gun clicked, I was upset. After that, I stacked the deck. I would *never* miss again.

CHAPTER 8

"X"-mas

We weren't really looking forward to "X"-mas. None of us were, including Judy. I involved her as much as I could, but I decided we were going to Indiana for "X"-mas. I didn't do that to be mean to her, but I just couldn't stand to be here without her.

"X"-mas was on my mind, of course, so I asked Judy to go Christmas shopping after Thanksgiving. I still wanted her to get that old feeling, and come home. That was my motive, to get her home for me and the girls.

We went a couple of times "X"-mas shopping; I'd get her out as many times as possible. I talked to her on the phone on Thanksgiving; we were working some plans out. After that, we made a date, and I picked her up. The day this was scheduled, and I was like a kid in the candy store. I didn't want it to end. I'd put my arm around her, to guide her through the icy parking lots. I was elated, but I knew the 'date' would eventually come to an end.

It was just like when we were married. We picked out clothes for Cheri and Sharon, and we would go out to eat afterwards. I was so excited the entire time, looking for that chance to hold her hand, put my arm around her, just like a guy out on his first date.

I didn't want to ruin the moment and I was a perfect gentleman. It was great when I could 'guide' her. I don't know if she knew what was going on, or if she caught on to my secret plans of getting us back together as a family in time for the "X"-mas holiday. That would make my "X"-mas, if she said she was coming back. I would've cancelled my plans to go to back home if she did that.

I set it up with her that she would have Christmas with the girls before we left. I didn't want the girls to miss out, neither did Judy. The girls would get upset a lot around the holidays—she'd jump at the kids; the kids would get mad at her. The girls would say, "Doesn't she understand? It's the first 'X'-mas without her."

After Thanksgiving, I went outside and put lights out. It was hard, but I wanted to do that, for the girls. Also, we were putting some "X"-mas decorations up, to give it that "X"-mas look. The girls were baking cookies, and they were trying to make new things. I wouldn't keep Judy from coming here. I'd encourage what the kids would want, and they wanted her to make cookies with them. One time, I came home and seen her at home with the kids, and it felt great. I couldn't eat the cookies, but God, I felt good; it was just like old times.

We all had one common goal. They'd all do the same things that I would. We wanted her to come back, to come *home*.

Although the kids would lose their patience, it wasn't so much the youngest, but the oldest. Cheri had it built-in that she was the boss of the house. She was now the mother of the house. When the original mother would come over, they would clash. Judy wouldn't like how Cheri would be with Sharon; she wouldn't like it either.

Sometimes I minded Cheri being the boss, but other times I didn't. There really needed to be a woman of the house, and I'm glad it was Cheri, and she was there to do that. She was the neater one of the two.

It was Judy's suggestion to go Christmas shopping, not mine the first year. This continued year after year until the girls got married. I looked forward to this every year. We would go through the same ritual of going shopping, and then going out to eat. I cherished the time that we would spend together. We shopped, and then we would go eat out afterwards. We would go do this a couple of times, four to five times a season. We would buy Sharon's and Cheri's birthday gifts as well.

Friends would say, "Ignore her;" that's what their advice would be. That's easy for them to say, because they weren't directly involved in the situation. They don't know what it was like for me. Joseph would tell me not to go "X"-mas shopping, and Kathy would, too, and also Beth. But they weren't the one married to Judy—*I* was.

I could have been cruel, and told her to go by herself to go "X"-mas shopping, but that wasn't the point. I was there to win her back.

Judy got upset with me. I took the ring off. Judy wasn't pleased with it, even though she was married to another guy. I don't remember why I took it off that day. We were eating after shopping when she noticed.

I thought the cookie making went well. We wrapped the gifts together. Putting the Christmas tree up that year was different. That one thing wasn't there—the lost piece of the puzzle.

It was always different writing the cards. Now it was just "Curt and the girls." Before, Judy would write, "Judy, Curt, and the girls." I had thirty or forty cards to do, and it was hard. I sometimes seemed like I was in a daze. My in-town and out-of-town letters were dropped in the mailbox; the stack of cards would make a *thump*, like the thump in my heart.

A couple of days before Christmas, we put the tree up. I put the lights on the tree, and the girls did the rest. They didn't make any comments about Judy; they didn't want to ruin the moment. That undermining thought within us all was kept silent.

We were preparing for our big day with Judy. She came over and helped make dinner. "Hurry-up, and get things done before she comes," everyone in unison said. We anticipated her arrival. She came in, and started cooking. We had started the turkey before she got there.

We had gravy, mashed potatoes, everything. The girls' cookies were the dessert for the day. Then the kids gathered 'round the tree and gave out gifts. I got Judy a blouse. She was shocked. She didn't anticipate it. She didn't get me anything. I think I also got her a sweater or two, like nothing had ever happened.

After everything was done, we'd sit around, talk, and spend time with each other, just like a regular holiday. I was just sitting back and enjoying the moment. For a few hours, it's just like nothing had ever happened.

Before, I'd always enjoyed the kids and Judy opening up their presents. This time, she was there. I kept everything else out of my mind. When she was ready to go, I said, "Do you really have to leave? Can't you stay just a little bit longer?" When she left, it was like the roof fell in on me. I watched her go out the back door, and then went to the picture window to watch her drive away.

It felt like torture. "X"-mas was over for me at that point. Now we had to pack up the car to go to Indiana the next morning. We only exchanged the gifts that we got together; I packed up the rest of the unopened presents in the car for Christmas day.

I was hoping for Judy to say something special, but all she said was, "See you later." Even on a regular day, that's all she would say.

As usual, I couldn't sleep too much, and I had my typical coffee, cigarettes and slushes.

The next day was "X"-mas Eve. We just got up that day, hung around, and left that afternoon for the "X"-mas Eve dinner. We never had both "X"-mas Eve and "X"-mas Day at Mom and Dad's, and this year was certainly different.

It was different because she wasn't there. *She* was the missing piece of the puzzle. The kids kept me up, and my parents were so happy to see me. On that over two-hour drive, going due east, I was anxious to see my parents. However, Judy wasn't there beside me like she always was. Now it was Cheri, reading a book.

When we got there, Barry was there, and we sat and talked until Dad came back from taking Mom somewhere. I put the presents around the tree, and sat and talked with my father. I put the kids to bed, and then we talked for a while and then went to bed.

I didn't sleep that night as usual, probably because it was my first Christmas without my baby doll. I felt empty. I had several cups of coffee and cereal. Mom was up already making the turkey. We opened up presents after Joe and Lilly came down, in the morning.

We all pitched in on getting dinner on the table and ate at about one. Candy came in the afternoon, and Lilly, too. We had a nice time, but something was missing. I was only half- there, without Judy by me.

I did call Don and Sally's around four o'clock so that the girls could talk to her. I was able to speak to her for a moment, and it made me feel great—it *made* my day. I had a really bad cold, and it only added to how I was feeling.

I wasn't really prepared to celebrate Christmas. It didn't seem like Christmas to me. Everything I did was for the kids, so they would have a good time. It didn't do any good to change me; I was already in the hole and I couldn't get out of it.

I just tried to get through the rest of the day. I kept myself busy talking to my brothers and parents, and helped do dishes and things like that, anything to pass the time.

I only smoked three cigarettes because of my cold, but I drank a lot of coffee. I had a drink with my family.

I couldn't ruin tradition.

After, we came home and unpacked. I felt down as usual. It was this way until I would see her again. I did what I could to keep the kids happy. I didn't smile a lot, only when I would see her again.

Over the holidays, Sally and Beth came over, but not Don because he was sick. Judy was supposed to come as well. Instead of coming over, she decided to go dancing. I was mad because she was supposed to come, and we were going to spend the evening together. It broke my heart. She decided that her dancing was more important to her than spending time with us. I would get down when things like this would happen, when she'd cancel plans or change them.

When the ladies came over, we opened presents, and the kids showed them what they got.

Also, Will and Andrea came to visit. That was nice. Then they left, and I was really mad, because she was supposed to be *here*. I even took the watch off, the one she got me for Christmas. When she gave it to me, I never took it off until that day. It was like having a part of her. I would never wear it constantly after that, just now and then.

I even had a watch that I stopped wearing. I don't have it with me, but I can't wear it. She broke my heart too many times. It meant something special to me, since she earned the money for it.

I started thinking that day about what if the tables were turned? What if I was the one that left, if I was the one that wanted the divorce? Her love wasn't as strong as I was. God, she was my idol. She was on a pedestal. I worshipped the ground she walked on. What else could I say?

If I was a rich man, I'd buy the moon for her. I'm not a rich man; I had to work for a living.

Would she have been as nice as possible to me? I think not. She probably would have kicked me out.

I used to be a lot happier when I was married to her. I signed on to be a father and a husband. I knew the responsibilities I was getting into.

When she left, I just became a father—'Dad,' as my kids would call me. I had to figure out my responsibilities myself; I had to work thru problems by myself. I didn't have her there to lean on, like I used to.

When you get married, you sign on to be a couple for life, and then I didn't have that anymore. I didn't have anyone to lean on for the day-to-day problems.

Any single parent knows that. The girls always had something going on. They were both in the band. They had their friends, and a swimming pool.

Once Cheri and Sharon started driving, I had to upkeep their cars as well as mine.

On top of that, Judy would bring her car here to get worked on.

There were a lot of things I had to do to just keep sane, to keep my daughters happy. They needed to be happy, regardless of how I felt. It was the number one thing on my list to do.

I always figured mine would come down the road. My number two thing on my list was getting Judy to come back.

If the girls weren't here, I would've not made the night out, when she left. I told my nephew that recently.

If I had no kids, I wouldn't have made it that night, either. That night we helped each other. Cheri knew that it was because of Bob, and she swore a bit.

The responsibilities kept me alive. I was different than a man who lost his wife, and had to raise two teenagers. He has *no* choice. I was different, because I chose to take care of them. I could've let her have them, but I didn't. They chose Dad. That's why we're so close today.

Even though I look back on it now, I still would have made the same choice to marry her. I loved her from when I said to her, "Hello."

On New Year's Eve, the first year, I felt pretty rotten. Sometimes we went out; often we stayed at home. You should have someone to hold on those special occasions: Christmas, Thanksgiving, and Sweetest Day. I loved holidays, until she left. Then they became just another day, and I just tried to get through it.

The girls were here together; Beth dropped her kids off. At midnight, I felt a lot of anguish and pain, and a lot of loneliness; I wondered what she was doing.

CHAPTER 9

Coming back home

I was hoping it would be a better year, for her to come back. It was on the top of my list. That thought was there twenty-four hours a day. Also, that day Beth told me that Judy wasn't happy in her life. Beth told Judy she better go and talk to someone that could help her, like the pastor, and if the pastor can't help her, he can recommend someone for her.

I felt good. Now I'm going to win; now I'm going to get her back. Wow! Someone will talk some sense into her; someone will send her home to help raise her daughters.

One day after the holidays, I got home from work around five-thirty. Judy was here, and I got to talk to her a bit. She was getting up to leave, and I walked her out—I had to move my car. She said she had to talk to me, and she would call me later.

I was feeling that it was going to be something good. I couldn't wait to talk to her. She called around midnight, and to my surprise, she told me that Bob was leaving next week, and that they weren't getting along. She and Bob were getting divorced. "He is nice and generous, yes," she said, "but, he isn't *you*." I felt drained and weird. I didn't know *what* to say! We talked till around one. She said she felt that maybe we can get together, but it will take time. Judy was finally considering going back to me. God, I hope she comes back!

That night I cried; I cried for joy! I love her! I will pray for our reunion.

I won! The girls will have their mother back, and I'll have my wife back. I was really happy; I probably didn't sleep that much again, in anticipation of her coming back. Just the thought of holding her—aw,

God! Doing things like we used to do, being with her, holding her hand, to give her a kiss on the neck, and her to hug me back. And the girls to say to each other, "Aw, they're at it again!"

I was walking on air, and I couldn't wait to see her again. My daughters really needed a mother, and I really wanted her. A part-time mother would never do. And they *wanted* a mother.

Many times, Cheri would argue with her, because she was mad at her, and then she would reminisce about being with her. Then Sharon would often ask her directly, "Mom, when are you coming home?" She would ignore it, or change the subject.

I never told my parents the whole story; I protected her. I didn't tell them because she didn't need the extra baggage when she would come back.

She was thinking of moving back in around her and Bob's divorce date. We talked about it; I was going to move downstairs, so she could have my bedroom, and put the girls together.

The next day, I was elated. I was walking on air. My dream was coming true! She was going to come *back*. It was one of the best days of my life, up there like the day I married her, or the day I met her. I knew there were more days like that to come.

That night, when I came home from work, I was in heaven again, top of the world, Mom! My family could get back together once more. I could put my arms around the one I love. It was a sleepless night, but one of anticipation. My kids would have their mother back; I would have my wife back. I worshipped the ground she walked on. Now, I look back and wonder how anybody could love that much.

I would buy the moon for Judy, and I often said I would die for her.

The next day, I came home from work, and she was here, just like it ought to be. It made me feel wonderful; *beyond* wonderful. Great, just like old times. I know we got problems to work out, but God, I don't think they are as big as she seems to make them. I know it will be hard for her, but I'll help her. Love has *no* barriers.

I feel mixed-up inside, because, I wonder, is she coming back for real, or is she pulling my chain, or is she tempting me? Or, is this just my mind doing this to me?

She didn't stay long that day, with all the commotion at the house.

Her nerves were on edge. I, however, went to sleep, because I'm hoping she'll come back. I prayed every night for her to come back.

The next day, I felt great, because Judy was here sleeping on the couch, but we didn't get to talk since the kids were around. Don got operated on, but he was ok. Judy was supposed to call that night, and didn't. I went to help Beth with her car, after midnight. Beth wasn't saying much, because she didn't want me to get my hopes up. I was depressed when I got back, and I got the bottle out and started to drink. My emotions are all screwed up. Good nite. I *need* her.

Next day, I seen Beth and told her I wanted Judy to go see a counselor, or a psychologist. If Judy wanted to come back, I wanted her to be happy, and I want to be happy with her. I was hoping if she seen a psychiatrist, she would straighten her mind out and want to come back, for me and the girls, and be a family again. Raising the girls by myself was tough. I put my mind to it; I owed it to my family.

Next day I talked to Judy. She said Bob left, and she was down, and she didn't want me to push her. She also said she was going to find a good psychologist to go to. I am hoping that the psychologist will bring her home.

On the next couple of days, I wanted to call Judy, but I didn't, because I didn't want to push her, since she asked me not to. Sometimes, I wished I didn't do the things she asked me to do.

One night, soon after that conversation, she called after one in the morning with a flat tire. I went out to help her. She gave me directions to her apartment. I drove out and fixed her tire, but I was looking for that opportunity to talk. She told me that she told her mother what had happened, that she was thinking of coming back home.

We were talking about her coming back, the kids, her father, and Bob leaving. I told her I'd give up my bedroom, and put the girls together and get Sharon's bedroom. We'd see how things work out. She thought it was a good idea, and something she could think about. We decided not to tell the girls or our parents, until we were sure she was going to move in.

Talking to her during those three hours made me feel absolutely elated, like a school boy when he asked a girl out for his first date. That night, we talked in her apartment, in her kitchen, over coffee. It was always over *coffee*.

After a while, we didn't have much more to discuss, so we parted company.

When I got home, I felt we gained a little ground. She is still in love with Bob, but she felt deep down that she is still in love with me. She also said that when things get rough, she thinks of me.

I got home, had more coffee and a cigarette, and hoped and prayed that things would go my way, not *his*. I am still in love with her. I got to bed around five.

Her mother, Sally, also suggested that she go and see a psychologist, and it did make it worse. The psychologist made her make a list of positives about Bob and me. She said that Bob was a nice, generous, man but he wasn't me. But she didn't want me to want her, and she was very clear of that. The psychologist was forcing her to make a decision, whether to come back to me or go back to Bob, and she felt, "Nobody cares what I want, and I want Bob; Curt is now just a brother to me." I was a little upset that he didn't say anything about the family or the girls.

After a couple of weeks, her sister put the kibosh on it, and said that she should take some time to live by herself, to find out what she really wanted, me or Bob.

One minute I thought I'd won, and that I was on top of the world; next minute I'm in agony all over again. I was so confused, so tired, and wishing my life would end. I'm existing in a living nightmare, and the best thing I know is death itself. For death isn't so bad, it is *peace*.

I didn't think of shooting myself that day, but I wanted to die. I didn't have my gun, since Joseph had my pistol and Will had my shotgun. And, my .22 rifle would jam once in a while, and had to be repaired. I thought of doing pills that night. I don't know what stopped me. The girls were home, too.

Also, that day, she told me she turned our wedding rings into another piece of jewelry. What a slap in the face that was.

Now it's a year later. You think all day of the torment you've been through in the past year. It gets good; it gets bad, like a yo-yo. I wish I could've slept that year through, and not have to contend with it. The problem was that I only had one-half to four hours of sleep a nite. I didn't get that much sleep. I went through a lot of vodka and a lot of cigarettes.

She's at the house eating with us. It was so sweet to have her there, and I was hoping and praying that I would have my old family back. That was not only for me, but for the girls.

The irony of it is, a year later her ex is telling her that he loves her, and her husband is telling her that he loves her. She is so confused.

I'm not confused about her coming back; I know what I want. I'll help her, because I'm in love, and if she doesn't come back, I'm lost.

The next day, she came over. We went to Don's for Cheri's birthday party. I felt like my family was back together. It was like we always were, for one of the kid's birthdays: cake, candles, singing, and gifts.

The song in my heart wasn't a melodic tune, just another sad song. I was careful that day, because I didn't want to ruin the moment, but I didn't want my heart broken, either.

After the party, everyone left and went home. Driving home on the freeway, I was glad that I got to spend time with her.

During the next week, she didn't call me much because she was with him. I didn't want to call when he was there. I honored her request; he didn't. I left her alone; *he* kept coming back. It was juggling things up, because it was messing her up and keeping her confused. Beth told her: "If you're going to go back to Curt, you'd better be sure!" Beth also warned me not to get my hopes up too high, but it was too late.

A strong love can be turned into a strong *hate*.

I hated life at the time. I wanted to move; I wasn't sure which state I was going to go to. I just wanted to get away. I didn't think of suicide at the time, even though she didn't know if she wanted me or not. I got the feeling I was going to lose. She went with him in the first place; he was new and exciting; I wasn't. When he moved back in, I felt misplaced and I lost—*it* shattered my dream.

Bob kept her like a yo-yo, moving in and moving out. In turn, I felt like a yo-yo. He would play her, like a violin, over and over and over. One day he left for good, when he found somebody else.

Her mother felt she was getting used by him. She even thought that her seeing the psychologist made her worse. She never elaborated why.

During this time I would go to work as usual, just to try to make it thru the day, hoping and praying that I would talk to her that night. All the time I anticipated that she would be here, or I would call that evening. When I would come home and her car wasn't there, I would be let down, but I still hoped she'd call me that night.

If she didn't call or come, I'd go to bed brokenhearted that night. When she wouldn't call or come see me, I felt like she was avoiding me. At times she said she was afraid of me, because she didn't know how to handle it, since I was so nice to her. She wouldn't expect it from another person. I wasn't the same like everyone else. It wasn't *me*.

I was so confused. One time I'd feel she was coming back, after that time she wasn't. I didn't know what to do. Why is she doing this to me?

I was smoking and drinking more. I went up to three-and-a-half packs a day. From a couple of drinks, I'd go to one-fifth of a bottle or more myself nightly.

Legally, he was still married to her. There wasn't anything wrong with him staying there, technically, but it was wrong to me. It wasn't fair. He wouldn't let her alone, so she could make up her mind, what to do. He wouldn't let her alone until he found someone else.

I would never wish this on anyone, even Bob. I *hated* him, and I went thru so much pain.

I'd drive by, and if his car was there, I wouldn't stop, and then I'd come home and start drinking. The booze would dull the pain, and get me to sleep.

I didn't ever intend for my kids or extended family to see me in this state. I always tried to drink when they went to bed. They knew what I was doing. I'd sit in the kitchen table, in my small white ranch, just drinking myself away. I really just didn't care if I'd even make it to the next day. I'd just pray that I would die, and that I wouldn't wake up. There are just some prayers God just doesn't answer. I wish Judy would come back very soon; I need her back.

It's an anniversary today. One year ago, today, we signed the disillusionment papers. Originally, I knew it was coming. She came and picked me up at work. I didn't talk to her much that day. It still feels like agony. I went through the civil war and I still wasn't winning.

She doesn't know what she wants, and I'm no further ahead than where I am now. Nothing's really changed, other than the fact that she doesn't live with me anymore. My loneliness is always at the forefront of my life. I am a substitute mom, doing the best for my kids that I know how.

Life to me right now is just a big joke. You work so hard to buy things for that someone special; you'll do anything for that person. Then one day, you're not good enough anymore. And you get kicked out of their life, and it doesn't matter what you do or say; you just can't change their mind. But you try; God do you *try*.

I made it a year, but I didn't know if I was going to make it through another one. To tell you the truth, I didn't know *how* I was going to make it another year.

I felt things were getting better, but I wasn't positive. I still had my death wish. Until she came in that door with her suitcase, I couldn't let go of it. I always figured if she could come back and really try, and if it didn't work out, I could then handle it. People said it wouldn't be the same. I said, "I'll make it the same."

She once said, "How do you know you could trust me?" I said, "All I need is your promise." I'm a man of my word, and she knew how I was with promises.

During this time, I didn't think of killing myself as much, but I didn't want Bob to get my girls. But now and then that act crosses my mind. Beth said that she would come back for the girls, not me, because she has outgrown me. At that moment I was dead; I knew it was the end. I knew at that point that it wasn't going to work out, and that she wasn't even going to try. I was done—I just wanted to die.

I felt tormented, like I didn't want to live anymore. But, I wasn't going to kill myself. I wasn't going to let Bob get my girls, or her.

I loved her, but I hated her. I *hated* the situation. If she is really thinking of coming home, she wouldn't sleep there. She isn't coming back, because she never calls me. She is using me to get closer to my girls. The girls have no mother, because she's not here. She is knocking out my love for her slowly, but surely. Right now, I don't care if she does come back. If she does go back with him, I'll let the door of hate open up.

One night, Judy asked Cheri what she thought about her coming back, and Cheri said, "Only if you're married." Cheri didn't want her to leave again, to leave *us* again. Cheri always wanted her mother on her terms, not Judy's.

Judy really hurt her. She hurt the kids. Each one took it personally.

I was the mother in this house, period. You can't raise a kid twenty miles away, when you aren't there. Many women would disagree with me, but that's how I feel.

One day at work, Bob called. I was busy at the time, so I said I'd call him back. A shot of hate went thru me, and I decided to call him back; he told me he was moving out, and getting a divorce. He said Judy should go back to where she belongs, with her family. Even *he* knew it. He said to me, "All she talks about is *you* and your darn kids." At this time, I told the girls I talked to him, and he would leave if anyone wanted to go there.

I still did pray about her, and hoped that maybe we could go out.

A brother?! That bothers me a great deal. I devoted half of my life to her and to my girls. What the am I going to do? I would kill myself, but I have the girls. They would have no *mother*.

My life is just a big empty space, something that needs to be filled between birth and death. It's just something I have to do.

I wonder sometimes if I should tell her to stop coming around and bother us. It's too complex; I didn't know if I should tell her to get lost and never come back, or if we should try to work it out. I was in such a state of confusion. Even though I prayed, it didn't seem to make it any easier. I was too impatient for God to wait to see what He had in store for me. I wanted her now, not tomorrow, although I would take her back tomorrow.

I thought about asking Judy's permission if we could move, and then I asked Sharon one night over dishes if we could move. She asked, "Why?" but I just gave her the basics. I'm not happy here. She just said she loved me. I thought, what was the use of staying here, if there wasn't anything left here to fight for?

One night I called Sally by mistake and she told me that Bob moved back in again, to pay the bills. Bob still wanted a divorce, but Judy said things were getting better. He was stringing Judy like a yo-yo, and she was stringing me like a yo-yo. I was distraught, but I wasn't going to give up.

The longer this all goes on, Judy doesn't call me. I feel like I'm getting used, only good enough to lean on when she has a problem, and love like a brother. Maybe this is the end for us, but I'm not going to give up, not yet. There still could be hope.

Sometimes I wish I could tell her to go live in the bed she made, but I can't get myself to do it.

Interestingly, Sharon told me that Judy said that Cheri doesn't want Judy to come home. Judy says Cheri won't let her, and it's because Cheri wants her to come home in the *right* way. Like Cheri said, we should be married before she comes home.

I didn't waste any time in my mind how our remarriage ceremony would be. I didn't even get that far, because I wanted her to just say she was coming home first.

Judy's just using Cheri as an excuse. She doesn't call or bother to stop over, and I was right about them getting back together. I told Joseph today about them getting back together, and he told me not to get my hopes up. But, how can't I? I feel one day we'll get back together again.

I finally got to talk to Judy. I feel she's coming home. I don't know when, but soon. I hope I'm not wrong again. It won't be the first time I did that. There were things she would say, like Bob's not me, and that would make me think. They also worked different shifts, didn't see each other a lot, and fought.

I had seen something on TV that talked about divorce. It said that people today forgot why they got married: that is to have children, raise them, and build things up when they are older. But today, it's different. They put the importance on themselves. That's why there are so many divorces. So, there's Judy putting self-importance over me and the girls.

Today was a special one-year anniversary for me. It was a year ago that I wanted to take the car out on the freeway where I knew there are more curves and hills—I thought I'd have a better chance of killing myself. I never thought I'd get paralyzed, or anything; I just wanted to *destroy* myself.

I wanted to start asking her out again, since I felt I had the opportunity. I had tickets to a show. I did ask her, but she said she was thinking about it. However, the night we were to go, she got the flu. Then the girls didn't want to go, but Sharon decided to go. After, Sharon and I went to get dinner.

Judy came over to the house, and we had coffee. We talked about her coming back. She said she wanted to have a conference with the girls, and discuss her coming back, so the girls wouldn't feel that I made the decision by myself. I believe if she comes back and gives me her word, I will have faith in her. We will take it one day at a time.

The next day, I told the girls that Judy was coming home. Sharon was so excited, although Cheri just had her hands on her face, and looked at the floor. I let them know that Judy wants all of our approval. Sharon said, "I want Mommy home." Cheri got tears in her eyes.

Cheri was skeptical. She was boss of the house, and she didn't want to give that up. She would have to relinquish her power in her house. She did want her mother to come home, but she just didn't want her to come home and leave again. Cheri wanted to cry and laugh at the same time, since she was mixed-up about her feelings. She also didn't want me to get hurt anymore. She could see what was going on with me. So could Sharon, but she was a bit more mature.

The best way I could explain it to the girls, and make me feel ok, was to tell them that Judy has been sick for the past year, and we shouldn't make her feel guilty about it. Also, I wanted Cheri to write down any questions she had for Judy.

I loved her so much. I loved her more than life itself, like my previous actions—my suicide cycle. I daydream about Judy coming back; I'm praying about it.

Judy and I went out to dinner, and had a long talk. She *is* coming home. She doesn't know when, and can't guarantee when. But she still doesn't know what she wants.

When we would meet, I wouldn't drag the past up, or throw it in her face. I wasn't going to do that, because it's dead and gone. I feel she'll be back towards the end of the month.

Sharon called me at work today. She bought a card for her, when she comes back. She's tickled, and absolutely elated. She wanted to make Mommy happy. She knew that Judy had questions and concerns, and wanted to alleviate them in her own special way.

I'm working late four days a week now. I don't know how it will affect things between Judy and me, but I hope I will accomplish what I want between us. I wasn't working as many hours. I would still be home to put the girls in bed.

I asked Joseph if he would help move Judy in the following weekend. He was so happy. He said, "I sure will; I'll be darn glad to help!"

I was thinking of how I went and got my cards read last spring. I remembered four things. First, someone with a suit case would be moving in with me; that was Lou. Second, I would have more authority at work; I had guys to oversee. Third, Judy's marriage wouldn't last more than a year and a-half. Fourth, she would be back, and she won't know why. When she does, I won't care anymore. And, I won't.

Judy called, and I asked her out to dinner and to a movie, and she said she'd go. I felt special and honored, but apprehensive, until it really happened. Until she was beside me, I couldn't put my whole heart into it.

I slept well, looking forward to tonight. She came in the afternoon, and we went to Gina's. It was like being in heaven—I was on cloud nine. I was like a young kid on my first date, hoping everything would go just right, like every date I would make with her. I enjoyed every moment.

Later we went to the movies. After, we came back to the house, and talked to the girls a little. I gave her some boxes to pack her things in; she left.

Judy mentioned at dinner that she wasn't going to move in next weekend, since Bob is the one pushing her to get out, and she can't grasp the situation.

I told her to take her time. I still feel that she thinks I'm to blame for her present marriage breaking up. Also, I couldn't accept it, and neither could her family.

A few days later Judy was over here, and I asked her out to dinner again. We had a nice dinner, and after we sat and talked.

Judy told me that Bob left a week ago. They went to see a lawyer and had a disillusionment paper filled out, but she didn't sign it because she wasn't ready. She also is not moving in with me and my girls right now, and maybe she'll never move in. She is going to stay by herself and see what happens. Until she decides what she wants, she's going to take one day at a time.

I was just floored. I was quiet and I really didn't know what to say. It was as if my whole world just dropped again. I was back on my pendulum and it was swinging in the wrong and opposite direction of what it should have been.

After I drove her home, we sat quietly in the car and talked about fifteen minutes. I couldn't believe what she said to me. Judy had my hopes up so high, and she tore my world apart again. She didn't understand why I tried so hard; she couldn't believe a man could love her like I did.

Then she said she doesn't have the feelings for me that a wife should have for her husband.

After I got back to the house, I sat in the car with the engine running. I was wondering if I should just close the garage door, get back in the car and lock myself in it, and let the engine run and go to sleep and never wake up—just end it all.

But, I felt I've waited this long; I can wait a bit longer.

She did say that she should have listened to me and waited a year before she got married to Bob.

I didn't feel like doing anything when I got in. I was drinking and praying. It was a night full of vodka and Squirt—heavy on the vodka, and light on the Squirt. I guess God still listens to brokenhearted drunks.

I was crying all night. I didn't even go to church that day. I didn't want to put on a front, when everyone else was cheerful. Everyone else was doing fine, but I was in a nightmare. I couldn't say I was fine when I wasn't.

The next morning, I sat here thinking of what Judy told me last night, and drinking, not caring about whether I live or die again. I just know that I love her, and that I want to get her to love me again.

I wonder what will happen next. Will Judy continue to go out with me, or not? Will Bob really want the divorce or a legal separation? Will Judy and I get back together? Or will I live my life a lonely fool, and be bitter towards women, afraid of getting hurt again?

In the evening, I told Sharon, in a broken voice, that Judy wasn't back as of yet, that she was going to live by herself, and maybe get an apartment. She knows how I feel about her, but she said she doesn't feel the same about me. She felt bad.

After Sharon got out of the car I sat there, thinking and listening to the radio. I wondered about yesterday, thinking about some of the things she said last night. If I wasn't such a nice guy, it would be easy for her. I thought to myself, *I'm just me. Yeah, just me, a fool, a stupid idiot, a bore. Just like an old pair of shoes, keep them around as long as they feel and look good. Throw them away when you get tired of them.*

I remembered that Judy said that she should have asked for half of everything and for the girls. I had said, "Well you really wouldn't have got that much after all the bills were paid." I never mentioned to her that I would have never given up on my girls, once I found out that there was another man.

Just think—I was finally beginning to feel good about Judy and me again. Now death is crossing my mind. Once more, I want to go downstairs and unload the option. I'm going to load all seven bullets; stack the deck. That way, it'd be done and over with. It can't be any worse than what I'm living.

I'm taking my girls back home, and tonight I'm going to pray harder than I ever have.

Next day at work, Joseph mentioned he had seen Kathy, and she said that Judy probably has no intention of working it out; she just needs the girls and a place to stay.

I saw Matt and I told him that Cheri only wants Judy to come back if she intends to stay. He said that Cheri sounds like a very put-together young lady, and what she really is saying is, "Don't come back unless you intend to be a good wife and mother, because you have already hurt us enough."

At work the next day, Sharon called me and told me that Judy told her that the reason she wasn't coming home was because we would probably fight and she would just leave again. I don't understand her way of thinking, because we never fought before.

The kids feel that their mother deserted them.

Judy was over today, and we had coffee and talked. I asked Judy out, but she said that Bob is coming over. I had a good time with her up until that point. I don't know if she told Bob about a separation instead of a divorce, but I'll have to wait and find out about that.

Judy left later that evening; I stayed home and watched the late show. Cheri came out and said something that bothered me. We talked about my niece's baptism tomorrow. I said, "Legally, she isn't my niece, but inside I feel like she is." Cheri said, "Yeah, I have 'X'-grandparents and 'X'-aunts and 'X'-uncles and 'X'-cousins and an 'X'-mother." I thought she was joking until she made the comment about Judy, but she was right.

It bothered me any time that Judy would mention Bob because I didn't know if they were going out or if he was staying over. The thought of them sleeping together just drove me nuts. For instance, did he sleep there last night?

I saw Xavier Jones at work today. He asked about Judy, and about how I am getting along. I told him that we date now and then, and that they went to sign for a dissolution, but Judy isn't ready yet. He told me to hang in there; that it would work out one day.

I've wanted to call Judy, but I can't. I'm afraid that she'll tell me that Bob will go along with her on a separation, instead of a divorce. I'm not ready for that right now. As you remember, when he left before, he came back, and I can't handle that.

I made plans with her to take her out. We went to Gina's Place. I was so excited to go, like I always was. She told me that Bob still wants a divorce. He felt the girls and her family never accepted him, and they should have taken things slower. He is going to date her now and again, but I know he won't let her alone until he finds someone else. She also told me that he will move her at the end of the month. Before dropping her off, I asked her to go to another restaurant. She said she'd like that; it made me feel good.

I don't know if she's playing me, or trying to get closer to the girls, but I'm going to hang in there.

Mom and Dad were happy we were going out again. They were thrilled, and hoping it was going to work out this time. They never said a bad word about her.

Another time I asked Judy out, she declined. She came over one afternoon, and we talked about her week, and had coffee together. Cheri said, "Are you two going out tonight or not?" and Judy asked, "What is this matchmaking? Why can't we all go out?" I looked at the girls and said, "I'm a big boy; I can ask her out myself." The subject was changed then, and I was disappointed because she turned me down that night.

For Easter that year, we didn't go to see my family. We had dinner at home. Cheri made a nice dinner. Judy mashed the potatoes, and I opened up a bottle of wine. Cheri had some too; it was a really nice day, until Judy left early.

On a daily basis, the girls would be girls. They would be crabby, and they would argue. Judy wasn't here to see it, the ups and the downs, and the joys. She missed out. I regretted her not being here to see it; the things she missed out on. If I had worked as I did and not had to take care of the girls, I wouldn't have seen it either. But I did, because I was the one raising them.

You know, regardless how busy my life's anymore, I always find myself thinking about her, and what I should do to get her back.

I went to bed, disappointed, but I was still glad to have seen her.

On one of my many talks with Joseph, I told him that she rejected dinner one night, and stayed for dinner another night. He felt I was letting her have her cake and eat it, too. It would hurt when Joseph would tell me God's truth. It wasn't what I wanted to hear. Most of the time, it was encouraging. He said that one day someone would catch my eye, and that it would be too late for her, and she'll regret waiting.

It still wakes me up in the middle of the night, that how could I be a good provider, husband, father, and she doesn't love me? I was everything that a girl would want. I still can't handle that.

Joseph would comment that I was too nice and easy to her, with all that I've gone thru. It's just me—I *love* her.

The girls of course missed Judy, and I would tell them, "I'm trying to get her home, not just for you, but for me, too. I don't want anything more than just to get this family back together."

Sharon wanted to help Judy move into the apartment, but Bob and one of his friends were helping her. She was upset about that. I gathered from Sharon that Judy is blaming everyone in her family for her marriage failing. It wasn't true. I feel that I helped it along. Bob was afraid of me. Cheri didn't like him; Don didn't like him; Beth and Sally just tolerated him.

Then it backfired on me. I just kept trying to be *me*, because I wanted her to come back. Sharon and the girls said that they were glad they stayed with me. It made me feel good. If not, Bob and Judy would have been here at the house. The girls knew I'd never give up on them; they knew I'd never abandon them.

I didn't appreciate her blaming things on me and the girls for her problems. She left, and she got herself in trouble again with this guy. I didn't cause her to get a divorce again. Those two weren't really meant for each other.

I always wanted to tell her to go away, but I just couldn't. She had a spare key to the house. I loved to see her and talk to her regardless if I was winning or not.

There was another key that greatly bothered me, and that was the one he had, the one to her place. It upset me; it broke my heart. Here they were, getting separated, talking about divorce and there he was visiting whenever he wanted. Sometimes I'd drive past the apartments she lived at. I'd see his car there and I'd just die inside. She missed events because she would be with him. She didn't come to my niece and nephew's birthday party, for example. Her mom wasn't crazy about that, her leaving early and all.

Judy felt we had two families, mine and her parents. I think she was jealous of the great relationship that we had. Don and Sally were like second parents to me; Lou and Beth were siblings. I loved my nieces and nephews, but the key element holding it all together was missing: *her.*

Church was always comforting to me, especially when the pastor said something that touched my heart. He said, "God gives you what he wants you to have and that isn't exactly what we want, but it is what we need." It made me feel that Judy wants Bob and the girls. God didn't give Judy what she wanted, and God let me have my girls, but not my Judy.

The girls would go see Judy at her new place, and in early May, Sharon asked her to go to Coaster City. She didn't know which weekend that would be, but at least she said she'd think about it.

Mother's Day was coming up. Judy was over for a slush, and we were talking about our week. She said she was sick and tired of hearing about Mother's Day, and how this really never bothered her before, but I feel that because of how the situation was, that was what was really bothering her.

I still decided to order her a corsage, even though we weren't officially together. I thought it would work in helping to bring back some of the old feelings.

That Saturday before going to work, I picked up my new glasses and stopped at the florist to pick up her corsage. I worked from ten to three that day. It wasn't mandatory, but I had some cars to work on at the shop, and not much to do at home. I wanted to keep my mind busy, but accidentally I drilled the gun thru the palm of my hand and that hurt.

I came home, weeded the garden and other things, and later that evening Beth showed up. We talked a while, and Beth said she was staying away from Judy and was upset with her. Judy told her that she didn't want to be married to me anymore. In addition, she wishes the family would let it go. Beth felt that Judy was blaming everybody else with her problems, and that none of this was my fault. She also said that she just wants to be like a sister to me. That *hurts*.

Because for me, we were once married, and I can't look at her like a sister and I was never able to and still *can't*.

Later, around ten, I went to her house, and surprised her with the white rose corsage. It was beautiful. She was surprised. We had coffee, and I invited her to Mother's Day dinner, and told her I would pick her up at seven p.m. She agreed.

The next morning, after eight a.m., Joseph called. He jokingly wished me a Happy Mother's Day, and asked me if I had read the comics yet. It was for me, and about the last year, he mentioned.

I already was going into Mother's Day with some hesitation, because of last year, when Mother's Day was the last day we spent together as a family before the big divorce. The comic was about two of the characters going to buy a card for a dad who's *both* mom and dad. It was *me*. It was *my* situation. No holds barred, direct, to the point. It was the truth. Like I told Judy, you can't be a mother not living in this house; you can't be a mother living ten miles away, period. You are still their mother, just not an acting mother.

That day, I showed them the comic strip. They both exclaimed, "That's it!"

Interestingly, since that day, Sharon and Cheri have on occasion bought me Mother's Day cards on that day. I just got one this past year from Cheri. The girls have written messages as, "You're both my father and my mother." It'd make me feel wonderful, but sad in the same way, for what once was.

After everyone came down, we drove back home. Beth stopped by to get her kids, and then we went to pick Judy up for dinner.

We were all so excited, especially me. The girls were very nice to her. We were all cautious, trying to say the right things and being careful of how our words and actions were being perceived. We didn't want to upset her.

We had a nice meal together, and a great time. It was a real casual night, the conversation flowed well, and the atmosphere was lighthearted, not serious at all. All was well, and I was thinking, "I hope this works!" There was a fair amount of people out.

We had a full course dinner—no expense was spared. This was a special occasion, and I was going to make it special and memorable for all of us. It was great. The only bad part about the evening was packing things up and going home.

I took her home, and walked her to the door. I wanted so badly to hold her hand or kiss her, and I knew I wasn't getting either. But it sure would have been nice. Although, the perfect gentleman that I was, I would never have forced myself on her.

Then we went home and I wrote as usual and went to bed.

I vaguely thought about that day one year ago, and I wasn't going to let it ruin my day, not this time.

Two days after our dinner was the one-year anniversary of the day we got divorced, or I should say, the day she divorced *me*. I was thinking of last year at this time, how I was talking myself out of suicide, but I wasn't going to let Bob and Judy have my girls. I still didn't want to be here. I didn't want to be where I was at. I made a promise to myself that I was going to raise my daughters. The thought of putting a gun against my head again was *not* an option.

I might think thoughts, of course; everybody does. I'm careful of what I say, and my actions. You can't take those back. Once something's said or done, it can't be undone.

Judy was over at the house, so I asked her out. We went to eat. I picked her up that evening at seven p.m. Judy asked me to back her up on disciplining the girls and I said, "Sometimes I'll back you, and sometimes

I'll back them, depending on who's right." She also mentioned that she went to the psychologist, and she told him she was living by herself, and deciding on who she wanted. I would cringe when she would say that, but there was nothing I could do. God, how I need and want back her love.

On the brighter side, I enjoyed taking her out. It made me feel like a man again. I felt like the head of the house, taking my wife out. I was trying to win her back. Compared to Bob, I didn't want to go out just to find somebody. I wanted her, plain and simple. Dropping her off after a date is hard. I want to hold her and kiss her, but that's not possible; it can't be.

Once in a while, we'd pass Judy, as Cheri would be driving. It was nice having her close by, but it still hurt that I just couldn't pop in at any time.

My smoking would kick up at times, to one-and-a-half packs a day, and I would still be drinking, and sitting there wondering at night if she'd ever come back.

I would pray often, just about every day. I wanted her to come home to me. I'd pray at church, and I'd pray in the car, and I'd pray at work. I'd always ask God the same thing—bring her back to me. I'm *sure* he's going to answer my prayer.

I tried not to drive by her place all the time; I didn't want her to think I was always checking things out. I wanted to only know if *he* was there.

One evening she brought her car over, since she needed some help with it. She was a bit standoffish, and in a hurry; I didn't know why. Then I figured it out—*he* must be over. She pointed out the dent in her fender and left. I didn't want to know if he was there, but I had to find out. I mustered up the courage to drive by, but I was going too fast. There was his car. I was floored, and I was also crying and swearing at the same time.

I got home, but couldn't tell the girls. Later, Sharon asked what was wrong, and I told her that I was sad, and felt like I lost. She felt I was too nice to Judy, and shouldn't be.

It's too late on that; it's all too late. He's up there; I'm here. After the girls went to bed, I drove by again, and the lights were out, and his car was still there. I just don't believe it. I've just got so many mixed feelings right now; I don't know what to do.

The next day, his car was still there. I was livid. My day was ruined. It was completely screwed up. I'm sure he didn't sleep in the spare room, either. I told Joseph about last night; he knew something was bothering me. He felt I was going to get her back, but now he didn't know. If she would just stop seeing him, he wouldn't come around as much. I can't stop him or her from doing what they're doing. I *wish* I could.

I'm still having health problems—my legs hurt; my skin is bad; I feel awful. I am *so* depressed. I don't care anymore about anything. I don't have love. I have nothing. I don't want to live with this skin. I want my heart attack, so I can die soon.

Sharon told me she talked to Judy today, and asked if she signed the divorce papers yet. She said I can ask her myself. I got to see Judy that day. She said she had signed them. They would be divorced by our anniversary. I didn't know if that meant mine and hers or his and hers; I didn't care. All I knew was that she was one step closer to being mine again.

I also had other things on my mind. Lynn would have been still alive, if he hadn't been killed. Being back with my mom and dad kept me busy for the holidays, but not enough to not think of my sweetheart. She's <u>always</u> on my mind. Johnny looked a bit older. Joe, Barry and I went down to the woods. I hadn't been there in ten years. How everything has changed, but not my love for her.

Judy is really driving me nuts, and so is my skin. I don't know what to do. I don't know why God is punishing me. I'm a good husband and a good person, just not good enough for *her*, and right now I don't know for whom else. I guess I'll just have to see what she wants to do. This is killing me.

I am going to keep praying. I know God will answer my prayer one day, even if it is after my death.

At church today when the pastor shook his hand with me, and said, "Peace be with you," I felt an overwhelming sense of peace within me. It felt great. When my thoughts are stuck on Judy and my skin is bad, I don't feel at peace; I feel lost. I'll never have a complete sense of tranquility back. When I'm with her, I feel a lot better. I want and need her so very much. I don't know if God will ever give her back to me.

Friends of mine came to visit tonight. They asked about Judy; I told them we visit now and then, date, and go out to dinner. I told them I'm still in love with her. They didn't know that she got remarried and was getting divorced; I felt to keep that to myself, and not to hurt myself. They said to do what I thought I should do, and not listen to everyone else. I agreed.

I just don't know what I'm going to do anymore—I'm lost in misery, pain and love; I might as well have another drink—the booze would help.

Judy was here today; Cheri asked her to go to a movie with her, Sharon, Stacey and Rhonda. She jumped at the chance to go, and is going to do whatever she can to go. I'm glad.

She told me on her drive home, that her court date has been pushed back. I was glad to know that her court date was sooner than I thought. She did mention that she would be single by our anniversary. At the time, I didn't know if that meant mine and hers or hers and his. Whew, all I knew at this time was that it would be closer to *ours* not *theirs*. What a relief!

When Beth would come over, sometimes she'd mention that Judy had company. Cheri would say, "Guess who?" and then I would respond, "I bet I can guess who!" I took the long way to get gas that night. I felt bad. A pain lingered within me. I passed by their place. There was his car. I shuddered.

Judy came that night around eight. She didn't stay long; she was in a hurry. I wonder why. He gets her tonight, too, and here I am—all screwed up.

It was mid-August; I went to work as usual and Joseph thought that I didn't look good. He suggested that I leave Judy alone for a while, and not chase her. Maybe then she'll come back. I don't know, and I'm afraid to try his theory.

The next morning, I know I shouldn't have, but I had to drive-by. I drove recklessly to work, hoping I'd get killed. I didn't, but I wish I had. Life is just a waste of time, and I don't really care about what happens to me anymore.

I feel that if he's still there after the divorce, I want things changed—it's not *fair* to me. On her days off, he's there with her. She only sees me when she needs me. I want my house key back, and I don't want her here anymore. I don't even want to know what she's doing.

Judy stopped by. Bob was up at Judy's, and I know that Cheri wasn't happy about it. She was perplexed that they were getting a divorce, since they were always together. I just didn't care what they do anymore, since I couldn't do anything about it anymore even if I wanted to. Sharon was upset at me for being so nice to her all the time. I couldn't help it; that was who I was. Sharon hugged me and told me, "I don't like to see you this way. One day, you'll read your book and ask yourself, 'Why did I do that for her, for what?'"

I cried, and told her she was a good kid. That night, I smoked one-and-a-half packs of cigs and moped over three very large drinks.

Judy had called the next morning. It greatly pained me to be nice to her. Joseph asked at work what was the matter, and I told him, about me driving past Judy's, and how the girls felt.

Judy just wants a brother-sister relationship with me. That can't be for me. It has to be all or nothing. I don't want it another way.

On Father's Day, Sharon and Cheri got me small gifts. It wasn't the same without Judy. Beth came by that afternoon; we had coffee. Beth felt that once they are divorced, he'll stop coming around. I wasn't so sure. It felt like a game to me. He's just waiting to get back in again.

Beth also said that Judy mentioned if someone would ask her out, she'd go. As long as she doesn't get attached to someone, I'll keep trying. If not, I'll go to slam the door shut.

Looking back on today, my donuts were nice, and I liked my gifts. But my *special* gift wasn't here. I spent the day without her. It was another holiday alone, with donuts for Sunday dinner and a bowl of cereal that evening. I'm just going to go to bed.

The girls aren't happy, and I'm not happy. If Judy was here, life would be different. I'd love to have her back; I've just got to keep trying to get her back. Things will be different when she's back.

Our anniversary date is coming up. I don't know if I should order flowers or pick them up, or have them delivered. I don't know how to get them to her. I think it would be a nice gesture. The day before that,

Judy stopped by. We talked about her upcoming divorce, her weekend and mine, and the girls. I asked her to go with us. She said, "Ok."

Judy also said something interesting. She wondered why her life was so messed up. She didn't know what the man upstairs was trying to tell her. (Maybe He's trying to tell her that she belongs here!) I can't remember what I said, or even if I said anything at all. Maybe God is trying to show us that we took each other for granted, and I didn't realize how lonely she was when I was at work.

In the end, God gave us this pain, to try to get us to wake up in the way we should. I needed to understand her, and her to understand me. I feel Judy does realize that God wants her to come back where her love is, and just waiting for her to pick back up.

Our wedding anniversary. I had errands to do throughout the day. Judy's flowers were delivered around four o'clock. Beth had stopped at the house; she mentioned that Judy is still deciding who she wants. Judy desires her freedom, but she still needs someone to take care of her.

She also wishes for money. You can't have all that with one person working. You have to give up things. Beth asked Judy, if she would turn the clock back five years if she could and if she knew what today is. She answered, "Yes," to both questions.

I picked up Judy around six-thirty, and she was surprised I bought her the flowers. She said, "I don't know what I'm going to do with you." I told her, I got them for her, because I love her. "Besides, you'll enjoy them," I said. She answered, "Yes, much more than the ones you got me last year." When she finished putting them in water, we went to see a movie.

After the movie, we went out to eat. During dinner, she remarked how her life has been in the past year. She was like the woman in the movie—the man had the kids.

We ordered steaks, and she asked me if Beth gave me a lecture about asking her out, since Beth gave her one, too. Beth wanted to know why Judy is leading me on. Beth told her that she told me, that I am "someone special" to her, but that she said to Beth, "I don't love him."

I then said, "Yeah, that's funny. I'm special to you, but I'm in love with you."

Judy stopped for a moment. She didn't know what to say. She probably didn't expect me to tell her that.

She told me about some guys that come to see her at the restaurant—one looked like me. Beth told him about me, and he said, "If he looks like me, he's got to be a good guy." I laughed!

Then she talked about Beth and said, "You ought to marry Beth." I don't love her like I do Judy; she isn't my type.

Although I feel, sometimes she is after me.

I said, "You keep coming up with these people who remind you of me, including your 'X'-to-be's first wife's next husband." She countered, "But, he doesn't wear glasses!"

I then changed the subject, seeing that I wouldn't be able to get anywhere.

We then went back to her place, and I wondered, "How many divorced people go out on their anniversary?" She said, "Not too many." I had to agree.

I walked her to her apartment. I wanted to kiss her so bad. I felt she wanted me, too. I knew she was still married to someone else, so I didn't try.

Since one of my brothers was in town, she asked what time he was leaving tomorrow. She wanted to come down but didn't know how she'd be treated. I told her he would be his quiet self, and she said she would come.

She ended the evening with saying she enjoyed the nite very much and that makes me happy! I'm ecstatic! That's the second time in a row that she said that.

I got home around eleven-thirty. My brother was there. I told him that Judy might come down tomorrow. He said he'd be good to her. I told him I love her, and I still want her back.

Reflecting on the evening, I thought of Judy. As we were coming in-and-out of the movie, I put my hand on her back to guide her. It was really hard for me not to put my arm around her. In fact, I had to catch myself a few times.

I don't have the fight in me, as of yet, for those small, beautiful gestures, but I'm going to keep trying.

Maybe I'll get what I'm waiting for. Maybe she doesn't love me now, but perhaps the love she once had will come back. If I'm still special to her, then that love has to be in there somewhere. I want it out in the open again.

Judy did come the next night, and it was fine.

At work on Monday, Joseph asked me about my weekend, and I told him it was pretty good. Joseph said I was cheerful for once, all day.

She got divorced from Bob. This is a good day, since it's the end of the month. I did call Judy today, but no one answered.

In the evening, I went to Beth's. She said she talked to Judy today. She seemed to be ok. Judy and Bob went dancing after they came out of court. They didn't stay for long, since it upset him. He wanted to be by himself.

Judy went dancing tonight. She's still waiting for that rich man.

Now I got my chance and I *want* that chance.

Hope to see her on the Fourth of July. It's my opening to get the family back together.

Judy said something about her working and dancing her life away again. And that I started then quit before I was doing good.

I wondered if this is one of the hints I asked God for, to give me the wisdom to win her back.

If she says something like that again, I know that's what I have to do to win her back.

We'll see what happens.

Matt would come in every Monday. I would look forward to it. I bought my tools from him. He became a Christian, and he knew a lot about the Bible. He was my supplier in more ways than one—he helped out on my job and was also my spiritual advisor.

When he'd come in, he's put everything in focus. We'd sit there, and I would tell him what's going on and how I felt about it. We'd talk about my girls, and I'd remark how great they were, and seemed to be.

Before he left, most of the time he'd pray with me. I always looked forward for him to come in to keep me in-line.

When he'd be on vacation, I couldn't wait until he got back the following week.

When I was going thru my suicide thing, he'd help me out. He was another one of my angels. He was an amazing guy. The last time I seen him was at Joseph's wedding.

Joseph went thru what I went thru, but maybe he wasn't as in love as I was. I was head over heels for Judy. I am still tickled when she calls.

There's still something in me for her. I'd like her back, but I'm not going to chase her. I can't.

I'm not going to put myself thru that again. That would kill me.

If it came down one day that she and I are free, she would have to chase me, but, I am also open to meeting someone new.

I always thought I was a pretty strong guy. I know other people are worse off than me whose problems can't really compare to mine, and other people are less worse off than me, and other people are still standing.

In the heat, I wouldn't feel well. Sometimes, I think this is all caused from the stress of the situation. God, I am miserable, and disappointed in myself and how my life turned out.

'I was hanging out with my in-laws; I hung around my family. On the other hand, things with Judy and anybody she was associated with became fractured. Things weren't the same between her and her parents, her and me, her and the kids, and her and my family. It was never the same, and after all the cracks and splits, it couldn't be put back together again to the way it once was.

Beth told me that Judy has been hurt about how the girls have been treating her. She said she went home last night and cried. She said she was going to call me and tell me off. I knew I'd get blamed for it, even though it wasn't my fault. Like I told her, I'd back her when it was right, and back them when it was right.

She also mentioned to Judy to stop leading me on. She said, "He knows we're just friends." *Yeah, friends. I'm her friend and I'm in love with her. I know one day she'll be back.* Beth said, "Maybe she will be back. But that could be years away." I told Beth I didn't have years to wait. In that case, I must close the door on her, sometime before Cheri's graduation.

CHAPTER 10

Big day!

Judy walked around the corner and said, "Hi." I told her that I don't know if I can get off Monday for River's Edge Park.

I wanted to know why she didn't stay last night—she said the girls don't have time for her, so she left. I mentioned that they go to visit her, but she's never there. They feel she doesn't have time for them. She replied that she couldn't stand the apartment, and she doesn't like to stay there.

She talked to Beth a bit, and told the girls she was going. I felt awful. It was always those inopportune moments that made me feel uncomfortable.

She'd always find an excuse to leave. At home, where she lived, she'd leave. She'd do that with Bob at her apartment. She doesn't know what she wants, but *we* do.

Beth came in the next day. I told her, if it wasn't for me, the girls wouldn't even give her the attention she gets. I try to do things to get us all together, life go to River's Edge. And now she might back out.

Beth said she don't like the way Judy talks to me, and talks down to me. I don't like it either. What can I really do? I just keep hoping and trying.

The girls have been really frustrated with Judy. I felt she got her second divorce to get closer to the girls, but they feel she isn't doing what she was going to do, which is to come home back here. Cheri feels I do enough for her, and about her divorcing the family, she can just go her own way.

I want her to come home, but I can see this is splitting up the girls from Judy.

Another thing bothering them is that Cheri saw Bob at her place. It's not helping the situation, either.

I felt that at that time, deep down, Judy was sorry for what she had done. I know she said that she didn't fight for half of everything, and also for the girls. She had too much pride.

At work the next day, Sharon called and wanted to know if I would like to take the young ladies out—Cheri and her. I said "Yes," and told Cheri to see if Judy wanted to go. She wasn't home, but she called later, and Cheri invited her to go. She wanted to join us. We picked her up, and went out to eat. We went shopping after; the girls both bought a sun catcher; Judy bought Sharon a blouse.

I told the girls that night that I was proud of them for being nice to Judy; it meant a lot to me.

At work the next day, the manager told me he didn't see any reason why I couldn't take Monday off. Yowza!!

I talked to Judy recently; she said that she doesn't have any doubts about going to River's Edge with us. Thank God, because I really want to go, even though I'll leave the guys out a bit on Monday.

Judy called to see if I wanted to go shopping with her tonight, but I couldn't since Candy was still here. She was disappointed to go by herself, but she seemed really happy to go to River's Edge with us. I'm so excited, and so glad that we can all go and have our family together again.

I wanted her to come see Candy, but she didn't want to stir anything up. She is afraid if my side of the family won't accept her like they once did. They might not at first, but I know that eventually they will. You can *bet* on that.

Well, today is the big day! God, please forgive us for not going to church. Hmmm. I will be spending the next two days with Judy.

I didn't sleep a lot, in anticipation of the big day, but that's ok! It's finally here, and we're going to get the car loaded up and get on with our trip.

Judy came in; the girls were still getting ready. We got gas, and left.

We drove straight through, and then got to our hotel. We went to eat at Johnson's Restaurant. I was thrilled to be on this trip with her, me and all my girls. It was peaceful to me, and there was *completeness* about the situation. It felt right. I was all right, for once in a real long time.

Judy and the girls were all laughing and joking together. I'm glad to see the girls including her.

While we were eating, Sharon said to Judy, "See how much fun you'd have if you came back." I wasn't sure what her response would be, but it went something like this: she laughed and asked if this was a plan, and I laughed and said, "Not really." After that I didn't know what to say. We were trying to bond again and get to know each other again; I'm not sure where she was coming from.

After supper, we went back to the hotel and the girls were swimming; we sat and talked. She asked if Beth gave me a lecture on bringing her to River's Edge. I told her, "Yes." I also mentioned that I might listen to people, but I do what's best for me.

She also said that Beth gave her one and to quit leading me on. Judy said she told Beth that she is honest with her feelings for me.

The girls then came back to the motel; we went down to the lounge for a drink. We talked about the girls, and all the usual pressures that are compacting around me—work, the girls, and especially *her.*

At that point, I threw my heart out. A typical Sagittarius, I threw it out there on the table. Right here, right now, these are my cards, straight up. Do you want to be on board or *what*?

I said those three words to her, those three beautiful words everyone wants to hear from the one they hold their deepest admiration for. In addition, I told her I want her back. Of course, I didn't know *how* to get her back.

We talked about a few other things, and left the lounge. We walked a few blocks, got some coffee, and brought it back to the motel.

My answers were on their way. She said her life was so screwed up right now, that she doesn't know what she wants. She can't guarantee me anything. She knows she can make it on her own, even though sometimes it's hard.

She didn't understand why I still loved her, even after everything. She added, "Maybe I don't know what love is." I told her, "Maybe you don't, but *I* do." She knew she could talk to me; she knew she could trust me. I told her that's part of love.

We then walked back to the room. The girls were there, but we had to get a new room, since the air conditioner broke and there was no way this night wasn't going to be less than perfect.

Cheri and Judy slept together; Sharon was with me. I watched my girls, smiling to myself that everything was going to be ok. Better get some sleep for tomorrow.

I felt better that night than in the last year and a half. I'd just stand there and watch her sleep, just like old times. I even covered her up once.

Big day at River's Edge! We rode many of the rides, coasters, you name it, and we even seen some shows. It was a joy to be there; there was a joy in my heart that I hadn't felt in a long time. I put my arm around her a couple of times to guide her; it felt great.

This was the first time I rode a roller coaster. It was exhilarating. A few months after the separation, she agreed to come on the trip with us.

Sharon remarked as she was running through the puddles, "Mom, this is the way it should be," but Judy hesitated and never answered. I was trying to woo her back and didn't succeed. We stayed at River's Edge for a whole day and the prior evening, and we had the best time.

After the big day, we drove home. She helped me unload the car; I put her suitcase in hers. I then closed the door. It was after twelve o'clock at night; I reached in to touch her chin, and thanked her for going along. I meant to kiss her cheek, but she turned, and I accidentally kissed her on her lips! I was ten feet tall, and climbing. She then said, "You're welcome," and left.

What a great vacation that was, let me tell you.

At work, I told the guys about the trip, and Matt said, "I know she'll be back."

I also remembered that Cheri said something to Judy on Monday, which was, "This is the way it should be; Mom and Dad together with their kids." I don't remember exactly what she said in return, but she did mention that she's happy she came along.

CHAPTER 11

All this craziness

I did talk to Judy a few days later, to see if she remembered about our date. Later that week she had forgotten when I called her about it the night before. It hurt—she knew I was disappointed. Bob was probably coming over and staying the weekend. I just don't get it.

It really tore me apart over the weekend, him staying with her. She says I smoke too much. Look at her, with what she's doing. I feel like a fool; I feel like an idiot—I'm the guy everyone tramples on. I just wish I wasn't here. I just wish sometimes I'd move, and get away from this place.

I dreamt of her, that she was kissing me and wanted to come back. She said she'd come back on my terms. I told her that she'd have to love me more than ever before. And no more dancing, only if I can go with her. I also told her she'd have to tell me about our problems, and not bottle them up. She kissed me and said, "Ok, I promise."

I had several other dreams—one was that Sally said she had her daughter back, and that they (Sally and Don) were quite happy about it. God, how I wish these dreams would come true.

There'd be other great moments together—one time we were at home and a song I liked came on. Cheri grabbed me and started to dance with me. Then Judy looked at me surprisingly, and I asked if she remembered this song. We danced together. God that felt good.

Every time we would not talk for a while, and then she'd call, I'd melt like butter in a frying pan. And then there was that, "Hi there!" when I'd see her. I guess that's what true love *is*.

I went out and got drunk soon after she dusted me on our date;

I wasn't feeling good, so I guess it wasn't the only reason. I just feel trampled by everyone.

Sometimes at the stores, the girls would give Judy a hard time. Not necessarily meaning to, but because they were young. It would make my evening go downhill, especially since I'd be trying to make it a better evening for all of us. Sharon would snap at Judy, or Cheri would make a comment. I'd try to fix it, but sometimes I couldn't.

Judy cancelled our date again—she had hurt her ankle, and was off all week. I couldn't be upset at her for that. Still, I was let down.

That night, around one o'clock, I was listening to the radio. And John Denver's "I'm Sorry" was on.

My feelings are true to these lyrics. I'm sorry I let her out of the house. Maybe all this craziness wouldn't have transpired. Maybe she was unhappy for a long time, perhaps for years; I don't know. I just couldn't read between the lines. All I know is, I love her and want her back. It's that simple.

That weekend, I went to Mom and Dad's. We had dropped Cheri off at Will's, and got to Mom and Dad's in the evening. We had dinner; Dad and Sharon went to bed. I told Mom that I was dating Judy now and then. She told me to be careful, and to watch myself. The second fall might be harder than the first.

The next day I drove home. During that long drive, I always thought of her. It was a solo trip. She stopped late in the evening, and I asked her out for Friday. She said she was busy Friday and Saturday. I felt let down, and on Sunday, I have to go back to get Sharon.

Interestingly, that night she brought up our divorce. She said that people told her that divorce is a fifty-fifty deal. I never thought of it that way, personally, and it wasn't fifty-fifty because *I* didn't want it. I asked her if she has figured out why she ever divorced me. She responded, "Neglect and money." I asked her to explain her statement, but she didn't. She wasn't in the mood.

It seems to me like she's dating someone else. If she is, maybe it's time to close the book on her, but then again, she may be blaming me for her divorce from Bob.

I don't like this back talk; I don't like her tone of voice. I'm worried; I'm upset. I don't like any of this. If things don't work out soon, I'm going to stop it all: this story, seeing her, helping her, saying her name, and talking about her.

My old Judy has died. She is a different person now. Like I said, I feel used. She just wants to get closer to the girls. When that rich man comes along, she'll be gone again.

Beth told me tonight that Bob is mad at her. He wants to know where she is and who she is with at all times. Screwy, isn't that? I guess he left in a hurry last time he was there, she added.

I know it. Someone else is in the picture.

Joseph told me, that Kathy told him, that Judy was dating other guys. Beth must have told her. She should have told me, but I guess she didn't want to hurt me.

I was thinking of Judy, and what she said about money. Yes, it's true; I don't have a lot of money. But I am a man who is rich in the love for his daughters.

I saw Matt Madden again. He was on vacation last week; I always miss him when that happens. I told him about Judy dating other guys and her sharp tone. He said, "Curt, God is on your side; just be patient."

Judy called me at work today, and she was upset because she wanted to pick Cheri up tomorrow from her uncle's house. Cheri said, "No," since I was going shopping with her tomorrow night. I tried to calm Judy down, but I don't know if it did any good.

Joseph was on my case again tonight. He wants me to back off Judy, and date other girls. She dates, so why don't I? She'll only come back when she's ready and wants to. No sense waiting on her.

Judy was over the other day; Sharon and her friend were downstairs playing in Judy's sewing material which she left here. She gave Sharon misery over it. But it really isn't Judy's. If she wants it back, then take it. If not, then what's here after the divorce is mine, and the girls can use it.

Well, it's the third week of August, close to my loved one's birthday. Sharon told me that Saturday doesn't suit Judy to be taken out, since Sunday afternoon would be better.

I was really upset when I heard that, since I would be back picking Sharon up. You see, after all, Saturday is her birthday, and I was the first one to ask her out. I replied in anger to Sharon, "If she thinks I'm going to work on things for her while she's out with another guy, she better forget it." I thought to myself, *I do everything for her, try to help her out with the girls, and this is what I get.*

After Cheri came home that night, she could see after delivering Don's birthday present (couldn't forget Don), that I had tears in my eyes. She asked what was wrong, and I told her. She said, "Dad, we've been telling you that for a year now, so forget her, because she's not worth it."

I told the girls, "Let's leave for the weekend." Cheri and Sharon decided we would go to Coaster City, and leave Saturday morning. We're even going to bypass Judy, and ask Sally to watch Sadie. I know it'll make Judy mad, but I just don't care at this point.

She wants me to take care of some things this weekend while she's out with another guy? No way. Let one of her boyfriends do that.

I can't believe all of this. I was going to finalize plans for her birthday today. I even bought her a necklace. I also bought fireworks in celebration, too. I was going to make reservations for her birthday, but I'll wait till tomorrow.

This is the third date that Judy was cancelled now, and each time, they were set up a week in advance.

She's changed. Maybe throughout this whole situation, God is trying to tell me something—I *feel* that He is. Maybe Judy isn't coming back, because she needs a lesson. Maybe things will work out; I don't know. Maybe what I feel for her anymore isn't love, like what I used to have for her. Now it's just my hurt talking.

The next day I went to work as usual. In the evening, we got things ready for Coaster City.

Before I went to bed, I wrote a note for Judy, explaining why we were leaving town. I put the note and her present in an envelope, put it on the counter, and went to bed. We'll have to see what happens.

The next morning, I got up early. Cheri was upset with me for leaving the note and present for Judy. She felt I shouldn't give her a present at all, but I know in my heart that I had to.

That morning we drove to Coaster City. There weren't as many rides as River's Edge Park, so to me the girls didn't have as much fun. The girls tried to be cheery and keep my spirits up all day; I was glad for that. I'm sorry Judy wasn't here to see our girls growing up.

We went back to our motel, and went to sleep for the night. But I stayed up and cried for Judy to return.

The next day we left Coaster City around one-fifteen, and at home I noticed a message on the counter. My note was gone, and I also noticed my present was still here.

In the message Judy mentioned that she was upset, and felt the girls didn't care about her. She also felt I couldn't accept that we weren't together anymore. I didn't know what to make of it.

I went to unpack the car. When I came in, Cheri had read the message. She had a hateful look on her face, and in a sharp tone said, "She's blaming you again."

Sharon grabbed it and read it, and gave me a kiss.

I called Judy to see if we could straighten things out, but there wasn't an answer.

I called Beth, and told her what was going on. She said she'd be over. She got here an hour later. We went out to talk. She told me Judy has a boyfriend, actually, a few of them. She also told me that Judy hopes I don't get married, since she'd be out then. I told Beth, "That's right."

I told Beth that Judy needs to get things straightened up with the girls, since the longer this goes on, the more it will tear them apart. I told Beth what Cheri said; she wishes Judy would leave and just let us alone.

Sharon started to feel that way, too.

I tell the girls to talk to Judy, but they say that Judy won't listen.

I told Beth, if things don't soon straighten out, I'm going to have to bury my love for Judy.

Well, my nerves are bad; I'm smoking and drinking as usual. But I do need to go to bed.

After work the next day, Sharon told me Judy was here. And Sharon gave her a present, and so did Cheri. Sharon asked her why she didn't take the present I got for her, and Judy said it was because of the circumstances under which it came. She added if I really wanted to talk to her, I can call her.

I didn't do anything wrong in this. In a way, you could say I stood Judy up. It wasn't meant to be this way. Now she knows how I feel and that she doesn't like it any more than I do.

Oh, I found out that her boyfriend has money, which is important to her. This guy is in his forties, loaded, with a boat. Great.

In my prayers before going to bed, I asked God for help, to straighten this mess out with Judy. I got one, and was able to do that.

Judy had the girls over for supper tonight. But I didn't get a chance to talk to her.

I told Beth that I am seriously thinking of bowing out gracefully and giving the ball to Judy. I told her I talked to Matt about it today, and he thought it was a good idea. I didn't tell Judy that I might go out with someone else a few times, to see if it would wake her up. Maybe it won't; we'll see.

Beth mentioned she told Judy about me going out with other women. Judy just stared back at her in discontent.

Well, she can go out, so why can't I?

The next day, Beth called, and said she has a new boyfriend. She wants me to meet him. Actually, she wants me to watch her kids this weekend, so she can go to meet his family, and I said, "Sure." She told him about me, and he said I must be quite a guy. That felt good.

I told her I still hadn't talked to Judy.

You could say in a way that I stood Judy up on Sunday. However, our date was for Saturday, not Sunday. She's taking me for granted and I do feel bad. I hope we can clear this up.

Cheri had gone over to Judy's; I really hope she never walks in on Judy and one of her boyfriends; it would be pretty bad. I'm sure Cheri would just explode on her, verbally.

I'm still hoping and praying that we work this out. We'll have to see.

That weekend I was invited to a picnic. I wasn't sure if I really wanted to go. I drove all the way down to Gennistown, but turned around and headed back to Burchin. My skin was bothering me, and I just couldn't get it together to go. I stopped and had coffee in Burchin and then went home.

My skin is falling apart, and so is my heart. Judy's turned me out again, and I don't know what to do. Every time I think of going out with someone new, Judy's memory hits me like that tree did on Rt. 165.

That evening, Beth and her guy came home to get Justin and Stacey.

I could tell by the look on her face that she had a great weekend, but not me. My life is all screwed up.

I saw Matt again at work. He always asks how things are going. I told him I'm going to ask other people out, if I see someone I'd like to take out. I also said, I'm still asking Judy out, and going all formal when I do take her out.

I think he was glad to hear this.

Matt did feel that she'll have to make the next move, but if she doesn't want to be a mother to the girls, it's best if she leaves this area and moves somewhere else.

That night, the girls didn't go with Judy when she asked them over, since they already ordered pizza.

I still sat and thought about her, and put my trust in God. I'm putting more faith in Him, and I know he'll work it out someday.

At work the next day, Bob Jordan and Suzie the secretary were giving me a lecture on Judy. They told me to stop worrying about everything. Things will be what they will be. Judy said to put it in God's hands—I guess there's not much else I can do.

The Annual Fair's coming up, and my mom and dad and Joe and Lilly are coming in this weekend. I've talked to Beth, too, and I guess Judy wants an apology for the mix-up. We'll have to see what happens.

I've had these strange dreams lately. First, I was with another woman; we were at my parents' house.

In another dream, I went to talk to Judy, to see if we could get back together. She was locked in this room. Someone went and unlocked this room so she could come out to see me. She didn't come out, so I went in. She was sitting on this big rock. We talked a little, then she said, "I don't know," in response to I'm not sure what, then she got up and jumped off the rock. She turned into a small dog or cat when she hit the floor, and started to run away. Someone caught her and said, "I told you she is a little mixed-up, now do you believe us?"

I'm not quite sure what these dreams mean, if I should stay or go. I do know that perhaps these dreams occurred since I was wondering about these questions.

My family did come in that weekend, but I didn't go to the Annual Fair. Joe and Lilly stopped by, and she asked about Judy. I told her I didn't feel right about what was going on, since she hasn't talked to me for about two weeks now.

My heart still aches for her. Since I've put it in God's hands, I do feel better. It would be nice if she would come back. If not, I'll accept things the way they are. I still feel Judy didn't give me a chance, and she's using me. I still hope and pray that she comes back to where the love *is*. If not, I have a warehouse of love to get rid of.

At work, a lady I know stopped in today. She said her and her husband split three weeks ago. He took the house and the kids, and kicked her out. She didn't say what the problem was and I didn't ask. She asked me to take her out sometimes, but her husband is an old friend, and I just can't do that to him.

Lately, the money issue with Judy, which that was one of our problems, really has been bothering me. I always did the best I could, saving up and buying things cash.

As far as taking her out goes, I really don't have the extra cash right now. That has to go into paying the bills, and taking care of Cheri and Sharon.

I still hadn't talked to Judy about her birthday mishap. The girls were being picked up by her today, and were having dinner at Beth's tonight.

Cheri mentioned to Judy that I was going to help her with a project she was working on.

When I heard this, I told the girls to tell Judy to call me when she wants me to work on her apartment, like moving something or hanging something up. For three Saturdays I've tried, and it hasn't worked out.

Beth even mentioned it to me. Well, she can call me, can't she?

I went to see Dr. Banks today. He asked how things were going with my "X" and me. He mentioned that my skin has been in turmoil since my divorce.

He said, "It's funny how two people fall in love, decide to get married and raise a family and live their lives together. Then one day, something happens and it's gone. And most of the time it is over the little things."

He also said, "There is a very thin line between love and hate."

He suggested that I quit worrying about things between Judy and the girls, and everybody else.

It's easy for people to say that, when they're not in the situation. I know they care, but they're not hurting like I am.

Later that evening, I went out with Dylan. He said to back off from Judy and wait; this is easier said than done.

At church that Sunday, I prayed again for Judy's return. I got a tingling feeling all through my body. I really believe God was listening to me. I don't know His plans, but I'm sure He was listening.

Later that day, I went back to The Club. I had a really nice time there. I met a great lady. She was in her fifties, and if she wasn't, I would've asked her out. She'd been divorced about eighteen years.

She felt Judy is uncomfortable with me because she feels guilty. I'd be dumb to take her back. This nice lady said to give other women a chance, since many of them would love to have a nice guy like me for a husband. She also said that Judy feels guilty since she let someone else get in-between her and her children.

I appreciated her time, and her comments made me feel so good. I slept better that night than in a long time!

I saw Matt Madden again. He was glad that I sounded and looked better than I have in a long time. He said he can't tell me whether or not I should wait on Judy; that's up to me. I'm a person too, and should be treated like one, not someone to fall back on. He said I was to keep the faith, and go out with a girl or two.

He's a good man, and I appreciate him listening to me, and his great and timely advice.

Finally, after several weeks, I was coming home, from work and there was Judy's car in the driveway. I wasn't sure what to do. I went in, and nothing was said for about thirty seconds. Judy said she came down to give Cheri a perm. We made some small talk, and then I went downstairs.

After, I came up, and the girls weren't in the kitchen.

I asked her why she didn't take my birthday present. She said that she didn't like the circumstances.

We talked, and got things straightened out. I asked her if she'd like her present now. She said, "Yes." I laid it on the counter, and it sat there while we talked.

She thought I cut her favorite tree down, just for spite. I said, "No."

She also said, I should go out with friends and not sit here.

She then said that she asked the girls to go to the ice show next month, and asked me, too.

I was pleasantly surprised. I wanted to say yes right away, but I pretended I was thinking. Then I said, "That sounds nice, ok."

We also talked about a lot of things, like I'd like to take her out, and spend money on her, but I don't have it.

We talked about the kids having the cars and other things. I did acknowledge that I told Beth I am tired of trying to get her and the girls together. Because every step I take to help her, she turns around and takes two steps backwards with the kids. Later, Kathy called, and we went out for coffee and talked.

The next day, I was thankful to God for sending Judy here, and that we were able to talk and work things out. There was that old Judy in her talking to me tonight, and I was grateful. I'm putting my trust in God with this situation.

CHAPTER 12

She acquired a "friend".

Beth called Judy, and wanted to go with us to the holiday show. Judy told her she just wanted us to go. She asked me to intervene for her. She cheered up when I told her I'd talk to Beth. She then said, "We're not even married, and you're still getting me out of trouble." I have many times, since our divorce done things like that. She doesn't seem to get it that I do it out of my love for her.

A few days later, Judy was over to trade cars with Cheri. I added some oil to the car, and then I went with Cheri to see Reba McEntire. I enjoyed the show very much, but would have preferred Judy being there.

Later, Beth was here with her guy. She asked me to go to Joe's with him while she worked. Beth told me that Judy went out with Beth and a friend of hers the other day, but that's all that was said on that.

The next day Beth's car wouldn't start, so Kathy took her to work, and Cheri went with me to see what the problem was. We got it started and dropped it off at work for her.

The next day, Beth called. She said she called Judy after midnight, then early in the morning. No answer. Beth said Judy is really upsetting her lately.

She's doing things that Beth never expected. She's been out every night, with a different guy. She thinks she's with some of them. I know Beth is telling me these things little by little, not to upset me. She knows I can't take it all at once.

She brings her boyfriends around for Beth to meet; Beth feels none of these guys are for Judy, but she knows she can't tell her that.

I told Matt Madden about this, and he said it sounds like she doesn't know what she wants.

Another day, she was crying because she was at the house and her car wouldn't start. It wasn't in park. Oh, I hate it when she cries, because it makes me feel so bad. We got it cleared up, and she went home, and I called her later. I guess Cheri upset her, and Judy yelled at her. I wanted to go up there and help her. She said she was ok, because through this, she acquired a *friend*.

My heart hit the floor. I thought I was getting closer to her, and I really wasn't. She's using me again; who are these guys that she picks up, anyway? It's none of my business, but it hurts anyhow.

It came time to go to the show. We took my car; Judy paid for gas. On the way up and back we talked a lot with the kids. The show was nice and I wanted to take everyone out to dinner afterwards. I wasn't sure where to go, but we picked a nice place and went in to eat. I wouldn't have it any other way. It went great. I got the lobster. Everyone seemed to have enjoyed themselves immensely.

We came back; she got into my car to go home. She wound down the window and started the car. I put my head in to kiss her on the cheek. (Hey, she said that her life was so messed up lately.) I intended to give her a light kiss, but we ended up kissing each other. What a moment! It was magical; it was great!

I know she wanted to kiss me as much as I did. I said, "I still love you." She said, "I know." We said, "Good night." She then backed out of the driveway. I never got complete satisfaction, because she would never say it back.

I did feel on cloud nine, though, that night. I was about five feet off the ground, in fact. I was so thankful for that night and that kiss.

The next couple of nights, I had those dreams again. In the first one, Tim and I went to a bar, but it was in the basement of a house looking like Grandma's. In the second dream, I was talking to Judy. She said, "I saw Bob the other day. We had kissed a few times. She added, "If you want me, you'll have to pay more attention to me, than he did." As we kissed, I said, "You got it!"

As my birthday approached, Judy offered to make the cake, and that made me feel good. Cheri told her that the party was Sunday at seven, and she snapped back and said, "The cake will be there, but I don't know if I will." So, for a few days, I worried that she might not come.

That Sunday was my party. Judy came around six-twenty. She told me, "Guess who is engaged." I didn't know who she was talking about. She said that Bob is. I was glad, since then I knew he wouldn't bother her. Not right now, at least.

I wanted to say, "Honey I told you, he couldn't love you like I did."

Later, Sally, Beth and other family came. After we had cake and opened my presents, everyone left.

The next day at work, I told Matt Madden about my birthday party. He was glad Judy came. I also told him about Bob getting engaged. He smiled, and said, "One down," and I thought, one to go! Yes!

Judy told Beth that she wished I would go out with someone else. She said that she dates other men, so I should date other women. I would only take out women who were my close immediate friends or relatives, such as my daughters or my niece. At a wedding, I would usually take Cheri or my oldest grandson.

Next night at dinner, Cheri asked who's playing at The Music House. Sharon said, "Randy Travis is, and Daddy is taking Mommy." Cheri replied, "Blah." I guess she still doesn't approve.

It's been three years since I hit that tree on Rt. 165. It's still alive. Part of me is still living, but part of me died.

I asked Judy about seeing Mel Tillis; she said, "Yes." I can't wait!

I talked to Beth. I guess Judy is upset over Sally coming to my party, since she didn't see Judy. That's not my fault.

At church today, the pastor quoted a passage from Mark. But I forgave her. All I want now is to have her back; I just want my love returned.

Cheri talked to Judy and she mentioned about us going out Saturday night. I guess our plans are still on; that's great. I'm even planning on getting her a corsage for our date, since she cut me short on Sweetest Day.

Wow! The day of the big date! I picked her up around seven. We went to The Squire for dinner, before going to The Music House. Everything was going great, until I mentioned that Sharon didn't feel good on Tuesday. From then on, I could feel the hostility.

After the show, we went to Gillente's and had a drink. She then started on the situation with Sharon. I tried to explain to her that there really wasn't anything wrong with Sharon, and if there was, I would have let her know about it immediately.

Boy, did I get flack over this. She felt I was pushing her out.

I cried on my way home. I felt she was just picking anything she could to widen the gap between us, because she has no intention of <u>ever</u> coming back. She also mentioned to me, more than once, that she has expensive taste. That sounded in my heart in a hurtful way.

The next night, I had one of my dreams again. Each dream had me opening and closing locked doors and relocking them. I'm not sure what this means, but maybe I should keep these doors shut and let things alone.

I told the girls that Judy made a fuss over Sharon being sick. Sharon reminded Judy again, what was said to her, and I gather things got straightened out.

I wish Judy wouldn't get so mad at me and blame things on me. Sharon said, "She only does that Daddy, because she loves you." I said, "It sure doesn't sound that way to me, but I still love her anyway." Sharon said that I should tell her I love her. I said, "I do, but it doesn't do any good." She added, "Well, Daddy, one day you'll be happy again. You should look at your life as a circle. Cheri and I fill up one-half, and Mommy used to fill the other half. You lost one wife and still have us; Mommy lost two husbands, but she doesn't have anyone."

Sharon is wise for her age. As they say, "out of the mouth of babes comes wisdom."

I told Joseph about how Judy takes things. He said. "She doesn't realize how nice you are, and if you were someone other than yourself, you'd be a real idiot." I guess he's right.

Prayer is the only thing that keeps me going. I see no dawn over the horizon, of Judy ever coming back.

Beth told Judy recently that her current guy is too self-centered. She shouldn't be going out with him, anyway.

At church, the pastor talked about I Corinthians 13: 4-7. It hurts to hear it, since I am patient, kind, and loving, and I'm not resentful, and I feel right now that she is none of these things.

I had another dream about Judy. Her brother came by, and told me that Judy was worried about Sharon, so we went with Cheri to find her. Sharon was also in this dream. We were back home, walking upstairs of this old apartment building. We found her apartment, and I knocked on the door. She opened it, and grabbed and kissed Sharon.

I told her, I just wanted her to know that Sharon was ok. She put her arms around me and thanked me. I also told her not to keep her boyfriend from me. Even though I don't like it, there was nothing I could do about it.

We were standing in a hall, and three girls came down the steps. She was to go out with them, but she told them to go ahead without her. She looked at me, then put her arms around me, and kissed me tenderly for a long time. Then I woke up.

Next night, I was talking to Beth. She says Judy feels guilty about everything. Judy feels we should just all accept it. I don't think she's accepted things, and neither have I.

I really enjoy being with Judy, but you'll never know how much anguish I go thru: being afraid to touch her, and being afraid of rejection.

I'm a really sad person. I remember when Judy said she was unhappy in our marriage. Now that we're divorced, she's still despondent. I just don't get it.

CHAPTER 13

Calling her 'Judy'

Judy couldn't pick the girls up from dancing, because she had a date. Boy that made me mad. I can't afford to take her out, because I have to keep a roof over the girls' heads. Now she's going out with someone else, instead of me. Darn.

Sharon had a doctor's appointment. She called Judy to take her, and Judy said "No," since she was busy that morning. It made Cheri mad, and really hurt Sharon. I told Sharon to tell Judy, and Judy changed her appointment. I know they were hurt.

Next day, I was talking to Judy about Sharon's birthday party, and she'd make the cakes. I told her that Cheri wanted me to call "Judy," since she wanted to talk to me. Uh-oh. I shouldn't have said that to her on the phone, but it was too late to retrieve it. Judy said, "What, what's this, Cheri calling me 'Judy'?!" I tried to laugh it away, but it didn't work. She cut me off and snapped, "Well, I guess we've been on the phone long enough." Then she hung up.

I was hurt, but I knew she really wouldn't understand. I told the girls long ago they could call her what they wanted, so that's what they chose to call her.

The girls cornered me later and asked me what was wrong. I told them. Cheri said, "Too bad." Sharon added, "There's nothing wrong with that." I told them to be ready for questions tomorrow.

Next day was Sharon's birthday, and Judy came over to help. We gave Sharon her stereo. She thanked us both.

A few of Sharon's friends came over. After we all ate, Judy asked why the girls are too busy for her. I told her she needs to ask them more often to do things together, things that don't even cost that much.

About us, I told her that she and the girls have me wrapped around their fingers, and I love doing things, especially for her. I told her, "I know I shouldn't, but I do care about you." She didn't say much in response to that.

As she walked to the door that night, she told me in a broken voice that as a mother she thought she did everything right, but the girls picked their father. I put my hand on her arm, and told her lovingly that, "You were a good mother and wife." She replied, "You said it, I *was*." After I knew she was ok, she left. Later, I went to bed.

The next day, I thought of what she said, and that I should have told her, "You can be a good mother and wife again." But if her response was negative, I think I would have lost it.

That same day was the party. Don, Sally, Beth, and Judy came over. We had a nice time. I really wanted to ask her to go to New Year's at The Music House, and I wanted to know if we are spending Christmas together this year. I did ask her to The Music House tomorrow night. We'll see what happens.

The next day, we went to church, and after dinner, I took Sharon to Terry's Ice Cream.

Later, I went to pick her up. We went out to eat first. Judy knew the waitress, who was from the dance group! She told her that her life has went downhill since the last time they seen each other. She introduced me as her "X". I didn't like that. She told her, "We're still friends."

We went to the show. Then, we went to her apartment to look at Christmas catalogs for the girls. We decided to go "X"-mas shopping together. I can't wait.

A few days later, we went to Judy's brother's house for Thanksgiving dinner. I was so excited as usual to spend the holiday with all my girls. Things were going great, until Beth talked about her night with her boyfriend. They were out, and then Judy came in.

At that moment, I was upset. I couldn't let it show, since I didn't want people to know. I wouldn't want to ruin everyone else's dinner. Earlier that day, she'd asked me to help her get some stuff out of her car. I wanted to say, "Let your boyfriend do it."

I was hurt, knowing I do everything for her. I'm in anguish. I try to get her to go out with me, and look forward to it. I can't try to piece this back together myself.

After getting thru dinner, we all packed up and went home. I just tried to get thru another holiday and go to sleep.

That Saturday morning, I got up and got some work done in my garage. I had to get to the hardware store for some tools. I feel better now that I found what I needed. I did have to back track though, to take care of all of this.

When I came home, Cheri said for me to call Judy. I did, and asked her why she didn't tell me she had off. She said she went out last night, and called off today.

So, we made arrangements to go "X"-mas shopping that evening. I picked her up. Things were going well—we bought clothes for the girls, got Cheri a new tape recorder and even a clock radio for her birthday.

At one point, Judy commented that, "You have more money to spend for "X"-mas than I do." I said, "I don't know about that, since I have two teenage girls to take care of." She then got sharp with me, and said, "Don't rub it in." I apologized and told her I didn't mean it that way.

We ate at Charlie's, and came home. I was tired. I didn't let the girls know what happened.

I looked in the mirror, and could only see a miserable person looking back.

I want to be loved and I'm hoping that my kindness and love would bring her back, just like I hoped it would keep us together. But it hasn't. What am I to do now?

I wish she'd spend more time with the girls, but she must think she is more important to just be doing things for herself. There's more to being a mother than bringing a baby into this world.

The next night, the girls mentioned about Judy taking Cheri to Harristown. Judy said she was to take her. I then told Cheri, "I told her we'd all go."

Then Cheri said, "She used to do a lot of things, but she's not married to us anymore." It hit me like a brick. Then Sharon said, "Yeah." I told them not to talk like that, but they're right. She did divorce *us*. She's not fully a part of our everyday lives, like eating dinner together.

We work around her to get her to be with us and do things with us, but it can only go so far.

Well, today is a big trip. We have to get going early. We picked up Judy, and headed up. We went to Cheri's doctor, and everything turned out ok.

Being that I wanted everyone to relax afterward, we stopped at a restaurant to eat. Judy and I sat on one side of the booth; the girls were on the other.

My coat was near hers, near the wall, and I gently reached around her to get my cigarettes out of the pocket.

She then said, "I could've gotten them for you." Sharon chirped up and said, "He just wanted to put his arm around you, Mom!" She was right. I smiled, with a 'yes'-type of smile.

Later, Judy commented that she didn't know why she went along, since she really couldn't answer the doctor's questions, and we couldn't get any shopping done, either. Sharon again said, "Use your head, Mom! We just wanted to be with you."

Again, she was right. I'm glad she went with us and I hope she gets that old feeling again, and she'll realize that she belongs with those that love her the most. I had a wonderful day.

The next day at work, Sandy said I looked great after having a day of rest. We talked a little about our exes. She's still in love with hers, after three years, and after two, I am still in love with mine. Aren't we a pair?

Next night, and the night after, Judy wasn't going "X"-mas shopping again. I took a friend of the girls' home, since she was visiting. I then paid bills, and went to bed.

The next day, I didn't believe it! Judy has plans for New Year's! If I didn't let my fear override me, it could have been me going out with her!

However, she just might have cut me off, like she has before. I knew not to wait so long. My love is cooling for her.

I can't believe this day. I then went to the post office, then to Dr. Banks, and stopped in at work, to check on Joseph. I chatted with Joseph a little, and afterwards I went home to wait on Judy's phone call.

She called, and wanted to go shopping. We went to the mall, and after that we ate at Charlie's. While we had coffee at the mall, Judy said she did go out with some guy, but she's not interested.

At Charlie's, this guy Anthony came over (I met him last year while "X"-mas shopping), and said, "Hi!" She called him over, and they talked about dancing. She introduced me as her "X" and friend. Again, she knew I wasn't crazy about that. After he left, she told me she didn't know how to introduce me; she was right.

That evening, I asked her what she wanted for "X"-mas. She said, "What money can't buy." She wants to be close to the girls. I can't help much more on that. She said that, "If my girls were closer to me, my life would straighten out." I can help, if she comes back. As far as our lives straightening out, mine will in time. I hope and pray it turns out the way I want it to.

Another night, she took Cheri "X"-mas shopping. When dropping Cheri off, she didn't even come in to say, "Hello." That kind of action bothers me, like she's allergic to me or afraid of me a bit.

At work today, I found out that that my workplace might close. It was hard to go Christmas shopping tonight, knowing what I am aware of. I guess God will just have to work it out somehow.

On the 20th, I had a great time wrapping X-mas presents with Judy. We didn't get them all done, and she said she'd wrap the rest of Sharon's presents while I visited Mom and Dad.

She also mentioned that Bob was getting married on January 9th; I was glad.

She's coming down X-mas Eve, and staying with us until the morning, to watch the girls unwrap their presents. I can't wait!

The evening of the 23rd, the girls and I drove back to see my family. We got there about ten o'clock. It was great to see Mom, Dad and Barry.

The next day we stayed at Mom and Dad's until one-thirty, visited Joe, then got on the 'pike and came home. We got here around six; I called Judy around seven. She said she was busy wrapping presents. She called around nine, and said she was going to her mother's, and she'd be there later.

CHAPTER 14

Judy and her boyfriend

At eleven-thirty, I called Sally's. Sharon was disappointed that she wasn't here yet. Sally said, "'They' left here forty-five minutes ago, and went to Beth's." I asked who "they" were. "Judy and her boyfriend," was the response. I broke down inside, and began to cry.

I asked Sally how long she knew about this; she said about three weeks. She apologized for letting me know now. I called Beth's. She said they left fifteen minutes ago. Beth felt bad, too, and told me she's known about this guy for one week. She knew it would ruin my X-mas, and it did.

Judy came here after midnight. I was glad to see her, but it hurt. I finished up the presents; we arranged them and I filled a stocking for her.

Sharon slept with Judy in my bed; I checked on them several times that night.

Next morning, I was happy knowing she was here, but sad at the same time.

She wasn't looking forward to X-mas, but she knows deep down it was there because of me.

We went to Christmas dinner at Beth's; she was cool to me.

Later, we came back to our house. Sally and Don, my aunt, Beth and her boyfriend followed.

Before Sally left, she said, "Please give Judy more time!" She thinks we made a very big mistake, talking Judy into going to a shrink, because Judy is now more messed up than she ever was.

At the gathering, Beth let me know about Judy's boyfriend. Sharon yelled out to Beth, to quit talking to me about Judy, since I only get upset.

Beth also said that Judy and he are going away in January. Judy told Beth she was upset that Cheri's party would be around that time, and it's going to upset her plans. Beth didn't like that.

Later, Sharon said Stacey told her that Mommy has a new boyfriend, and that they were at Beth's last night. She said, "If two can play that game, you need a girlfriend."

I also asked Cheri why she didn't tell me. She said, "You know why." She added, "I'm enjoying my life right now, like you said I would. I don't care about her anymore, and I don't care if she comes back or not."

I decided to call Kathy and see if she wants to go to the New Year's Eve party with me. She said she'll call me on Wednesday to let me know.

Joseph's glad I asked her to go, but, boy, he's not too thrilled about Judy.

After X-mas, at work, I had seen Matt Madden again. He was sorry for me, X-mas turning out the way it did. He told me not to try so hard, and not to worry so much. I said, "But God helps those who help themselves." He said, "But, your help doesn't seem to working." I guess he's right.

Kathy said she'd go with me. Great! I have a date! I called Beth, to tell her not to say anything. She agreed. She was so happy that I was going. I called Kathy, to tell her what time I was picking her up tomorrow nite.

It's New Year's Eve! I'm excited. After work, I stopped at the store to get some goodies for Sharon, Justin and Stacey.

I picked Kathy up at eight. We both had a really good time. I did drink a quart of slush, though!

Kathy came up with an idea, to tell Beth that she didn't go out with me, since her friend Charlie called, and she got her cousin, Barb, to go out with me instead. She told me about Barb, so if I was asked, I would know what to say. Kathy came up with this idea, because Beth told Stacey, and I think the girls figured out who I was taking. This would put doubt in people's heads.

I'm hoping this will get to Judy and start to wake her up, and that she may return. I'm going to play it, like Joseph, Matt, and Kathy suggested. Let's see what happens!

That night, after I took Kathy home, she invited me in for coffee.

We were sitting and talking and she got this book out, a fortune-telling book. She did my cards for me.

Before we started, I had to make a wish, and you know what I wished for.

Interestingly, my wish card came out. Although, according to the book, it said that it would probably not come true, at least not in the near future. That hurt.

I got home around three a.m. The girls were all in bed; Justin was in mine. I crashed and went to sleep.

Next day, not much transpired, except in the evening, Cheri was having Beth stay over. It was already late and Cheri went to follow her home before coming back. They were out till three a.m., and boy was I upset, but glad that they were safe.

That day, one part of Kathy's book reading did come true. A lite-complected blonde would call me or write me. My sister Candy did. One down!

A few days after New Year's (January 3), Sharon was talking to Judy. Sharon told her about her nite, and Cheri's, and mine. Judy wanted to know who I took out. She told her that she and Cheri weren't sure. Judy stated that it's about time that I date, because, she dates other guys.

Judy also told Beth that she wished I would go out with someone else. She said that she dates other men, so I should date other women.

Personally, I would only take out women who were my close immediate friends or relatives, such as my daughters or my niece. At a wedding, I would usually take Cheri or my oldest grandson.

I was afraid she'd say that. I was expecting a different reaction. I feel really bad, sad and mad at the situation. I'm just going crazy. I'm just going to drink coffee and smoke some more.

The next few days, I didn't eat much, and I got this feeling that she's never coming back. I haven't seen her since X-mas, and I just don't know what to do.

I just don't care if I live or die again. Life is just something to do, to fill in the time between birth and death, nothing more. Don't get me wrong, I'm not at the suicide point, because I need to raise my girls. I just don't care about life anymore.

At work the next day, I was thinking about applying for another job.

I don't know how things will work out with the crew, but I'm going to apply anyway. We'll see what happens.

The biggest decision to make right now is with Judy. What's she doing? Can't she figure it out that all I want right now is *her*? And that I'm not doing these things out of friendship? Doesn't she get it? Why won't she give me a chance? I am *miserable* and lonely.

The next day, Judy stopped in to help Sharon return some X-mas items. I gave her a late X-mas present: earrings and a necklace. She really seemed to like them. She said she'd talk to me later.

I took the X-mas tree down, and then I went and got a haircut. Sharon called from Judy's, to say she was going to a friend's house. She'd call after. Cheri went to Beth's.

I was by myself, and upset. I wanted to see Judy again.

Sharon called that evening, to have me pick her up. She said that Judy had to take something over for her boyfriend. Judy asked Sharon to go, but she didn't want to.

I was really upset after I heard that, and hit the bottle when I got home.

I felt pretty good after I had about five extra strong drinks of vodka in me.

I feel good when I see her, then I dread it when she leaves. I'm cheerful one moment, and feeling awful the next. She's always running thru my mind. Like asking her out—I'm always afraid she'll reject me.

I still wish I wasn't living. I pray for Judy to return. I'm happy to have my girls, but I am a lonely and tormented man.

CHAPTER 15

Tears

Today I would call it the "house of tears." At church, I had my usual tingle while praying for Judy. Afterwards, I got a feeling that something was brewing. I took Stacey and I back home, and then Sharon told me that Judy invited her and Stacey for dinner. I was disappointed, since I wanted to invite her to dinner—I had chickened out.

I was talking to Judy when she picked up the girls, and I told her about a show that I took Stacey to. She said, "Yeah, I enjoyed it, too." I could have fallen over. I knew at that point that she must have been there with her boyfriend. I was going to invite her for dinner, but didn't. Then they left.

I had seen Beth later. She explained that Judy invited herself out with her and her boyfriend. She danced with a lot of guys; she wasn't quite like she was when she was around Bob.

Friends of ours were there, and snubbed Judy, and made her cry. I certainly didn't like to hear that; however, I don't blame them for feeling like they do.

She also mentioned that Bob was at the dance club, and he has been real hateful to her. Beth says she falls too fast. I felt I'm good enough for her between boyfriends, but that's about it.

When she left, I went and got drunk. Cheri was out. I was a low, low drunk because I felt Judy would never be back.

Sharon was back then, and I asked her about her day. She replied, "Just like before, when Mommy has someone else around I get ignored."

I then said, "You mean, Judy's boyfriend was there?" She said, "Yes."

Oh, I was really mad at Judy and I was mad at Sharon. I didn't know why she didn't come home. She said she didn't want to walk in the cold.

I yelled at her; I cried; I said things I didn't want to say. She cried; we cried together.

I later sat down, and she made me coffee. She said I needed it more than anything to drink. She was right; but I can't seem to do anything to get Judy back.

After three cups of coffee, I felt better, and I asked Sharon what he looked like. She said, "Like Bob, but older."

Then Cheri stormed in, even yelling at Sadie. She was really upset. I asked her what was wrong. Her boyfriend doesn't want to see her anymore.

I told her about Judy's boyfriend being at the house. She knew he'd be there, that's why she didn't go. She also didn't want to let me know about him being there, figuring I'd be upset.

Next day at work, I told Joseph about her new boyfriend. He didn't think much of it. If God doesn't want me to have Judy, I wish he'd send me someone else.

Matt believes if God wants it to be, he'll let it happen. He also said that if she's happy, I should pray for her happiness. He gave me a Bible verse to read. He also mentioned that she doesn't know what she wants, since she's had four or five boyfriends.

Today is my older daughter's birthday. It seems like yesterday that I held her and fed her from the bottle. Now she drives a car, keeps this house in order, and chases boys.

That following Sunday was her birthday party. Sharon and I went to church. We also had steaks for dinner, and then headed up to Judy's. Several of her family members' cars were there, but not her boyfriend's car. I'm glad, because I don't think I could've handled it.

Will was there, too. After everything, Sharon walked to her friend's house. Then everyone else left, leaving me, her and Cheri.

She told me about seeing our friends, but not about how upset she was. She felt it was funny, how some of our old friends don't talk to her anymore. "I know," I said. They don't know how to handle the situation.

I wanted to ask her out for again, but I asked God for a sign.

I talked to Judy a little, put my coat on, and wanted to leave, since I didn't want to meet Charlie.

I went to the bathroom, and heard a knock, and a man's voice, so I decided not to ask her out. I asked God for strength. I went out to the living room, and she introduced us. He was a bit leery, and so was I.

I extended my hand. We shook hands; we said, "Hello."

I didn't say much to him. What do you say to someone that might be your predecessor that may take your love away from you?

He didn't look at me that much, and just talked to her. Cheri and I left. We were quiet going home. I told her soon after, that I can't help it that I love her. As long as I have you girls, maybe one day she will love me again and want to come back. Cheri wanted me to keep trying; I'm glad she approves.

A few days later, everything was in a disarray. I was at work, and Cheri called me. Judy had come over, and Cheri was mad at Sharon. Judy sided with Sharon, but things escalated, and she sent them to their rooms. The girls got mad. They felt she had no right to do that, since she doesn't live here anymore. After counting to ten, Cheri came out of her room, and yelled at Judy. She told her not to go running to me, or call her boyfriend. Judy said there wouldn't be these problems, if they went with her.

A few minutes later, she came back in and they all got mad again.

Judy was blaming me again, for *her* problems.

Judy told the girls I want her back, but she can't come back. It didn't bother me at the moment that she said that. Sharon told me this, but I asked why, and she didn't say.

I told them I can't help how I feel about their mother.

I was on the phone with them over an hour, trying to calm them down.

I told Joseph what happened, but he said that she'll probably never get closer to the girls, unless she comes back.

I feel sorry over the way everything turned out. I'm sorry for the way our lives have been turned upside down, and into different directions.

I shaved part of my beard off and kept the mustache. I need a change. I only did it for her, and I guess I just wanted it off; if I grow this again, it will be for me and my girls.

I feel Judy won't be back now; she's gone from me. I'm lonely and heartbroken. I do feel more at peace with myself, but I do still love her.

If anybody would have told me three years ago that we wouldn't be getting along I'd call them a liar. I just can't believe what happened to my family. I don't understand it, and probably never will.

I feel we can never be, with her blaming things on me, when she can't get along with the girls. She keeps tearing away at the wall of love I have for her. There are only a few stones left. It might be the best thing if she stays away from me.

When I see her again, I'll be able to tell if there's any love there.

I was driving to see the tax man, and on my way there, I seen Judy. I tooted my horn at her, but she didn't see me. I was pained inside.

He was even surprised that we didn't get back together yet, and was sure we could've worked it out. He said that most women figure they're missing something, because they have more free time on their hands, and most men don't.

I feel Judy never thought married life was the way it turned out to be. She really never loved me as I did her. I don't believe it when people say you grow apart. Nonsense! If you love someone, you make it a point to grow *together*.

I noticed I was low on cigarettes, and that I didn't buy them last week. That's good. That was a first in a long time.

Beth was talking to Cheri later that day. Cheri told her about the big fight. I don't know what Beth said, but Cheri responded with, "She is only my mother by birthright, nothing else." Beth changed the subject.

Sharon reminded me tonight of Matthew 19:9. It talks about if a man marries someone else, that person is committing adultery. I read it, and told Sharon, "I know that." I told her, "I read my Bible, and I read it a lot more these days."

At night, when I tucked her in, I told her to say her prayers. She said she doesn't do that anymore. I know she used to pray for Judy to come back. Since her prayers weren't answered, she gave up.

For me, I believe God will work it out one day. I know He will; I have faith.

Joseph let it slip that he seen Judy out. He told her she has to give up the idea of being the girls' mother, and just be their friend. He also had some other ideas. She'll have to work on it and give it time.

She asked Joseph if I was moving out-of-state. He told her, "No." I told him, "Yes, I would. The house doesn't mean that much to me." On the other hand, I would like the girls to be able to finish school. That's the only reason I'm still here.

The next day, I went to buy candy for the girls, and also candy and a card for Judy.

After picking up Sharon and Stacey at the movies, Sharon said, "Dad, you know Beth had a birthday party, and we weren't invited? Grandma set it up and she asked Mom, and Mom asked if she could bring Charlie." That wasn't said in a nice tone.

Sharon added, "Stacey said Beth told Cheri about it last week. But," Sharon said, "I don't think so, because Cheri would have told her."

That really bothered me. Great. Now Judy has me and the girls kicked out of her family, and Charlie's in. I hope she's happy.

Later, I asked Cheri about it; she didn't know about Judy being at the party. She just knew that Beth was to stop at Grandma's for cake and ice cream, same like Beth told me.

Well, I wouldn't have wanted to be there if Charlie was there. I'd like Judy to be happy, but not at our expense. I want her back, and I'd like it, if she and Charlie would split-up, and she decides to have the love I have for her, not an infatuation like I hope her and Charlie have.

At work, Joseph asked me if I got Judy anything for Judy for Valentine's Day. I told him, "Yes, a card and box of chocolates." He asked, "What kind of card?" It says, "Someone special." He said, "That a boy!" and gave me a smile.

At six, after work, I drove to Stacey and Justin's to give them their Valentine candy. I stayed for a bit. As I turned off Rt. 165, I prayed to God for strength for whatever happened.

I went to the lot, and Charlie's car was there, so I wasn't going to go in. I pulled out my key for her car, and decided to place the box of chocolates and card on the driver's seat.

I went home, and when the girls were there, I gave them their boxes of candy.

Judy had left cards for the girls, and I had some for them on top of the TV. The girls left me cards—Sharon's on the dishwasher, Cheri's on my chest of drawers. Funny, they were identical.

At work the next day, Joseph asked me how the gift and card went. I told him it didn't. He said he seen Judy at the restaurant; she didn't say much since she was busy.

I told him I had a dream last night, that my Bible kept flipping pages, and kept stopping on page 316. He said I should play that number tonight.

He called later, and said he won two-hundred and ninety-two dollars for a fifty-cent ticket. He tried to make me feel silly about it, but I was happy for him. He even gave me forty-two dollars for the tip, minus the fifty cents. Nice.

These forty-one dollars and fifty cents is the unexpected money I was said to receive, by Kathy's book reading. Two down!

Judy called. I said, "How are you?" She asked me the same, and wanted to talk to Sharon. She told her she was dropping off some cold medicine tomorrow. Why was she alone tonight? Did they split? These were my questions.

Another one of Kathy's book reading came to be. I was to have business dealings with a couple, and they came in today.

Next day, I was driving up Rt. 165 (I passed my tree!), and Judy was coming towards me. I waved, but she didn't see me. I felt ignored.

Later that evening, we had eaten. Nobody liked what Cheri made. At eight, I was in the restroom. I heard Judy talking. I came out to see what was up, especially since I didn't know what she thought of her gift.

I asked her if she wanted coffee. She said, "No." She was talking to Sharon, and her back was towards Cheri. She wanted an apology, for the other day. I told her I would help her if I could. I don't know what to do with the girls.

I knew she needed to hear that, and she knows I'll do what I can.

She seemed happier when she was leaving, and she was supposed to see Sharon at one the next day. To me, she said, "I'll see you tomorrow." I was glad for that.

She's always fighting with Cheri, who is as stubborn as herself. I hope I never learn what it is like to fight with someone like myself.

But then, I do know what that's like. I had a loaded gun to my head (the second time), so I was fighting with myself. I was making a decision to pull the trigger or not to pull the trigger; to live or to die.

After the girls went to bed, I prayed for Judy's and the girls' happiness. I hope they reach a compromise. Judy didn't say anything about her card or gift. But she did say she seen me driving; she was already by me before she seen who I was. That at least made me feel better.

A few days later, I was on Rt. 165 coming home, when the car coming towards me looked like Judy's. I was about to wave, when I saw she wasn't driving. She was in the passenger's seat. I think it was Charlie driving. I was too upset. I didn't even see her face. I was hurting, bad.

The more time passes, I think Cheri is right. Judy should move away and let us forget her.

Matt and I were talking. I told him what Judy said on Saturday. He says I have to give the problem to God to work out between Cheri and Judy, and me and Judy.

Judy is going to have to accept what she did, and how it affects everyone around her. We all paid for her decision.

I need to continue writing. Although I write my notes every night, I'm lagging by forty-seven days.

I finished shaving off the rest of my beard tonight. I feel much better.

Cheri noticed that Stacey's and Will's birthdays were coming up. She didn't know if we were getting invited or not. I told her not to worry, since we might not be invited to any party.

I know everyone was upset because Charlie was invited to Beth's party, but not us. It's ok; I love Stacey as my own. Now, I feel we're not a part of Judy's family as we used to be.

I have been staying away from Don's, I admit. I love Sally and Don; they are the best mother-in-law and father-in-law anyone could ever ask for, and we have such mutual respect for each other. However, I'm afraid things are splitting.

Joseph told me at work that he had seen Jason at church yesterday. (He was a guy that used to work with me). He asked Joseph about me and Judy. He told him I should forget about Judy. "She will come back when Curt doesn't want her," he said.

I would dream constantly that someone would be shooting me. As I was lying on the ground I would say, "Thank you." They were putting me out of my misery. It was always a different person, man or woman, and I never seen their face clearly. It might have even been me. I know they were astonished that I said that.

I keep blaming myself for Judy's actions, although I can't be responsible for someone else's actions, just mine. I can only take what I have and do the best I can with it—I have no other choice. She's picked her road, and it doesn't seem to be running in my direction.

Tonight, I had to get outside. I rolled the trash can out, and walked down to the mailbox at the end of the street. I pleaded to God for help and freedom from my pain of loneliness.

God, I felt so much better.

Cheri was in bed when I got home. She got out of bed and kissed me goodnight. Afterwards, I dozed off.

Next evening, Sharon was going to a friend's house. Dylan wanted to go to The Club. I decided to go there from about eight to nine-thirty, so I'd be home in time. I had about four drinks, and really needed to go.

When I got home, Sharon was there. She just got here two minutes before I did. She had called Judy to take her home. Judy was wondering where I was. I didn't tell her where I had been, that I was just running a little bit later than expected. I went to bed. My eyes were hurting, and of course, the booze didn't help.

How could I not go out tonight, for more than a few drinks? The divorce papers were filed in court two years ago today.

I went to church today. No special feeling, but I was a bit antsy, considering that we had to go to Beth's for Stacey's and Will's birthday party. I was concerned about it. When we got there, Judy's car wasn't there, just Beth's and Don's.

Sally asked why my beard was shaved off. I told her I was tired of it.

Beth told Sally, that Judy would be there later.

I wanted to see her, but I didn't, so after the party, I was the first to leave. I was hoping not to pass 'them' driving back to my street.

When we got home, Cheri was making spaghetti. She asked if Judy was there. I said, "No." She mentioned that Judy probably didn't want to run in to me. I wished that they would just get along.

I told her not to tell Sharon, for now, that we were going to see Mom and Dad for Easter. I only stayed for Judy at "X"-mas, and got a slap in the face. She *really* hurt me.

I'm not going to stay again.

A few days later, Joseph said that he seen Judy at her apartment, and talked about the girls. She had lots to say, and he just listened.

He believed that Charlie might have keys to her apartment, and he may be living there. Cheri might realize it, too.

Joseph admitted that Charlie looks like Bob.

I don't even want to hear or talk about Judy's mishaps anymore. I'm tired, and I have enough troubles of my own.

I was shaving tonight, and trimming my mustache, but I got mad and cut it off.

Cheri mentioned a boy that she's going out with, and said she'd like to see if he comes after her. I thought, "Sounds familiar." She'd like to go out, but she's afraid she might see him and she doesn't want to see him as only a friend.

I thought, "Sounds familiar, too." I told her, I don't like to go to places since I might see her with Charlie. And, I can't handle it. In two years, you'd think I could. Last week and the week before, I had seen Judy and Charlie going towards driving and I couldn't even deal with it.

I then said, "When she comes here, I enjoy every minute of it." I didn't think she'd understand, but she did. She was glad that I could at least do that.

At work, I told Joseph that Judy was a good mother, actually, a darn good one. However, the bad stays on your mind, and it takes a long time to get over that, for most people.

When people hurt you so much, that's what really sticks in your mind, regardless of how much good they do. With Judy, I'm not like most people. I'm not normal. I am aware of that.

That following Sunday at church, I got that warm, tingly feeling when I prayed. Judy must've had the weekend off, since after church we went and got donuts, and her car wasn't at the place she worked at.

All that evening I was playing records. One of them I listened to was "Where Do I Put Her Memory?" by Charlie Pride. After hearing a few songs, I lost control of myself and cried. I was glad the girls were in their rooms, so they didn't hear me.

At work the next day, my spirits were up. I don't know why; just because. Kathy called to have Joseph call her. She seemed pretty happy. She asked how I was. I said, "Happier than I've been for a long time. Still down at times, but my problem is, I'm still in love with that special lady."

Kathy said, "Oh, you'll have to forget her. There's more fish in the sea; I found that out."

I replied, "I don't want a fish!" we laughed.

After I told Joseph what Kathy said, he added, "Curt doesn't want a fish; he wants his wife back!" I agreed, and changed the subject.

This evening, I remembered something. Remember a curse I told you about? Someone did curse our marriage—an 'X'-neighbor. Judy would babysit their boys, and one day they got into it. Judy laughed about it, but I'm not laughing.

CHAPTER 16

Engaged again

My horoscope said I'd have a great day—it lied again. At work, Joseph mentioned he seen Judy. He said Judy said to say, "Hello." I told him, "Yeah, (right)." He questioned my tone. I explained that when she calls, she just asks for Sharon. Joseph countered, "Possibly she doesn't want to give you false hope."

I knew he had something to say. I said, "She's probably engaged." I knew it was coming, the way Beth talked. He said he talked to Judy, and she said she didn't want to give me false hope. She and Charlie are engaged or are going to be soon.

I was crushed and devastated again. I'm the lost guy. I could hardly keep my mind going on my work. I was in a deeper pit, and I couldn't climb my way up.

Joseph would say that Judy was leery of me. She was afraid of me. Perhaps because it was what she had done?

I was upset when Joseph said to her, "Don't worry about Curt; he'll be ok." Be *ok*? I don't think so. I still get hurt. Many times, I wish the pains I got in my chest would be the heart attack I want, but the girls would go to Judy.

Whoever reads this story will never know the pain I'm in. I hope that someone could understand what's in my heart, though.

I feel a little better that I got this down.

I'm smoking again, over a pack a day. Look what she does to me. I'm drinking, not eating right, not sleeping. This is another disaster. I didn't care if I woke up the next day or not.

A nice lady told me I was nice and easy to talk to. She said, "All good things come back to a person a hundredfold." I believe that, and read that in the Bible. I keep waiting for my good deeds to return to me; I'm waiting for that day.

Every time someone says how nice I am, I think, why Judy can't be saying that?

I might start sending applications again. Not here, but to get another job, to move away from the memories.

She'll always be in my memory, but at least I won't have to deal with her physical presence and being in this place. It's not a bad area to be, it's just that my life has to be better elsewhere.

Every time the girls had connections with their mom, I felt envious. I felt bad and left out that I couldn't be the one that could just call her up like they could; I couldn't do that. Our relationship was altered, and our conversations were, by default, about who was going to take Cheri or Sharon to the doctor's, or who was going to pick them up from school.

Our casual conversations were over. I couldn't, like Sharon, call Judy about getting her jeans fixed, or be like Cheri, asking for something to be hemmed.

She always would blame me when the girls would give her a problem. She did this because they weren't that close after she left and she didn't live here.

Cheri and Judy would always fight. If Judy would come back, or I would find someone, possibly that would change, because then perhaps she would feel that she wouldn't have to be on my side all the time. Also, if something were to happen to myself and Judy were to step in, possibly over time things would improve between them.

The relationships between the girls have improved, but have not become what I would like it to be. I would have to be there, in order for it to be that way.

She came in one night after fixing Sharon's jeans. After talking to the girls, she passed me and said, "I did my duty." I asked her, as she opened the door, "Why are you afraid of me? I never hurt you and I'm not going to." She said I've turned the girls away from her, and her mom and sister could see it, too.

"I don't see how," I said. This wasn't true. She had keys to my house; she could come and go as she pleased.

I felt she was always throwing that at me, in order to relieve some of the guilt that she had since leaving us.

She didn't know how to handle me, since I'm always nice to her. That's why she's not here. I told her that I can't help the way I feel about her, and she smiled.

Then Cheri came out, and they had a nice chat. Judy was so happy talking to Cheri. I'm so happy they were happy. I felt, "Honey, can't you see where your joy is?" I know it's going to work out; I *know* it.

Sharon asked when I would stop writing. I said, "When God tells me too." We were talking about praying and she said she doesn't pray anymore. I said, "I pray all the time. You have to pray, and you have to have faith."

I had thoughts today, of what I would say when Judy tells me she is engaged. I'll say, "You won't find anyone to love you like I do, but as long as you're happy, that's what counts."

But then again, will I really be able to say this, when the time comes?

I had seen Sally at her and Don's house, and she asked if Judy came around much. I said, "No."

At work, I seen Matt and told him what Judy said, about me killing her with kindness. He said her subconscious bothers her, and it would be easier for her to handle it if I hated her. But knowing me, it's not me.

It was Good Friday, and I was getting ready to leave work for home. One of my customers today gave me five dollars each for both of the girls. Wasn't that nice?

I was pleasantly surprised when I came home. When I pulled in the driveway, Judy was here!

She was with Sharon in her room. They both came out, and I asked Judy if she wanted something to eat. She politely refused.

I asked her if she would check on Sadie if we leave this weekend. She thought about it for a bit and said, "Why not?" She then left.

I looked at her ring finger, but all I could see was the ring her mother gave her for her birthday.

Later, I took Sharon to get something for Judy for Easter. Then she asked me to take her to Judy's. I did. Her car wasn't there, but Charlie's was. She got real quiet. I felt bad.

We went home; not a word was said. Later on, Sharon found out that Judy was home. Cheri went up there with her. Judy took her home. Sharon gave me an Easter bunny.

The girls got a basket each from Judy, and some money. I picked up candy for Mom and Dad and for Judy.

That weekend we went to see all my family: Mom and Dad, Joe and Lilly, Barry, and talked to Candy. It was nice to see everybody, but I wasn't here with my sweetheart—that's the hardest part.

Sharon hurt her arm bad and I had to take her to the hospital when we got back. Cheri was worried about me calling Judy, and I told her I would after we get Sharon taken care of.

At work that Monday afternoon, I called Judy. Oh no, Charlie answered. He must be living there, as I suspected. She wasn't there, but I told him to have her call me. She did. I told her what happened, and she was ok with it.

Kathy called at four-thirty, to talk to Joseph. After he got off the phone, he said that Kathy wanted to know if I knew that Judy was engaged, and they're planning a big wedding, and Beth is in it.

I didn't say anything.

Then Joseph said he hopes he's invited. That hurt!

But then he explained that he would object at the wedding. I was glad he said that then.

After work, at eight, I went to get the crutches off Beth, but there was this white car parked in front of Beth's. It was them. After they got out of the car, they were holding hands. My stomach hit the floor. I just continued driving by.

A block away, I broke down crying. I just cried and cried. I didn't know what to do with myself. There's my sweet angel, with another man. And there's nothing I can do about it.

I got home, got myself together and went inside.

About ten, a car pulled up. I looked up, above the sink. My stomach hit the floor again.

Judy got out of the car. Charlie was driving. She brought the crutches that I was trying to get earlier. She stayed five minutes, if that.

At work the next day, I told Matt. what happened. He said, "God may answer your prayer the way you want it. Then again, maybe it isn't the way He wants it. Sooner or later you'll understand why."

I couldn't help thinking about Judy all day.

John 14:14 states, "If ye shall ask for anything in my name, I will do it." Well, I'm going to keep asking.

I saw Beth a few days later. She said she expected the worst when I came in and seen Judy and Charlie.

I didn't say much about that.

Cheri was telling her friend April, that she doesn't get along with her mother, and how her parents are divorced. She told her that I helped her mother get out of her second marriage, and she now was on another. She feels I'm the only one she can talk to.

It makes me feel good that I'm a good father.

After church today, I noticed a book at a store about what women want. That struck me that before sixty percent of the marriages go bad, the wife wants something else.

No one knows what they want anymore. Today this, tomorrow that. I worked for many years so I could raise my kids, and then Judy and I could do what we want. But she's not here for us to enjoy it.

There's a special bond between Cheri and I, and I don't know if that would be there, our talking, if her mother was here.

Cheri also lets me be her mother. Her friends talk about what they do with their mother, and Cheri doesn't have that. It's not her fault.

There's Cheri, a motherless girl.

I think the girls would like it if I had someone of my own (like a girlfriend), but then I know they'd feel deserted.

I'm trapped in a way. The girls love me, and I love them and Judy. I am ensnared by her. I liked it that way. But, I don't like the predicament I'm in now. I love her, and she loves me like a brother. What can one really do?

All I know is, I don't like the shoes I'm living in, but I wouldn't want to be in the shoes she's in, either.

If I knew this was going to happen, I'd still have married her anyway. Here is my tip for those wanting to get married: make sure love is love on both sides, not only on one side.

I read Judy's horoscope today. It said, "End an unrewarding romance. It is having a negative effect on everything that you do." Well, it's definitely having a negative effect on me! And mine said, "A romantic partner is single again and wants to return. Think of what is best for you!" I wish!

That is the only one in the past two years that is right on. But, I don't want to rely on horoscopes; I want to rely on God.

I'd love for her to return. This is where the love is; this is where every mother and wife belongs. In the sight of God, no man shall put asunder, what God has put together. Only God can decide that question.

I'm just trying to talk to God, and understand Him, and to get Him to understand me and how I really feel toward the girl I married and need and want and *still* love.

On Sunday, I was listening to the preacher on TV, since my hand and arm hurt, and I couldn't sit in church. He was talking about meek people, and how they are gentle, mild, and patient. He mentioned that they work quietly, and don't get mad, and want to work thru problems. They will not cut and run, and will not drop a marriage.

I felt bad when I heard this.

I was snappy all day. I was hurting physically and emotionally. The girls let me know that Judy was getting rid of our old couch and chair. I guess Charlie was buying the new furniture, since she can't afford it. I don't want the furniture; I want *her* back.

I have faith; I know God loves me, but I'm still in love with *her*.

Perhaps God is telling me to find someone else, but I'm too dumb to see the signs.

I'm afraid to get hurt again, if I do find someone else. What if Judy wants to return? Then I'll feel that I betrayed her, myself, God or the girls. I can't handle that.

I told Tim that I just keep talking to God to get the answers. And I do talk to Him, a lot. Tim smiled.

We got to spend the other day together and boy was that nice.

I feel the devil is testing me. As of yet, I don't receive any answers that I fully understand. I wonder what I've done to deserve all of this.

I had a thought, that one time God asked me for help, and I ignored Him. Now he's taking His time helping me.

Mother's Day is coming up. Should I ask her to go to Mother's Day dinner? She bore our daughters, but I am their mother. She's not doing the job now, I am. Who should get the dinner, Judy or me? Both of us, to be loving and fair, but I'll still have to pay for it in so many ways.

I saw Matt again. Joseph told him how upset I was, and how every little thing was bothering me.

Matt told me to unload my problems on him. He told me to take some time out and take care of myself.

He complimented me, and told me how hard I work, and what a good father I am. He said it's quite an accomplishment to raise my daughters myself. It deserves many merits, and it's more than most men can do.

He really built me up. He's right! I am one heck of a guy. Judy might find someone more exciting, but not necessarily *better*.

Matt reminded me that even though I want her back, it may not be what God wants for me. On TV tonight, a person said that life isn't always the way you want it.

Sometimes you have to put the past behind you, and look towards tomorrow.

But my problem is that I want to put yesterday behind me and I want Judy in my tomorrow. G'nite.

I was crying on my way to work today. Tears ran down my face as I prayed for Judy's return. I prayed; I worked out my depression.

Part of it working out was the fact that Judy called this morning. I knew it made me feel better to hear from her.

I think the reason I don't hear from her as much is contributing to my depression.

Sharon was quite upset that she couldn't get a hold of Judy until before nine. She cried and was disappointed, since they were supposed to get together. I told her that she probably just forgot.

Cheri told me she was talking to a friend, and asked if she knew Judy's boyfriend's sons. I was surprised. I told her, "You don't need to know about them." She said, "I should meet them, since Judy is engaged."

I was floored! I asked her, when did she find this out? "A month ago," she answered, and Sharon knew it before that.

I was upset. Then she changed the subject.

That Sunday, it was Stacey's and Justin's birthday party. I went and got presents, and Cheri and I wrapped them. Then we went to Beth's.

Before we got out of the car, I said that if her boyfriend is in the house, we're not staying.

Cheri said, "I know he's not here."

Judy had already taken Sharon to Beth's after they went to the movies.

She was standing in the kitchen. She gave me a slight smile and said, "Hi." I returned the greeting.

After we put the presents with the others, I gave a 'hello' to everyone there, and went to the living room to talk to Don.

Judy came in a few minutes later. She asked if we wanted coffee, and brought me some. I saw some of her engagement ring. She didn't flaunt it, but tried to hide it.

I really didn't talk to her, because I didn't know what to say.

She looked so lovely today, and I heard her laugh, like she used to! It was nice to hear that.

I wanted to take her in my arms and hold her, and it hurt me deep inside that I couldn't do that.

When we left and came home, the girls said nothing about Judy for the rest of the evening.

I'm still feeling lonely and depressed, and I cried and prayed a few times over Judy.

I would love to have someone for me, if not Judy. I would prefer her, though.

Pete and Joy L. came to visit today. They almost got a divorce; but thank God they're working it out. I hope it works out, because I love those two, and they're part of the family.

I had seen Matt again. I told him that I get a good feeling, that Judy is going to return. Other times, I get the opposite feeling.

He said for me to claim it, in Jesus' name that Judy will be back. Matt said he and others are still praying for me.

Mother's Day is coming up. I wonder if Judy wants to go out with us, or if I should go see my mother.

I've been following Matt's advice, and I do say I feel better.

I did promise God today, that if He sends Judy back, I'll see that she goes to church, and I will try to get her to be a good Christian.

Judy brought Sharon in tonight, and I had a chance to talk to her.

We were talking of nothing important, and then as she was getting into her car, I called to her from the back door.

She still answers to "Hon." I asked her if she wanted to go with us on Mother's Day. She paused a few seconds, and said, "Yeah!" I was thrilled and so happy! Another chance! Taking *my family* out on Mother's Day! Yippee!

She doesn't work this year on that day, so she said anytime would be fine. I can't wait to tell the girls and make some reservations.

Well, I told the girls about our upcoming dinner with Judy. We were eating dinner, and Sharon told Cheri that Judy asked if we were doing anything for Mother's Day, and Cheri said, "I'm spending my Mother/Father's Day with him," while pointing to me." I told the girls we were going to go out with her. Cheri didn't seem to relish the idea about that, but will go along with it for me.

Throughout the day, it was good. I read the paper, prayed and made dinner.

Sharon was out with Judy at the movies, and dropped her off in the evening. Then she got out of the back to the passenger's side. I can't believe she has the nerve to come here like that, with *him* driving.

My day was ruined at that point. When she has a boyfriend, she seems to want to pick up with the girls where she left off. I don't get it.

When Sharon came in, she said they went out to eat together. I told her, "I can't handle it yet."

A few days later, Judy called. She said, "Is Sharon there?" I said "Yes," and got her. It bothers me that that's all she says.

I had such a bad day at work. First time I got this mad in two years, partially because Cheri was home so late, and mostly over Judy.

I was so mad I couldn't see straight. I threw Joseph's radio across the shop and tools all over the place, and then I fell against a car, and cried like a baby, and pounded the window with my fist. It took me a half-hour to get myself together. Thank goodness no one was there.

At home, I set the punishment for Cheri, and asked if she set a time with Judy. She said, "No," and neither did Sharon.

Sharon said Cheri didn't want to go.

The girls don't want to go, but we're going.

Tomorrow is Mother's Day. I didn't want to call Judy, because I didn't want to talk to Charlie. We'll have Sharon call tomorrow morning.

Wow, it's Mother Day. I'm so anxious to see Judy. I didn't sleep much. I went to church today, and prayed for Judy. Cheri, thank God, had called her to set a time for dinner.

The girls got dressed and we picked Judy up around two. Charlie's car was there. I sent Cheri in for her. We went out. She was cheerful today, and was happy being with the girls.

We got a table quickly and we were there for two hours.

I was so elated to be there with her. It was like my old family, the way it should be. But in reality, it wasn't. It was just a postcard of a family that was no longer really together. I was sad as usual when it ended.

You enjoy your time with someone, but you don't really enjoy your time with them when you no longer have them.

It was tough, because I was with her, but then I had to bring her back to Charlie.

It was the same way with Bob. That afternoon, she was *borrowed* for only a couple of hours.

I hated the drive back home.

She said, "Thank you," thinking it was the girls' idea, when it was really mine.

Later, we went to Sally and Don's. We were there for a half-hour when Judy and Charlie came in. I was hurt. I couldn't believe that she would do that when I was there. I felt and thought, *don't flaunt him in front of me; have some respect for me.*

She was glad we took her out and was proud of that, but I couldn't get past her standing there with *him.*

Sally offered coffee, but I refused; I just wanted to get out of there. I hadn't had vodka in about two months, and I didn't want to start again now. Judy was happy to hear that.

I did smoke. I had two cigarettes left in my last pack and I decided to quit this morning.

That all changed when I had seen them together. It upset my stomach; I hit bottom again. I felt like throwing up. I wished I wasn't there. I couldn't believe this was really happening.

We then left. I walked around the house like a lost pup.

Joseph called; I told him what happened.

He tried to cheer me up, but all I could think about was *her*.

I wish the girls were older and on their own, so that I could finish my life with a bullet. I was in the pits again.

I'd get there a lot—it was hard to get out of it.

I'm not jealous of Judy, just jealous of Charlie. I don't like him; he has what I want. I know the Bible says not to do that, but I can't help it.

The next day at work, Joseph asked me what I was doing and I replied, "I don't know; I don't care; I'm not here!" He replied, "I can see that." He tried to cheer me up, but at that point I really didn't care.

I don't want to give up. I really felt at dinner that Judy can come back. At Don's, when they walked, in I felt the opposite.

A few times today I felt like drinking again. I just can't handle all this stress and this awkward position that I'm in.

If they marry, Judy better not ask Cheri and Sharon in the wedding, because I can't handle it, and I'll need them that day more than she will.

Two years ago today, Judy killed me inside and divorced me. It still hurts because I love her.

In the last two years, I've tried everything to get her back. I've bought her flowers, remembered important days and included her in every holiday.

I've tried to make things better with her and her family, and also with our daughters. It seems to me I'm on the losing end of the stick.

Cheri's growing up, is older and is going on with her life, and so is Sharon. Even though she is growing, too, it hurts her more in some ways that Judy is not here.

I thought I'd have her back by now. The fact that Bob was out of the picture, I thought I'd be home free.

But now she's on to another guy, holding on to an arm of another. And as usual, he's got more available money than I do to spend on her.

Well, it has been two years; my feelings really haven't changed for her, but I will keep on trying.

I'm still surprised I can write like this.

When she made an appointment to see a counselor, she was already out. The small- town girl met up with the big city ways and wasn't strong enough to hold her own.

I had a rough night. Thoughts of Judy were running thru my head. Joseph and Mel were really worried about me. Mel felt, "Curt's the nicest guy you'd ever meet, but he's killing himself." My tools were all over. They felt that I've got too much in my mind.

How could anyone be the same after going thru what I'm going thru over Judy and work? Even Ben and Sheila are worried about me; I can't help that.

Joseph said that Ben inquired about how I could get so depressed. I guess I said, "I'll commit suicide this weekend, for something to do. I hate weekends!" I told Joseph that I didn't mean anything by it.

Next day at work, Joseph asked again what was wrong with me. He said, "I know your arm and hand hurts, but what is it?" I replied, "I don't know." I was stopped in my tracks.

That night, Cheri went to Judy's for dinner. Sharon was already there. This really bothers me, since last summer she didn't want bothered with the girls. Now that she has a boyfriend, she wants them there all the time. I'm feeling threatened, and I'm bothered by this. I feel abandoned, because Beth likes Charlie. And I haven't heard from her since the birthday party. Even Sally and Don like Charlie.

Mom called tonight. My cousin died of a heart attack. I was blown away, since he is only twenty-nine.

Mom called the next day. What a twist to the story. He shot himself in the chest. I would never downgrade him, like Tim did. I've *been* there.

When he died, Tim screamed, "Why did he do this; how stupid can he be! He was young and had the whole world ahead of him!" This *devastated* Joe. I got upset with Tim for being so *un*understanding, and I said to him, "Don't judge him until you've walked in his shoes, and I have." He looked at me and shut up, and never said another word. It brought the *reality* of the situation to him; he didn't want to think about losing *another* brother.

When talking to my aunt, I found out that she also thought of suicide in her life, as I did.

Next day, when we got to my family's house, I dropped the girls off and went with Barry to the funeral home.

I knew he killed himself, but there was that element of disbelief.

He was upset over his ex-wife. She left him and she got the kids. He was still upset over that. He left no note.

I asked, "Why?" but envied him at the same time. I remember him as he was growing up. He was a nice, good-looking guy.

I saw how this affected his mother, and I'm glad I didn't take it this far. I'm glad I didn't do to myself what he did. I could see what would've happened to my girls, my parents, and the rest of my family. I believe that God let this happen to show me what *not* to do.

I'm thankful for people like Joseph, Kathy and Beth, and my girls, for getting me thru this part of my life.

CHAPTER 17

The wedding

This morning was the pits; then came dinner time. A painter came to talk to me. He said, "I see your 'X' is getting married." He said that Judy had called his wife about making the dinner at the church. Then Judy called back, and told her that Sally was going to do it.

I told this guy I don't talk to her much. Inside, I wasn't there for a little while. I knew it was coming, but I didn't want to face it. It took everything out of me. I asked him, "When?" He said, "Sometime next month." I hit bottom; I just wanted to crawl in a hole. I felt a pain that you just can't understand.

I told Joseph, and he said in response, "She's not!" He said for me to relax; how can I? He's never been where I've been.

Judy better not ask me to let the girls go. The answer is, "No!"

He could see I was getting upset, so he changed the subject.

I feel God has forsaken me. I have faith that God will send her back. I remember what Bob said, that she'll never be back, but later he recanted and stated that, "She belongs with you and the girls." After two years, what have I gotten?

If this marriage goes off, I'll feel, here I go again. I will be in another long state of depression. I feel stabbed in the back.

I know I had to understand about cousin Joe, but, what if I get to that point again? Maybe, who knows? I can't think of a what-if scenario be right now; I'll wait.

I look at the price I paid for her to be happy. Everything is broken up: my house, and my heart. Things will never be the same. She also

215

put herself thru pain. I wonder, in the end, if all the prices paid were worth it!

At work, Joseph knew I was thinking of *her* again. He said, "She's been married before; it didn't kill you. It won't kill you again."

I didn't hate Charlie; I just envied him.

Joseph would remind me, that I had two girls to take care of, even though my life didn't mean much to me. He's right. My life doesn't mean much, so I'm trying for the hereafter. I think it will be much better then.

Joseph thinks I'm killing myself at work. I do my work, and help him. He doesn't understand that I need the extra pressure at work. It's keeping me going; it keeps my mind off of it.

That night, there was another surprise. Sharon called and said she was going with Judy to go look for a dress for the wedding.

I stopped her right there and told her in anger that she's not going to no wedding. She asked, "Why?" I told her, "I can't handle it right now." It shattered my hopes that she would come back to me.

After she hung up, I sat at my desk shaking. I couldn't believe what was going on. I didn't think she'd have the gall to ask for the girls to be in the wedding. She knew how I felt. This validated them getting married.

Joseph asked me what was going on. He said something; I don't know what. I didn't hear him. I was smoking like a train, and walking around the shop like a lost kid. I was miserable.

Then Judy called. She wanted to know why Sharon couldn't come tonight. I told her I'm not ready for her to get married. I told her my feelings on life, and how I don't care anymore.

She asked if Cousin Joe's death hasn't shown me something. I told her, "No," but inside I wanted to say, "Yes." He looked at peace inside, and that's what I want.

She told me to get over it by now. I had to get a hold of myself. She said the girls are worried about me, and it's not doing me or the girls any good punishing myself.

I told her I still love her, and I can't help that I do. I told her I pray to God that she never loves anyone like I love her.

Judy said something to me about the girls being in the wedding. She didn't like it that I was trying to stop it. The conversation was cut off, and she said she wouldn't pick Sharon up that night.

I felt that I had to let them in the wedding, because she might take me to court over it. It was useless at that point, since they wanted to be in it.

Later, Joseph was eating, but I didn't want anything of what he offered me.

Joseph wondered how things would have been, if I wouldn't have been so nice to her.

Later, the girls didn't say much. I know I have to talk to the girls this weekend, regarding when the wedding is.

You know, I was getting a peace about me. I haven't had a drink in months. I was working on quitting smoking. I'm smoking like a train again, and that bottle looks tempting.

On my way to work, I started thinking of Judy and started crying.

Later that day, I was talking to Cheri and I asked about the wedding. I told her I don't want her and Sharon in it.

She told me they're going to be in it. She doesn't want to, but she's going to do it to keep the peace.

She said, "We have to face it—she's not coming back. Sharon's already faced it." She added, "Daddy, you're going to have to face it."

I told her that I don't want them in it; I'd need them more that day.

I guess I'll let them be in it, because it will be the last thing I'll ever get to do for her.

Cheri is right: I got into another state of depression. I smoked all evening. I feel I've lost my last friend around here.

I've been thinking about how I could kill myself and have it look like an accident.

I cried inside all evening and prayed. I watched *The 700 Club*, and the evangelist reminded the audience to believe in God, and believes that what you pray for will happen sooner or later.

At the doctor's the next day, he asked me if I wanted more nerve pills. I told him I have to work it out *without* the pills.

He wanted to give me some more, but I told him I still have some, actually enough to kill myself.

My mind's been in turmoil all day over this wedding thing. I guess I should let the girls in it, if Judy asks me.

Why does she want them there, to show off? Make her feel better about Charlie? Maybe I'll just pack up for a few days and leave.

What about the girls? Maybe Joseph could stay here, but it wouldn't look right.

I might end up in court.

I feel I have to separate myself from Judy's family. I need to go and get my stuff from Don's and Beth's. I need to stay away. After all, no one calls me or comes over: I'm the *outcast*.

Sometimes I feel there's no God. Then something snaps, and I know He's there. Too many things happen that you can't explain. My belief is then reinforced.

I know God will return Judy—I just have to have faith.

I was talking to Kathy about Beth, and how I don't hear from her much anymore. Kathy feels the same way. I guess I'm not important. Judy is getting married to someone other than me—I can't *stand* that.

Cheri said she was going to Judy's that night. I don't know who, her friend or her mother's.

I went into my room, laid on my bed, and looked at Judy's picture. Tears just rolled out of my eyes. Then I heard Cheri talking and looked out my window. She was getting in Judy's car.

Later, I was reading my Bible, and then I cried hard.

I called *The 700 Club* and got an advisor. She talked to me; we prayed. She asked for a blocking for Judy's wedding, and for my girls, and she told me to talk to my girls about them being in the wedding. Let the Lord take over the problems.

That night, Cheri brought her friend Ann over to keep an eye on me.

Next day at work, I had seen Matt. I told him about my phone call. He said it was good advice, and invited me to his Bible study.

About the wedding, he suggested I ask the girls *why* they feel the way they do, before telling them *my* views on the wedding.

Next day, Judy was all I could think about. I don't know what to do about myself. My cousin keeps coming to mind, how he looked at peace.

I might try to talk with the girls tonight, but I don't want to get upset at them.

Maybe Joseph can talk to them, since I can't. I was thinking of drinking again, but I promised I'd let God handle the situation and the bottle's *not* the answer.

I was talking to the guard at work yesterday. He believes in everyone having one true love. He's been divorced for over twenty years and is remarried. He saw his wife again at his son's funeral last year. It's the first time he's seen her in all those years, and knew he still loved her.

I was dreaming lately of Judy and she gave me a long sweet kiss. It was nice. Thoughts of her were running thru me all day.

It's easy for someone else to tell you to forget about something or someone when they're not involved in it.

At work there was nothing pressing. I started to compose a letter in my head to Judy. I told her I want her to be happy, but she's not responsible for what I do from this day on. Also forgive me for still loving her. Once I promised to love, honor and cherish her, and I still do cherish her.

I feel abandoned and betrayed. I'm not happy about the wedding or the girls being in it, but I don't want Judy to be mad at me.

I fear I'll start drinking again. This is all messed up. I'm in constant turmoil. Death isn't the answer, but I'm afraid of the future without Judy. I don't want anyone else. I'm not even interested in looking. And if I wanted to, in today's world, where would I even look?

On Sunday, I listened to a few church programs, instead of attending. Beth brought Sharon home in the later afternoon. She didn't even say, "Hi."

Sleep is hard for me. I can't get up. I'm asking God for guidance in talking to the girls. Joseph felt Judy shouldn't have asked the girls. I found out I can stop her, but she'll be hurt. I still want her back.

I'm wondering if her brother's going.

At work, sleep was still lacking. I smoked my last cig. I blew my top at work; buddy Joseph took it. I apologized; he said, "It's ok." My nerves are bad.

Next day, I did the same thing. I told Joseph what happened; he said to take it easy. After that happened, I had to drive around for fifteen to twenty minutes to cool myself down.

Tonight, Cheri said Don had one of his spells and wasn't feeling well.

I'd like to trade places with Don. He knows his time is short, and he wants to live longer. I figure I have a long time, but I want to die!

A Tom Jones song was on an album I have, "If I Ever Had to Say Goodbye to You." It just puts my feelings out there. I'm not free. I'm just some poor soul walking around in this miserable flesh, just waiting for my chance to exit *out* of here!

Judy took Sharon to get shoes. She wanted me to see them, but I just couldn't.

Joseph was off today, but Eli, a guy I know, came down to see me. He told me to slow down and not worry so much. That is easier said than done. He said I'm rare, and I've got to find someone else. He added, "One-sided love hurts very much." He's right.

Judy took Cheri to buy shoes. I thought of her today. I envy her. She got to walk away from my skin problems; I have to live with them. Still, I don't blame her at all. I can't stand myself; why should she?

I heard another Tom Jones song: "A Woman's Touch." Without being able to touch her, my life doesn't mean much to me. I agree!

When I met her, I felt she was a blessing to me. I thanked God all the time. Without her, I'm a puppet without strings!

Tonight, it rained. When Judy pulled in to get Sharon, I didn't even look. I didn't want to upset myself.

I was folding clothes in the basement, when they returned. I was glad that I didn't see her then, either. One glimpse and I would go bananas.

Next day was Father's Day. Cheri was up before noon. On the envelope of my card she wrote, "To my special Dad." I needed that. The girls were later whispering about my Father's Day dinner. I couldn't wait. Sharon gave me her card, too.

I went to the grocery store, and when I got back, Cheri wasn't there, because she went for a bike ride. Sharon said she went to Judy's, to give Don his card. I was floored then, hearing Judy's name. I could barely eat my chicken and potatoes, which the girls so lovingly and thoughtfully made for me.

I was on my way to the garage, when Sally and Don were there. Justin said there was a Father's Day present for me at Judy's. They dropped Stacey off. Sally gave me a hug and a kiss.

Stacey gave me the present, a nice short-sleeve shirt. It said on the box, "To a wonderful uncle, who has been a terrific father. Love, Stacey." I was touched.

Next day at work, Trent, from one of our suppliers asked, "How's your love life?" I said, "What love life?" He was surprised that we weren't back together. I told him, of course, of the upcoming wedding and the girls being in it. He felt it might be for the best. He said, "You'd take her back, wouldn't you?" I responded, "Yes!"

To add insult to injury, Sharon asked if Charlie's son could come here swimming. What are they thinking? That this is what I want? No way! This can't be one big happy family! She even wanted him to come when I'm not here.

I was mad. First, you girls want to be in the wedding, and that really hurt me. I'm doing it for your mother, because I love her, but don't push me! And if this keeps up, I'm selling the house, and moving to the other side of the state!

I was mad, very mad at them, mad at her work. This must be Judy's playing in getting all the kids together.

How's this going to look, him living up there? She can help raise this boy, but not her own? What would people think?

Is this the block I've been praying for?

At work, Joseph was shocked that Sharon even asked me that, and said it must be Judy's idea.

Next day, I was supposed to be at a big party at Will and Andrea's. I wanted to go. However, while we were at a grad party, I asked Cheri if we were supposed to take Stacey home while going to Will's. Sharon said, "Mommy's bringing her." I said, "What?" Cheri snapped at Sharon when she said, "Mom." Then Cheri said, "Judy's bringing her home from Will's." The girls were still going to go, but I wasn't going to be there, while Judy was with Charlie. Do these people think I'm stupid or something? Don't they know I have feelings? I'm not made of iron!

I drove fast to Will's. The girls dropped some clothes off; Sally and Don were there.

Cheri wanted me to come in, but I couldn't chance seeing Judy.

I left and took the long way home, so I wouldn't see them. I was in pain. I felt like dying. I wanted to get drunk. I tried to pray. I took a nerve pill or two.

Cheri called later. She said Judy didn't come. Sally said she called earlier, and wouldn't be there.

Cheri knew I was upset. I told her they say it takes two years to get over a divorce; I'm not normal since it's taking me longer. It's been over two years and I still love her. Tomorrow would have been our anniversary.

She's said in the past for me to have my own life. But, I don't care too much about myself. Judy didn't like herself; now I don't like myself, either.

Next day was our wedding anniversary. Great. Andrea brought Sharon home in the afternoon; she was a bit put out by the whole situation with Sally. Will was upset, too. They feel Sally is pushing Charlie in. I can understand that, though, since Judy is her daughter. I wonder if Judy thought about today.

Andrea said that in the future that they'll have two birthday parties, and they'll invite us to her side.

Next day at work, Matt was in. I told him how things got screwed up yesterday. He said that if I left it up to God, he'd take care of it. But, I stepped in again. God can't give me anything I can't handle. He's sure God had something to do with Judy not coming there.

About the boy, he wanted to make sure I wasn't punishing Judy, but I need to draw the line somewhere.

Judy's wedding date is coming up. I'm depressed with my skin and this situation. I talked to God about how I feel. I asked Him for the return of Judy, and help with my skin and hip.

I cried; I thought of death again. I'm happy I have God to talk to about His love, my children, a good job, and a roof over our heads. But, I need my "love."

I only exist; that's it. I have maybe one good half-hour a day, and that is all.

At work, I talked to an old customer, and I told him my daughter drives my good car. He asked why my wife doesn't drive it. I said, "I'm divorced and have my two daughters". He felt I have a rough road ahead.

"Forget Judy; find someone else," he said. "But, easier said than done," he mentioned. Ain't that the truth?

It's been a year since Judy's been divorced from Bob. Now she's married again.

Cheri called at three-thirty p.m. to say Sharon and her wouldn't be home. I asked where they'd be. "Rehearsal," she said. My stomach hit the floor; I wanted to throw up. "For the wedding," I asked? In a low voice, she responded, "Yeah." I asked, "When?" She said, "Tomorrow, at seven-thirty p.m." I didn't know what to say.

Cheri said that Andrea called and mentioned that Will would be over in the evening. Will didn't want to go. That picked me up.

I'm afraid of tomorrow and tonight, because life is a lie. Everyone says life goes on, but not for me.

Like I said, death is running thru my mind.

The girls left about five minutes after I got here. As I was cleaning up, I broke down and cried like a baby. I pleaded with God.

I was so low. I started to drink and smoke heavily, putting down my first drink in months.

I sat in the living room, with my tape player on. I thought of shooting myself, and I got up to get the gun, but that wouldn't work, since Joseph's got my pistol and Will's got my shotgun.

Cheri came in, around nine o'clock. "Open some windows in here!" she exclaimed. It was raining earlier. I wondered where Sharon was. "In the car," she said. "We're going to Charlie's, and we just got a lecture from Judy and Charlie." I didn't want them to go, but if it meant that much to them, what can I do?

They came in around eleven o'clock, and went straight to bed. Cheri shut off the light at eleven-thirty p.m., without a word to me.

Sharon came in to me after midnight, and gave me heck for smoking. I said I didn't care. I'm not happy, and haven't been for two years. So why should I care now?

Sharon wanted to know when we were going on vacation. I told her we're going to Mom and Dad's place, but we were leaving tomorrow night. Since Judy's getting married, it changes everything.

She kissed me goodnight.

Next day, somehow, I slept fairly well, even though I really drank a lot.

I was busy at work, which helped, but on the way home, my thoughts began to run rapid. By the time I got home, I was a nervous wreck. I lost it then.

I started to cleanup, but broke down, falling against the bathroom wall, and crying.

I had vodka and soda later, to calm me down, and prayed.

I waited for Will, but he didn't show up.

At around seven-thirty p.m., I got gas and went to Kathy's house.

She smiled at me, and gave me a hug. She was surprised that I didn't know when the official date was, until recently. She said she was invited, but didn't go. I'm glad she didn't; it would have hurt our friendship.

We watched a movie, and talked about Judy. I told her I was afraid of losing Sharon.

I told her I quit drinking until the night before, and how I'm smoking again.

She told me to forget Judy, because everyone likes Charlie.

I got home around midnight.

The girls didn't say anything, only that Will couldn't come, because he had hurt himself.

Will should have invited me.

I'm glad Kathy took care of me. I couldn't have gotten thru the evening without her.

I'm hurt that the girls didn't even ask about me.

Next day, I got up. I didn't know why I slept so well; it must be because of the alcohol.

It amazed me how little people cared about how the wedding affected me, especially my girls.

At one point, I broke down while loading the dishwasher. I was so weak, I could hardly stand.

Sharon had come down and hugged and kissed me later.

Later, I remember reading something about how all the tears and heartbreak aren't worth the pain I have inside me at this time. That touched me because I knew that what was happening to me was small compared to my reward in heaven, but it didn't really matter at that point.

I feel I'm ready to die now. Judy's happy, so it's time for me to go.

The girls are as happy as they'll get. I have no joy left. I can't even sing along to the radio anymore.

I've had visions lately. I see myself standing, and then I get a close-up of my face. There's a crack, a gunshot. Right before I hit the ground, I get another close-up. My face is pained, and distorted. As my head settles in place, I have a smile on my face, and say "Thank you," in a happy voice.

A don't see anyone else but me. Do I shoot myself or does someone shoot me? I don't know to whom I'm saying, "Thank you."

I told Kathy about this, and she told me to get into a group session to talk since I'm destroying myself. I don't care if I am. I am slowly going crazy, or killing myself, but who cares?

At night, I did read my Bible and say a few prayers.

Next day, I found out that Will was hurt and couldn't go to the wedding.

Joe and Barry came in to town to buy fireworks. We talked about Joe's death. I told them that I understand what Joe did, since I've been there. I still get pretty bad, but not to that point anymore.

Joe gave me a small lecture, and said, "Just remember, we care about you." That comment really made me feel good. I needed to hear it now.

After they left, I just did some things here and there throughout the day, and worked on the pool. I read the Bible, and took a nap. Cheri came in to tell me about her time at Will's. When I was alone, I cried again.

Cheri left later, and told me not to go by the Crystal Inn. There's a sign that says, "Best Wishes Judy and Charlie." At first, I dismissed it. When I sat down again on the patio, my mind began to wander. I cried, prayed and ached. I ached over my heart, and my skin, and my love for Judy. If I had a gun, I'd use it. I feel abandoned by everyone around me, even my girls.

I'm not getting any answers. Things seem to be getting worse. However, I still seem to keep the faith.

She promised me she'd be here, but she never promised to stay, not forever.

A wedding vow is something to be kept not broken, at least not by me. My promise to her was that I would try to keep it, but it will have to end someday.

Will her promise to Charlie end up like Bob and me? We'll find out.

This Fourth of July was nothing to talk about. Last year's celebration was *so* good.

I saw Matt on July 5th; we had some time to talk.

He prayed for me and Judy's happiness at one moment, and I did feel lighter and a release.

Pat Roberts says, "If it hurts and pains you and you love them, you should stay away from them." I just can't do that.

A few days later, Cheri mentioned *her* name. My insides started to churn. Later, Sharon called. She told me of the mail. She and Cheri got a card from Judy. I started feeling sick again. I put up a good front, and asked where they went. She started to read the card, but I stopped her, since I couldn't take anymore.

Cheri had gotten a flat that day, and had to stop at a gas station to get it repaired.

We had to take the car over to the new apartment. I can't believe it's in town.

That poem, "I Wonder," that high school students read, was going thru me today. I honestly do wonder if she *ever* thinks about me at all, like I do her.

Cheri is going to enter the local contest. I'm glad for her. She's such a nice young lady. Her picture and name were in the paper. She didn't put Judy's name and address. I'm glad, since I don't want to answer any questions to anybody.

Sharon came home from Beth's today. As she was holding the ladder, she said that Sally came over to Beth's and asked them out to lunch.

She asked for some of her items back.

I told Sharon she can have them if she wants them.

Sharon was wondering why Sally is being so mean, and pushing us out of the family. Sally asked if I have a girlfriend, and she said, "No." Then Sally added, "He better get one."

Sharon was a bit put out by that. She was going to tell Sally that it was none of her business.

I told Sharon that everyone's happy with Charlie, and I'm someone that they used to know. It's easier for them. I'm hurt, but what can I really say or do?

I had to go to the doctor today. He wants to put me on more nerve pills. I'm taking the green one at night, but they put me in a fog in the daytime. He gave me another Rx for the day. I've been a bit on edge anyway, since I heard Cheri on the phone, I'm sure with Judy. I guess she's been back in town.

I am still waiting on you, Judy. It's a part of who I am. I'm waiting for you to come back to apologize. I want to see us together again, more than friends. I'll just wait one more day.

Even though I'm taking a lot of nerve pills, I'm still not sleeping that well. I have so much inward pain. I dream about her; songs remind me of her. I'll never hate her or forget her completely; I'm just still hoping that she'll return.

People can't understand this, but they're not me. My love runs deep for her.

All the songs that remind me of her, I'm hoping someday I can sing them without crying.

CHAPTER 18

After

I had seen Matt. He knows of my deep concerns that Judy wants Sharon to live with her. Charlie's son is there. They're always going out to dinner. He feels they're trying to win her over with monetary things. He feels I should tell her that if she goes there, it always won't be that way. I know Sharon really cares about me, and I don't think she'll go.

Since Cheri was in the homecoming parade, I had to go with her. After, I said a little prayer hoping that I wouldn't see Judy and Charlie. When I was giving Cheri the keys to her car, there they were with Charlie's son. She said, "Hi;" he looked away. I was floored. I was hurt. I smiled at Judy while looking at Cheri, and then I left. I came home.

The pain inside me was so intense; I wanted to get drunk. The closer I got to home, I knew it wasn't right. I kept myself busy, taking pictures of the car.

Sharon then wanted to stay over at Judy's, and I felt it wasn't my place to tell her, "No." I still pray for Judy's happiness, but I do remind God of how I love her, and how I long for her to return.

I had a bad night again. I wonder when all this will end. The nerve pills I took are making me sleepy, but I just don't seem to be sleeping any better.

I'm having weird dreams again. I'm cutting the skin and meat off the back of my legs and my back end. I am cutting to the bone, and taking a bite of it. A voice asks why I'm doing that. I say, "It will grow back." Then I wake up.

My skin is really bad lately. Even Sharon made a comment about it. Being in the car bothers me, because they don't like me there.

I wonder if that's why Judy left, because of my skin. Maybe that's what drove her away.

I don't know if anyone would want me like this. I don't know why life has to be like this. I'm waiting for the day for God to heal my situations, to end this pain. I want freedom, and if death is my freedom, then so be it. I haven't been afraid of it since my accident.

Today was a bad day at work. Everything went wrong. Joseph was upset; Nick was off. I couldn't get all the work done.

We had a high phone bill; then a salesman called. At that point, I had it. My nerves were shot.

I couldn't talk to the salesman; I started to shake. Nothing came out of my mouth. Joseph was in the office. I gave him the phone, and walked out. I was almost in tears. I walked around the block.

When I came back, Joseph wanted me to leave, to go for a ride, go home, and take the rest of the day off.

After, I went home.

I know the base of my problems is my feelings for Judy. I read my Bible, but it doesn't always help. If things don't straighten up, I feel I'm in for a nervous breakdown. At this point, I'm praying that God will pull the plug on my life. I can't take much more.

I had a rough night again, but word must have gotten around, because everyone was less demanding on me, and worked together better.

At least that's going smoother.

Cheri says she has tomorrow off. She wants to go to the lake. I then talked to Sharon, and she said she'd go.

This year, I can only take my vacation with my girls one day at a time. River's Edge was nice, under the circumstances.

The girls were joking, but I still had memories of Judy and the girls and me. It wasn't easy.

Later, the phone rang. Sharon answered it. It was Judy. She wanted to talk to me. I was very mad at her. But, as soon as I was talking to her, I melted. She avoids me, so I don't know why she wanted to talk to me.

She asked how I was doing, and was on my side about work. I felt good. She said I didn't need trouble at work, since my personal life was in shambles.

When she said that I thought, "Honey, if it wasn't for you, my personal life wouldn't be like this." I said nothing.

She wanted to know if Sharon could go to Charlie's company picnic. I said, "Ok." Judy was happy.

It hurts me to know she's with another, but I do want her to be happy.

Next day, I was up before Judy came here. I had a hard time because I didn't want to run into them. I couldn't keep my mind off of Sharon being around Charlie. I guess I don't want her to like him so much, so that if Judy would ask her to live with them, Sharon would leave me.

Sharon said there's a difference between loving someone and being in love with someone. I feel there's no difference. That popped out when we were talking about Judy.

My writings became intermittent. After she got married for the second time (actually, her third marriage), I feel I lost, so I didn't write every day. I'd still get my hopes up, but they weren't as high as they were before.

I was like a battery that didn't have any juice left in it, and I didn't know if it could be recharged. We didn't see each other much, either.

She also wasn't stopping at the house much. Sharon could just walk up to Rt. 165 to visit, or Cheri would just drive over.

There really was no need to see each other. She and Charlie had it all taken care of.

If there were any messages for me, she'd tell the kids.

Monetary issues: there were none. We had already agreed that she would pay half of Sharon's braces, and she did.

I didn't ask for any money from her.

It was another bad night. I talked to Matt. about Judy. He's glad she still cares, just not the way I want.

Judy was coming to pick up Sharon, so she could stay over before they leave for Sharon's trip. I was really tired, and I fell asleep in the recliner. I was awakened by Judy and Sharon. As they passed by me, my eyes partially opened. Judy was asking me if I had a hospital card for Sharon. I said, "Yes."

Judy went outside, and then Sharon gave me a hug and kiss. After that, all I could think about was Judy, and how she looked in her dark slacks and light blue top, holding Sharon's suitcase. I cried the rest of the day.

The next day, Cheri and I went out to see Mom and Dad, and we also went to stop to see an aunt and uncle, then to Joe's place. We took Mom and Dad out for supper.

I did go to work for a few hours, after Joseph was crying for help.

The next few days, my eyes were bothering me. Judy had brought Sharon home, but I didn't want to see her, since the pain of seeing her would hurt me right now, and I don't want her to see me in this state.

Sharon had a nice trip, and I'm glad she wanted to stay here, instead of at Judy's.

It's tough loving someone that doesn't want you, and worse, being afraid to see them.

Stacey and Justin are staying at Beth's this weekend. I guess Beth feels I don't want the kids here anymore. It's just her way of dealing with the guilt of being in Judy's wedding, as if she betrayed me. She doesn't call here or stop or anything. And, everything I did for her. Hmmm.

Judy's birthday. Happy birthday, honey! But it's not for me—it is lonely without you. I am in a lot of pain. I wish for my death soon.

Next day, I was at my doctor's. He felt I wasn't doing well at all, and asked for a shot for me. He said my stress is too high. He gave me more pills, and told me to go home and keep my feet up.

I was surprised that Judy picked Sharon up tonight for school shopping. It was nice, but bothered me, considering that in the past two years she's bought very little for the girls. She's pushing her money around now.

At the shop, everyone thought I looked better. I'm glad. I'm feeling a lot better lately, but not really sleeping better.

I had seen Judy a few days later when she was in the driveway one day. I said "Hi," to her, but didn't look, since I didn't want the pain to start again.

A few weeks later, Judy was here. She was sitting at the table talking to Sharon, but she seemed down and after a while she got up and left. I didn't know why she felt so bad, but later Cheri explained to me that she didn't have her help her choose her senior pictures.

I didn't know that at the time and I was really hurt. Later, I was crying and listening to sad music, like, "I Can't Help It (if I'm Still In Love With You)" by Hank Williams and after a bit I turned off the record player and went to the garage. I just couldn't take it anymore.

She's always blaming me for things whether they're true or not.

The doctor said he had a new treatment for me, of which I'm a prime candidate. He knows about all my problems with Judy and knows that's why my skin reacts the way it does.

The pastor at church wanted me to come back, but I can't go there. It's too painful. *She* got married to *him* there, and I'm not going there.

Cheri mentioned that Judy isn't buying much for Christmas, since she has so many people to buy for, and not to expect much. That hurt the girls even though they tried to fluff it off. It hurt them, but I made up for it.

Judy would still be defensive on things, even though she left us and didn't live here.

My birthday. Cheri took me out for lunch, and then the girls made me a birthday dinner. Sharon got me a toolbox and Cheri got me a gift card. They felt it wasn't a happy birthday. I just laughed and chuckled. Well, it was different.

Cheri got me a great card that said how much she valued me. I can't say how much that means to me.

Months later, it's the continuing saga. I haven't written much since my last birthday. I've become number to the situation. It is what it is, and can't be changed. But my feelings for her aren't changing.

I let the girls handle more of the situations between themselves and their mother, and I stay out of it. I think they were all getting older: Judy, Sharon and Cheri. Judy was realizing that the girls were causing their own problems, and I had nothing to do with it. They needed to solve their own stuff, and not take it out on me.

My nerves got worse, and so did my skin, but then it got better.

I am on day fifteen of my stay in the hospital. The doctors felt my skin condition was caused by too many mental and physical traumas and stress in a short time.

They felt that the car accidents, the big operation, and the divorce yielded quite a shock to my system, plus Judy's marriage to Bob and then Charlie. I was a *wreck*.

You know how you take those psychological tests every year, the ones that ask how many stresses you have been thru? Well, I unfortunately went thru too many each year.

They only let me out for eight hours that week.

I had to take all kinds of baths, use several creams, shampoos, etc. I got better every day.

The doctors felt that all of my skin problems are directly or indirectly related to my divorce.

I was in too much pain to think about Judy at the time, but not that tears weren't shed at other times.

Even though she hurt me, I still love her.

I still am set on a mountaintop, when I see her. And, I get knocked down when I see her with Charlie. We just answer each other's questions and that's it.

I still had an underlying hope to be with her, but it wasn't as high. I hope she's happy.

I'm not so happy, but I've learned to *accept* my problems, especially if I don't want to end up here in the hospital.

During my stay, I had two anniversaries: a work and wedding anniversary. Not much more than a thought about each one.

During this time, Judy got into it with Cheri, and Cheri hung up on her.

Then she came to the house screaming. I wanted to hear her side, before saying anything.

A few weeks later, we were able to talk about it, and Judy apologized to Cheri. I was glad, and it started them on to a better relationship.

Another year, but my heart is still broken. Mom told me that friends of ours got a divorce. I was sad about that one, as my own.

I got promoted at work, but it didn't help me and my nerves.

I was back in the hospital.

Judy bought a house near me and I don't care for that. If she's gone on her own, I wish she'd go away from me.

This past summer, Sharon, Judy and Charlie got into it. He was calling me names, and Sharon didn't like it. She headed home and hid from Judy several times. We talked when I got home.

She also told Judy that I still loved her. Yes, even after four years I can't think of no one else. It was an awkward moment, since I didn't know what she'd say. I was nervous; I didn't know if she'd use my love against me.

Judy asked Sharon how she's supposed to solve her problem of two men loving her? No answer.

She told Sharon that there are many other women who would love me.

I need to learn to relax more, so I don't end up in the hospital.

My mind keeps running back to the memories of her every time one of my girls mentions her name. At times, I'm happy to see her. Then, at other times I wish she'd move away and leave me and the girls alone.

There was a show choir dinner, right around Christmas. Sharon had invited me. She never told me that Judy was going to be there, so I wasn't prepared for that.

I went to the high school cafeteria, as instructed by Sharon. She told me to be there at five-thirty p.m. I came home at five o'clock, cleaned up, and went.

I went in and waited in the hall outside the cafeteria. As I was looking in there for Sharon, I stopped cold. There was Judy. All I could do was try to keep myself from passing out. I looked again. There was Charlie. My stomach turned, and I was weak in the knees.

Sharon was then behind me, and I turned to see her. I was so sorry I had to leave. I don't know whose eyes started to tear first, hers or mine.

I hugged her, and apologized. I told her I couldn't see them together just yet. I told her I'd pick her up later, and left.

I drove around for a while, and then returned. She never said anything about it. Seeing Judy was one thing, but, her and Charlie, that just totaled me.

This trip is related to my work and my problems over Judy. I might get released in a few days. I told the girls to keep it quiet, regarding my stay up here. Sharon told Judy I was here, and that it was about my nerves, which I didn't want Judy to know. Talking to Judy would have made things worse for me.

I guess Judy wanted Cheri to go out with her for Cheri's birthday, but Cheri didn't want to go.

This battling is just going on.

I know Cheri wants us all back together, as so do I and Sharon. She plays it her way, Sharon plays it her way, and I play it my way.

Although this house is filled with a lot of love, it's still lacking one major *key* player.

Fate has been cruel to us: Cheri's had her back problems; both girls lost a full-time mother; I've lost the love of my life.

I hope that their lives will be better than mine.

My skin problems are tough. I'm tired of feeling the way I do. I don't believe people know how I feel. I still pray for an end to this rotten life. I still have Sharon to raise, and I don't know if I can do it. I don't know if I can *outlast* this pain.

Although at times the light treatments help, sometimes it gets to me.

Well, I went to see the specialist again. She wasted no time to put me back in the hospital. The nurses remembered me as the nice guy that doesn't cause "'x'-tra" hassles, and does what he's told. He's divorced, has his daughters, and has a lot of problems in his personal life.

After I told my doctor how depressed I get, he wanted me to see a counselor, and then a psychologist. I talked to her and she thought I was doing well with myself, and I had the right train of thoughts. I need to be a little more patient and optimistic about myself.

As far as my feelings about death, every person in my position feels that way.

People in pain or people who work with people like me understand me. They might not agree, but they understand; that helps me.

I've cried many times and fallen to my knees to let the Lord heal me or let me die. I also cry over Judy, and I ask the Lord to return her to me.

Someday, I know it will work out. Sometimes I think it is useless. The love of my girls keeps me going. Without it, it's nothing.

Later, I found out that a lymph node had to be removed. It was tough. As they were stitching me up, they asked if anyone was here waiting for me. I had to grab the sheets and hold on as tight as I could to hold back the tears. God, how I wished she was here.

I imagined her walking in with the girls, and wondered how I'd react.

I fight back the feeling I have for her, knowing what was and how it could never be again.

I just want to hold and love her again.

I did get out of the hospital.

I guess Judy wanted to see me, but Cheri didn't think it was a good idea.

Knowing she cared would have helped me. Judy stopped by to see me a week later. We talked.

Then she came before Christmas. We talked about how Christmas is for each of us; it's hard.

Then she said something that blew my mind: She said she knew our marriage would have worked out, if she would only have worked at it more. At that point, I didn't know how I wanted to react. I desired to give her a hug, but I didn't. That whole incident killed me inside.

When I told her I forgave her for everything, she actually got *mad*, and I don't know why.

But, I still cry and pray for her return.

I've had several anniversaries since my last writing. I fought my way through every one of them, although they hurt me, just as the first one hurt.

Many times, I'm alone in this house. I try to examine my life. I wonder if this loneliness will ever end.

My first grandson was born, Casey. I can't tell you what a blessing and sanity keeper that is.

I started writing a few poems here and there. They helped express how I feel. I wrote them about Judy, and the loneliness I feel. Also, they are about other people that meant a lot to me.

I was reading a poetry book of Cheri's, and things just started coming out of me. The first one was our parents' fiftieth wedding anniversary or about my brother that died.

It's been almost two years since I've really written. I keep myself busy with Casey. I guess I've been burying myself with being busy.

I'm back in the hospital again.

No one knows what I endure, and how much more I'll have to. I am in mental and physical pain, and one causes the other.

My mental pain has made me into another person. And I know I'm very sensitive to certain things, like romantic or tender scenes on TV—I just can't watch them.

Later that year, Judy surprised me and told me that she and Charlie are splitting. Well, here was another opportunity for me, the one I was waiting for. I was hopeful, yet cautious at the same time.

I did see things coming for the last year. She lets him get away with things that I wouldn't have been able to.

I wasn't as happy about it as I should have been, since I could see the pain she was carrying; it was written on her face.

A few months later, she told me that Charlie was leaving for sure. I stepped up to the plate, and let my feelings out to her. I told her I loved her, and that my feelings had not changed. I would do anything she wanted.

She looked at me and said, "Curt, I don't think I could live with you."

I was floored.

I want her to come to me, to *want* me. I wish I could take her out, but I can't.

I resided myself to not having her again. I don't like to see her hurt, and you can't blame me for feeling so deeply about her.

Sometimes I think I must be one of the dumbest people around for caring so much. I can't help my feelings. They are not dead; rather, they are really alive and waiting for *her*.

I was back up at the hospital.

The more I hurt, the more tenderhearted I get. In pre-surgery, they asked me if I had family waiting. As before, I wanted to say, "Yes." But against myself, I had to say, "No."

It hurts, that I was there for her, but she wasn't here for me.

I know I'll live alone after the girls leave, and I'll die alone. I have little self-esteem for myself.

I lost my job that I loved. I lost the one I loved. My health isn't good.

I still pray for my heart attack, the one that is going to kill me.

I prayed I wouldn't wake up from the operation. Sometimes, I still can't see a reason for this life. Sometimes I think the "powers to be" are playing with me.

I always thought my love would bring her back. I always told her she would have a hard time replacing me. I was right.

It was strange with Charlie. He would linger on the situation. He would still see Judy. She wouldn't put a stop to it, either. They would go out.

Periodically, I'd take her out. We'd go out with Casey or the girls. I'd take her to all of the different places in the area. It was a different kind of dating, *family* dating. I was trying to get the family back together.

I was sitting back and waiting. I didn't send flowers, but I'd still buy her cards and candy for special occasions. We might have bought her a plant for Mother's Day.

I was visiting her today, with Casey. I asked her out. She accepted. We had a great time!

She told me that she and Charlie went to see a lawyer the other day. She didn't seem bothered by it, and I wondered what was going on.

I've asked the girls to be nice to her.

I told them, "I'd like to take her out, but at the moment, I can't afford it."

Sharon said, sharply, "Daddy, Judy is still seeing Charlie." She doesn't want to see me hurt. I don't want to hurt, either.

On this day, years ago, Judy divorced me. Not the most pleasant memories. I thought about it somewhat.

I had another nightmare again.

Judy and Mom were in my dreams, and Casey, and some other women.

Someone asked how we were getting along. Casey asked when and if she was going to marry me. She said that probably she would someday, but not right now, and she was seeing some guy. She knew I heard that.

I cried as I held onto Mom. She said, "Curt, forget her," and cried.

I fear she won't come back again.

I am a prisoner, captured by all of this.

CHAPTER **19**

Another guy

Judy wasn't feeling well, and I told her I'd make her something to eat and take her to the hospital if needed.

Then, Sally called, and told me that Judy's in the hospital and needed emergency surgery. She wanted her mother to call me. I was in shock. Sally told me to meet her at the hospital.

As soon as Cheri came home, we went to the hospital. When I had seen her, I felt like crying. She had so many tubes in her; I felt like they were in me. She depended on me; I am her crutch. Judy asked me to rub her back, which I was happy to do.

We then came home. Sally called the next day. I went to the hospital; she looked a little better.

As I was home alone later that day, it hit me! I've dreamt this before, her lying there with all the tubes in her.

Sally, in a loving gesture, said she knows we'll get together again. I hope so.

Every day she was at the hospital, I would drive to visit her.

In the middle of all this, I had to go to the hospital again. I went up this morning, and thanked God that my hip is fine.

Then, I was getting ready to go see Judy. Cheri commented that she was talking to Judy the other day and said to her that I would be up at night to see her. Judy replied sharply, "Well, he doesn't have to!" And she responded, "He wants to, to make you feel better. You don't have to watch what you say, like around Charlie." Cheri was upset, and I was sad, for just trying to help her out.

I keep having this vision. I see myself lying on the floor, dead, with a little hole in my head. I hear people telling of my death. People said, "He shot himself in the head."

I believe this is occurring because of my inner fears that Judy and I won't get together. After all these years of waiting, is this the way it will end? I don't know.

Sharon had seen Mrs. Morgan the other day. She said, "Wouldn't that be nice, if your mom and dad got back together?" she said, "I'm not a child anymore. It wouldn't work out. I would have to move out."

It didn't bother me that Sharon had to move out; it was just that I wanted Judy back.

During this time, she was able to get out of the hospital, and go back to her home. I would go over several days a week, wash her clothes, sweep, and do other chores. She dusted, did dishes, and cooked. I did this for a while, until I got discarded again. I didn't go, either, when Charlie would visit.

I would take her out to eat with me and Casey, to woo her back, but it obviously didn't work.

A few days after my appointment, I went to her house to help with some chores. After I got done, we talked. Judy said, "Sharon tells me you're writing again." That floored me because I didn't know she knew I was writing.

That was my personal writings, about all of us.

She told me that she didn't want me to get the wrong idea. She thinks of me as a brother, and she didn't know what she wanted. What a slam!

She didn't care what Charlie did and she appreciated me, but wanted me to say, "No," once in a while. But the way I feel about her, I can't. I wanted her back, and, I wanted to continue trying.

I have felt that she always wanted to have me around as an insurance policy, just in case things didn't work out with someone else.

I was upset about what was said, but the next day she called. She wanted to know if I was hurt about last night. I was, but I didn't want to tell her that. I wasn't going to let her know that I felt bad. She would have gotten upset.

What a tough day. A big wedding anniversary. It would have been celebrated 'Curt'-style, taking her out to a great dinner, a beautiful corsage, and pink carnations sent to the house.

But instead, I kept focusing in on that daymare that I've had—lying there dead with a hole in my head.

Sometimes I think the hole in my head is a symbol of an old saying, that you "have a hole in your head." People tell me that, when I tell them I still love her.

It's a picture of what I must do—get her out of my head, or blow her out of my mind.

I also thought of what Bob had said, about coming back home. Charlie had said it, too. Ironic, isn't it? I wonder if she ever thinks about these things.

But, what if she and Charlie get back together? What then?

These past three and a half weeks have been the happiest in years. Spending time with her is great. I'm sad when Charlie calls when I'm there, because he's a rival to me right now.

I wish he'd go and get the divorce, so I can get my family back together and get on with my life.

So, I say good nite tonight, on the passing of this anniversary, and go have something to drink.

I've started walking a lot at night, to clear my mind, and talk to God. I'm asking for the wisdom and patience to win back Judy's love. I'm afraid I won't win, and I'm not sleeping much, and I'm smoking more.

The thought running thru my head now is that I'll lose. I have to tell Judy that this will become the end of it, friendship and all. I don't want to see her anymore, and she can't call when I'm around. I don't want her here anymore. The only way she can come is if she wants to work it out and make sure she stays in my life.

I can't stand to be rejected again. She needs to decide soon, before my love for her is gone. If she rejects me, there just won't be anything left of me. It will just drive me insane.

Every time between the guys, she says she doesn't know what she wanted. Now three times she's throw me away. This one more time will be the end.

So many years—it's 3a long time to wait for somebody. I want to be loved; I need to be loved, but I'm getting more and more anxious and afraid each time.

Judy called today. She said Charlie is going thru with the divorce. She told him, her or his girlfriend. Now I know why she was so out of it the other day.

I'm sad for her, but I will pray for her and our situation. I should have told her what's in my heart, but I didn't want to push her. I'm really in such turmoil, more than I've been in some years.

I walked tonight, and talked to God to give me the strength to go on.

I'm tired and afraid, that I don't know how to win her love again, and that I won't be able to carry this cross that God has given me much longer.

God, I love her, and I really want her to marry me again.

A few days later, Sharon woke me up, and said, "Dad, Mom's in the hospital." That woke me up with a jump.

Judy had called and was having pains. After all day we found out she had an infection, and God, I'm glad she's ok.

Cheri was talking to Judy tonite, and Judy was a bit down. I guess Charlie took his girlfriend camping this weekend. Judy was upset, and Cheri told her not to worry about it. She also felt when Judy left Charlie a few years back, that Judy should have never went back to him.

Cheri's never said it, but I know she would like to see me and Judy back together. Well, you know how I feel about things. Of course, I'd like to be the one who fills her lonely hours.

My birthday. I got quite a surprise at work. A guy came into the shop, and said, "Happy Birthday!" He gave me a fancily-wrapped bottle with six balloons attached.

There was a card with it, and it said, "Your friend." I thought after a while, the only person that could do this was Judy, but I wasn't sure.

She called tonight, but played dumb. I did get it out of her. I really liked it. That I received a gift from her made me feel wonderful—it came out of left field. I felt like she wanted me back, that we still had something there.

I was in the kitchen when the phone rang. Sharon answered, and yelled for me in a broken voice. It was Judy—Don died.

I was surprised that Sally asked me to be a pallbearer. I mean, I was but wasn't part of the family. He was my father-in-law, and somebody that I admired, and we were good friends. He was a good grandfather to my kids.

A few days later, Casey and I were over at Judy's. She said she was talking with Sally, and told her that I was always there when she needed someone, and Charlie wasn't. Of course, I was there—I love her. Like I've said, I'm her crutch when she needs someone.

Sally said she'd rather see me around than Charlie. That comment made me feel good. I didn't know how to react to that, but it was nice to hear.

I lost my canine friend and pal, the one that saved my life. I was with her when she passed on.

Sadie's health was rapidly failing, and she was almost blind for years. She'd run into a corner, or between the stove and fridge, and couldn't find a way out. I felt bad. She had a hard time walking, and then she quit eating.

Sharon took her to the doctor's, but there wasn't really anything they could do. I didn't want to put her to sleep, so she was at home.

The girls kept a watch on her all night. They left in the morning, but I continued to keep a watch on her. I was checking on her, but as I put my coat on and went back to check on her, she was gone.

I closed her eyes, petted her, and cried.

The girls came back home and I left them with her for about an hour. Then, we buried her and after I calmed myself down and I went to work.

I was going to leave Sharon a note to bring her to the doctor's this afternoon and put her out of her misery, but it wasn't in God's plan.

Casey doesn't understand what happened, but I brought him to where she is, and I told him he could talk to her at any time.

No one knows what she did for me. Even Don loved her, too.

Little did the girls know what I went thru and what I'm still going thru. It's devastating to me, watching Judy play the field and choose other men over me. Not only does she date them, but she marries them, and I try to court her in-between. It never seems to work out.

What a nightmare I had. It was bone-chilling. Casey and I walked into this room. Judy was laughing and talking with three to four other women. I can't remember what was said. I said to Judy, in a sharp voice, "Sounds like you're married again." She answered, calmly, "I am." I said, "You've only been divorced for two weeks!"

She said, "Yes, I met him two weeks ago, and he swept me off my feet." In a loud and shaken voice, I responded, "You didn't give me a chance! Well, that's it! Forget everything—me, the kids, all of it. I can't take it anymore. That includes anything with my girls, weddings and all. You're out."

With tears in my eyes, I grabbed Casey and went outside to my car. He was at the outside of the trailer.

Judy ran after me, and in a calm voice said, "I'll talk to you tomorrow, when you're calmed down."

I started the car and said, "There is no tomorrow for us. I don't want to see or hear from you again. It's all gone."

I woke up, shaking.

Sometimes I feel my bad dreams are trying to tell me something, or it may be my fears. I don't know. It makes me wonder what will happen to my love and me.

Looking over this year, it wasn't my worst or best year. As I have my toast, I hope and pray for a better new year. However, as long as I'm lonely, I know it can't be.

I'm ready to leave this year, happy that it's over. I'm still lonely, even though I have the love of my girls and my grandson.

As I lie awake tonight, I try to make sense of this painful life of mine. Life was so much simpler when I was younger. Mom and Dad told me what to do, and I worried about the dumbest things, and they were always there.

I grew up, got married, and life was much tougher. My worries were many. I leaned on Judy, and she leaned on me. We were there for each other. With the big "D", life got *much* harder. My worries increased a hundred-fold. Now I have no one to say to me, "It will work out; it will be ok." I need to have someone to hold me, and tell me, "It *will* work out; it *will* be ok." I'm tired of being alone in a crowd.

I talk to God a lot. Although I feel better, it doesn't take the place of a hug, a hug that I desperately need. That voice of reassurance that I need—that human touch, if you will.

Sometimes, in this lonely, painful life of mine, I pray for my death. For some reason only known to God, I'm still here, fighting day-by-day to make it through.

Sometimes it seems my lot is to be the nice guy. Then I get kicked in the behind by the same person I'm trying to be nice to. And then I turn right around and try to be nice all over again.

Although there are a few people out there, who do like me for being nice, I sometimes wonder if it is worth it.

Living in this godforsaken body is a living nightmare, let alone having people kicking me all the time. It would be easier taking the kicks if my body wasn't racked with the mental and physical pain I have to endure.

Things were really bothering me today. I realized it was Lynn's anniversary. The current problems I'm having overshadowed my hurt for Lynn; I'm embarrassed that I forgot. Now I feel so drained.

Years ago, Judy left. I declared, "God sure gave me a mountain to climb, and I'm still trying to climb it. I don't know why. I try to be kind and honest with everyone. But I've gotten beaten down, and put in last place. That's me, Curt the fool."

Life gives you many things, and takes them away. It took my Judy away. I will always cherish the time we were together, and the good memories I have.

I don't understand my purpose in life anymore. I have no real reason to stay at my job, and I don't stay around other than for Casey and the girls.

I have to be happy with what I had, and expect no more. I am set in my ways, and I can't seem to change. Nothing can change that but me, and I don't know how.

This guy came into work today. Surprisingly, he told me that I am a generous, hardworking, gentle and caring person that deserves a lot more that I've been given. I have not been treated fairly by others, but sometime in the future I will receive my reward. In addition, I will receive the greatest gift of all, when all is said and done.

245

It was the first time I had met him, and I never seen him again.

I am all these things. I know people admire me for raising my girls.

He said I probably love someone that doesn't deserve my love. There wasn't much else said.

Judy did tell me years ago, that she didn't deserve my love.

I can say, in the past two weeks, that we'll never get together again, and I'm wasting my love on her.

It's been many years since I legally ended my marriage, but it wasn't the end of my love for her. I don't feel like I do in the past. The intensity isn't there. I still want her and love her, but I have finally come to terms with myself. I still dream a lot about her. I don't cry as much anymore.

Since Valentine's Day, she has been insulting to me, and maybe that's why I feel this way.

On my New Year's drink this year, I still get down about Judy, but I don't cry as much like I mentioned, and I enjoy talking to her when I see her. I try to play fair where the girls are involved.

Sharon is getting along better with Judy, but Cheri has a way to go.

Cheri has to have a serious operation. I haven't written a lot this year, since I'm all screwed up over it. I'm also going thru a lot of turmoil. What if I lose her? What will I do?

Judy, Matt, Sharon, Sally, and Cheri and I went up together to the hospital. Sharon and Matt took their own car. It was hard to see her have to go thru this. I was lost, even though I tried to be tough for everybody.

She told me she loved me before she went in. She had her surgery and came thru, but it was tough to see her afterwards. Judy and I stayed up there and it was awkward a bit, but I was so glad to be there.

Here I was, taking care of my baby doll, my love. Our oldest was having intensive surgery, and I was here to hold it all together.

Judy made the remark that she felt odd with me in the same room. I assured her that I was a perfect gentleman and I still am. I just really wanted to hold her, but I couldn't.

The next morning, we went to see Cheri. Judy and I spent a lot of time with her, and I enjoyed every minute with Judy. I was puzzled that she brought something up which I had heard before: Sally would say, "Judy, I hope you're not leading Curt on." Judy would reply, "I'm not; he knows I love him like a brother, and that's all."

A brother, hmmm. I take care of you; I tend to you. I'm there when you need me. I take care of the girls. When I want you, you regroup me as a "brother." Thanks.

I wanted more but I wasn't getting it. My feelings have changed somewhat. The need is there, but not as strong.

I will continue to hope and try, and love her from a distance. Unfortunately, she's turned me out again.

It's New Year's again. I'll have my New Year's drink, and toast to Cheri for being here with me, and helping me be here. And to Judy, for being in my life, little that she is. But, she is <u>still</u> there.

My birthday again. Cheri and Sharon took me to dinner. It was a surprise. Joe, Uncle John and Aunt Stephanie were there. And, of course, Joseph.

Mom and Dad couldn't make it, or Barry. But it still was a great time!

I got nice cards, some money, and some other gifts.

You know, everyone who gets past a certain point complains about it. But actually, I feel great. Maybe it's a state of mind.

I've heard Judy has a new boyfriend, and the girls say she's gaining weight. Go figure. She met Tony, the neighbor guy. As usual, I walked away.

You know when I heard about it, it didn't bother me that much. Things are changing for me.

I was up at Sharon's last night, and there she was, walking in with her new boyfriend. I realized I didn't care much for her anymore.

As I left Sharon's apartment, I said to myself, "I lost and that's all there's to it." If that's who she wants, I don't care. It really doesn't bother me.

Wow. All those years to get over her—that's a *long* time.

If you think this story is over, it isn't. It will only be over when my life is done, or I'm happy again. Until then, I'll write something now and then.

"A New Year's toast to loneliness..."

CHAPTER 20

Changes

An obvious strain to me this year was when Dad had his heart attack. He blacked out. I'd drive out all the time to see him. There's nothing they can really do, except monitor his medicines.

At the urging of my girls, one night as I was visiting him, I hugged him. He walked me to the elevator, and that's when it happened.

I don't ever remember doing that before, not even as a child. After that night, it's been easier to give him a hug. Next, I'll tell him I love him. I'll have to work up to that, to give him a hug.

Well, Sharon's getting married. Sharon and Cheri have been asking me for a week, about what I'm going to say when I give Sharon away. I wondered what was on Judy's mind.

When she gets married, I had planned on saying, "Her mother and I," in response to, "Who gives this woman away?"

There was just that one choice. She is our daughter. I always wanted to include her in that response rather than to not include her, but secretly I always wanted to see the look on her face when she heard it. During neither time I got to see it, since I was facing the preacher. Secretly, I got a smile out of it. I don't know if she wanted me to say it, but I believe she was happy that I did.

I told the girls not to say anything, until Judy hears it in rehearsal.

On the big day I was to reply, I was to step back and sit with Judy. Before I got to step back, Sharon turned to me and gave me a kiss and a hug.

I got a lump in my throat, knowing my life was changing again. I held back a tear during their vows, remembering the day Judy and I said our vows to each other. I repeated those words to myself and cried inside.

Judy was beside me, and I wanted to hold her hand, but I couldn't—it wouldn't be right. When we danced at the reception, I got that old feeling back and I remembered how much I loved to dance with her. However, none of the other feelings were there.

That year I got a service award from work—it's one of the only things that have kept me going all these years.

Matt, Sharon's husband, got into a terrible accident. I didn't even have it a year. He slid into the oncoming lane, and the car smashed.

Matt was badly burned. They were transferring him to another hospital. We didn't know what to expect.

He looked awful. I don't care about my car; I just want him to be ok. Cars can be replaced, people cannot.

Over time, things were better. He recovered. He's really lucky, I'll say. So, we all thought that was enough, and Cheri was trying to get her wedding together.

Then Judy sprung one on us. *She* was getting married. And, on top of that, *she* wanted a big wedding *and* the girls in it. They both told her to forget it.

She was worried, how *I* was going to take it. They told her, that I felt her and her new beau Tony should just go away and get married, and that I didn't care anymore. So they did go away. I don't remember the day or month, just that they got married this year.

Good 'ole 165. First, it almost took my life, and for the third time it took away my wife. How ironic, that's where she met Tony. God, it hurt, that all those things happened there.

Well, Cheri got married. I said the same thing to the pastor that I did at Sharon's wedding.

I did get that lump in my throat again. I'm truly glad to see the girls get married, I am. I do have Casey, but now he's with Cheri.

It's not that the girls are far away, it's just that no one will be here but me. It's really going to be lonely for me.

At Christmas, I went to Cheri's first to open up presents, then to Sharon's for dinner and more gifts. Judy, Tony and Sally were there. Will stopped by later. It was like one big happy family, except for me.

Christmas is for kids, no matter how lonely I feel. I didn't even feel like putting up a tree this year, but I did it for them.

Well, it's the end of the year. I'm looking forward to next year. Between Matt's accident and Judy and Cheri getting married, I hope next year will be better.

I got a thank-you in the mail today. It was from Judy. She let me know she really liked the flowers we all sent her. But, it also said that she's glad our family situation is at a happy-medium.

Well, she didn't write "Love, Judy," but, I knew what she meant. You see, Judy had to have a similar operation that Cheri had. Of course, I'm glad she made it.

And yes, like she said, I'm glad she made it, too. Our family situation at a *happy-medium*? Well, that I wish would change.

The next day, I had this strange dream. It was misty and hazy, in the graveyard, near where I'm from. I was hovering a few feet off the ground, and looked down in front of me. To my right was Lynn's grave, and to me left was a double gravestone. I thought it was Mom and Dad's. I didn't see anything written on the stone. Right in front of me, besides Lynn's gravestone, was:

> In loving memory
> Curt L. Statten
> December 10, 1945
> February 18, 20--.

I couldn't see the last two numbers. I tried to look closer. It seems like the numbers were moving fast and then barely moving. Then, I seen an '06, and then an '09. It kept flip-flopping.

Maybe, I'll make it to 2006, then to 2009. Then, maybe not.

Maybe this is God's answer to my prayers, when this will be over. Maybe I'll get that heart attack to end this. Or, maybe the devil is playing with me.

I always said, I probably won't retire, and get to see my social security check. I joked about it for years, even to her.

I would mention, that my first check will come and I'll open the front door, reach out to open the mailbox lid and fall dead on the front porch.

Cheri had a baby, Dante. I'm so proud of my three grandsons.

What a tough day. My good buddy and pal Lou died. He was one heck of a brother-in-law. We had our problems: I was neat, he was messy. I'd try to get myself together; he drank and smoked too much, and it really interfered in his life.

Lou moved to Washington and was injured. After his car accident, neither of us could see each other anymore, and he was getting remarried. After I seen him, he was so happy. I couldn't take the pain, and after that last phone call, we couldn't talk anymore.

He may be gone from his world, but not from my heart.

She stuck with him until he died. He lasted about a few years until his body collapsed. On his birthday, I always think of him and what a great friend he was.

That year, Christmas was different. Cheri and her family went to visit in-laws. Sharon and I set my tree up at Cheri's, for when they came home.

Dinner at Sharon's: her family, Tony, Judy, Sally, Monica and me. Matt's brother also came. Judy and Tony got me a few tools. It felt weird that they did that. She got Will something, and since she loves me like a brother, she got me something, too.

I sometimes really get lost and upset and I pray to God to send me someone. I guess he doesn't figure I need someone yet. Or, I need to live my life alone. A toast to Cheri, Casey, Dante and Alan, and to another year.

Cheri and Alan did come back home, and we had a second Christmas. It was great.

In May, Justin came to live with me and attend school this fall. It's nice having him around, with everyone else gone.

I lost James Johnson. He was a good friend and co-worker. He had a heart problem, but it was cancer that claimed him. I was very sad. He was kind and gentle. I will miss him. Rest in peace, old friend.

In August, I took a vacation to the lake. We had a great time.

In December, unfortunately, I lost Dad's sister. It really had an effect on Dad. His health hasn't been great lately, so Joe and I looked after him.

I was really nice to have family together on Christmas. We had dinner at Cheri's house this year. I told the girls to tell Judy not to buy me presents this year. It made me feel uncomfortable last year. Judy understood.

Well, it's New Year's Eve again, and I'm not feeling great. I hope I feel better the next day. I spent a lot of time working around my house, so I wouldn't feel so lonely.

It started in the afternoon, when I started feeling sick and dizzy. At work, Marie and Hal sent me home. Hal took me home.

I changed, went to bed, and threw up in the middle of the night.

By the next morning, my arm was hurting. It had swelled up. There was so much pain. By the next day, they had to take me to the hospital. They kept me overnight, then for several days. I had lots of IV's. They found I had a serious infection in my arm. Even when I came home, I had IV's.

It took weeks to recover and to get back to normal life, even to drive a car.

It was tough. I handled it. I had to give myself shots.

Later, my roommate called me. He was a priest and a former paramedic. He told me that the IV's I was getting were pretty heavy stuff. He said, "You were on the edge, and were a very sick person. You were at the fifty percent mark, of losing your arm.

So now I knew I was really sick—waking myself up, calling for Dad, saying crazy things and having wild dreams.

This all happened a few weeks before I ended up in the hospital. The kids told me to go, and I didn't.

You know, I don't even remember being in that kind of pain, even though I had my big accident, when the doctor gave me one thousand to

253

one odds that I wouldn't make it until eight that morning after putting me in intensive care at five am. This situation was *so* much more painful.

Joe called me and told me Dad was having chest pains. He's in the hospital again. They're giving him medicine to help drain the water around his heart.

I lost another person today, Cameron, another friend from work. He had a tumor removed, but they found several tumors in his large intestine, and he didn't have long to live.

Sharon called and was all worked up. Matt was in another car accident, and was bruised up. He was in the hospital for a few days, and thankfully he'll be ok.

Changes at work again. Our manager was leaving. I was upset because he was a good man. I'm sad to see him leave. Then Craig came in, but he didn't stay long. Then they hired Mike.

With all these changes, and things I went thru this year, there wasn't much time to think about Judy. I was too worried to just get thru the day.

The hospital visits were stressful enough, and there were so many work changes. Matt was in his accident, Dad had his heart issues, plus I lost James and Cameron. My mind was so full of so many other things; I didn't have time to think about *it*.

She was there, but not in the forefront of things. I had other immediate concerns coming to the front position, that I just placed her on the back burner.

I'm sure sooner than later, she'll be back up front again. Time will surely tell.

On a lighter note, Cheri called and said, "Can you be my date to see Kenny Rogers at Bentley's Theatre? We're going with Judy and Tony."

Here's how it went: Judy and Tony picked up Cheri, then me. We went to dinner and to the concert. It was the first official family "group date." Dinner was at The Steak Place. I ordered a rib eye. It was a full meal: potato, salad, rolls, the whole works. I needed a full plate to get myself thru the evening. I wanted to be here, to see Judy, but it felt unusual seeing her with newest husband.

It should be me sitting there next to her, and then Cheri and Alan.

It was a strange and different family situation. Here I was out with my daughter, my ex-wife, and her new husband. That wasn't the end of the oddities that night. Just wait until coffee. Same side of the road. This time it was Jantley's. On the way back, we met Will, his new wife, Sheila, his ex in-laws, me, my ex-wife, our eldest daughter, and Judy's new husband.

They sat in front of us, and Carey suggested we all go get coffee. We sat at a big, oblong table, and I was on the end near Cheri.

I was looking at this whole thing, and thinking to myself, *who* could believe *this*.

I mean, I really like Tony; he's good to my girls, my grandsons, and Judy. But, he's taking *my* place at *her* side.

This whole thing was funny. I got to the point that I had to start laughing about this, and not crying. I had to, in order to get thru. There was nothing else I could do. I feel God throws in these little comedic things to get us thru the tough times.

After a while, we all got up and left.

When I got home, I got ready for bed, and thought, what a wild and crazy evening.

A week later, I was hurting. I was cold, and I threw up all night. My right leg was hurting. I had to crawl to the bathroom, and then back to bed.

I had Sharon call the doctor. She took me to the hospital, per his orders. They kept me for eight days. I'm glad I didn't wait this time. This trip is related to my work problems and over Judy.

A person close to me was going thru a divorce. The spouse had gone to a lawyer, to draw up papers. I was hurt and mad at the same time. I knew how this person felt. It crushed me to watch the events replay themselves like they had in my own life—getting served with divorce papers, dealing with the kids, having to decide how and where everyone is going to live, and especially, *why*.

I told this person, "Please *don't* waste your time, like I did, until it's too late. *Don't* waste *your* life, waiting for that person to come back!"

It made me <u>angry</u> of the pain that the person who wants the divorce is inflicting on their family.

I felt, this person doesn't care about anyone else right now, but *themselves.*

Now about Judy, she calls and checks up on me, every now and then. I asked her if she knows about this situation. She replied, "I know divorce is a tough subject between you and me." She added, "I know I hurt you." Then in surprise to me, she said, "I hurt, too."

She mentioned about this person, what they have had to put up with.

I can't remember what else was said in our conversation. However, I was out of it, and quite dumbfounded.

After what happened to me, and what she said about hurting me, do you know how many years it took for her to admit she hurt me? Almost as long as I've waited to hear that from her, although I told her years ago I forgave her. Maybe she is starting to forgive herself.

I reflected on Lynn today—his birthday. I practically think of him *every* day.

But this day is special, knowing there are others beside myself who are thinking of him, and there are others who gave their all—right *or* wrong.

He wasn't a saint, but he was my brother. We loved each other. All I've got is a cigarette lighter and a memory of shaking his hand before he got on that bus, the last time I would ever see him alive again. I will *always* remember that. That final handshake was not only between brothers, but between men—the Marines took a boy, and made a man out of him.

I cry when I think of him, and most of the time I visit him at his grave. My voice still shatters as I speak about him.

When I go to his grave and talk to him, or hear the *Battle Hymn of the Republic* or the *Marine Hymn* played, it shakes my whole being and tears me apart inside. I know I can be soft-hearted, but I have a right to be this way.

Thirty-four years with the company today. You know, thirty-four years is a long time, but, I like what I do and I do it well.

On Father's Day this year, I went home to take Mom and Dad out to dinner. She wasn't feeling very good, so Dad didn't want to go out.

I've been driving for a week now, so I picked up Casey, and I took him to the doctor; I had to get some growths removed.

Then I went to see Dr. Banks, who's helping me. Daphne was thrilled to hear that I'm coming back. I'm going to continue working on Frank's cabinet. Casey and I finished it today.

I went back to work. I've been here a long time, but, I like what I do and I am good at it.

The person getting a divorce called and said that they are going to try to work it out. I'm glad. If it doesn't work, they tried. At least this person won't be wondering, "What if?" like I did.

I took Casey to Park of Fun and we had a great time. Every time we go, I shed a few tears, of the memories of my family being there, and what this day is and what Memorial Day means to me—what my family has given up for this country.

My grandson Jacob was born today. I was so proud when I got to see him—my fourth one!

We got to go to the Vince Gill concert with Sharon and Matt, Jeremiah and Casey, and Judy and Tony. What a great time!

Then the next day, I got out with Cheri and Alan to see Travis Tritt. Judy and Tony came too. <u>Another</u> great time!

I was listening to some of my old records today; one of them was "As Time Goes By." As time does pass by, I really do believe that the music I listened to as a youth is and was a picture of my life.

I listened to music that talked of loneliness and heartbreak and that is how my life's been for years. I guess I was meant to be a loner. I should have looked at myself when I was young, and possibly changed my life, but, it's too late now.

I wished I had someone that loved me besides my daughters, my grandsons, and my family. I'll probably spend the rest of my life lonely and heartbroken.

However, I did have the chance once, to be loved by a wonderful woman, and God, I still wished I was loved by her.

The music of my youth tells my life, especially the song, "Sea of Heartbreak." That's how it went for me.

When I was younger, I was always drawn to lonely, heartbreak songs. I listened to Jim Reeves, "Welcome to My World," and another song, "I Missed Me," the A-side of "Am I Losing You?" I also listened to songs by Ray Charles. And, there was another tune, "I'm So Lonesome I Could Cry," by Hank Williams. That's me, lonely to a "T".

If it wasn't for my girls and grandsons, I wouldn't have anything to live for. I still dream of being happy again in this life, but time is running out.

I went home the day before Christmas. Things are a little tougher at home, because the doctor said that Dad's not going to get any better.

New Year's Eve

My usual writing at the end of the year. Casey and Dante stayed with me and we went to Sharon's to light off the fireworks to usher in the New Year. The boys, Sharon, Matt, Justin and I all enjoyed the fireworks. It seemed everywhere you look, they were all over the place—Happy New Year!

Unfortunately, in December and January, Dad was in-and-out of the hospital. It was near his end-time. So, they put a hospital bed in the living room, with twenty-four-hour oxygen.

He has good days and bad, and worries about things he can't do anything about. I went back to help him fill out a living will, but he won't fill out a regular will, either. Mom isn't much help. He said, "Your grandpa lived to be eighty-two and I plan to live longer than that." He's seventy-eight, and he'll be seventy-nine in August. I'd love to see him be eighty-three, but only God can answer that.

I feel bad. I only see Dad six times a year, but he has given me so much. I look forward to our talks.

He was the mighty man, who used to toss me around like a rag doll, and became a weak, frail man.

I can't stand it that he can hardly help himself up and out of a chair; it hurts me deeply. I'm scared I won't be able to hold myself together.

It won't be like when Lynn died. Judy helped me, and I helped Dad. Who will be there for me now?

This year, Lynn's birthday is on a Saturday. I thought of Lynn all week. Not that I don't think of him every day. I broke a few tears, like I do now and then. You'd think I'd come to terms with it by now.

Cheri asked if she could show her kids the really tall snowman that Tim, Lynn and Ray Smith made in the back yard when we were kids. I remember the good times and memories of Lynn. I wish he could've come back alive and well. Yet, in spite of all his devilishness, he had a sense of honor and sacrifice and pride in his country, right or wrong.

I will never forget the last day I seen him. I remember how he stepped on the bus, turned around and shook my hand. I didn't know it at the time that I shook the hand of a man, and a very big man, in my eyes.

My boss for many years, retired today. He had surgery, so he decided to retire early and move. Everyone is surprised that he hasn't come and talked to me yet. He doesn't like to wear his heart on his sleeve. We really do respect each other.

A little after eight, I was getting an item out of the top of the garage. The ladder I was standing on slipped, and even though I dropped the item and tried to grab the support with my right hand, I lost a grip and fell five feet against the fender of the car. I landed with my back to the car on a bag of empty pop cans. Thank God—that broke my fall.

I felt for broken bones and my left shoulder hurt a little. I laid there for ten minutes before I got up. I went into the house, splashed some cold water on my face, and put some sports crème on my shoulder. I called Sharon, and she came right over. She felt that my arm didn't look right, and took me to the hospital. My left hand was numb by then, and boy did it hurt when they took my blood pressure and took me to get an x-ray.

The doctor told me that I dislocated my shoulder, and gave me a prescription for the pain. Boy, I slept well that night. I have to wear this sling for about a month, and go to physical therapy.

The phone rang, and woke me up. It was Mom. Dad was talking to

Joe and Johnny, then threw his arms up and went out. They called 911, and took him to the hospital.

The next day, they put a pacemaker in him.

I took Casey with me to visit Dad and put flowers on Lynn's grave. On Father's Day, Casey and I went to see Dad.

On the Fourth, Sharon, Matt, Jeremiah and Casey and I went to Matt's mom's house for a cookout, and set off fireworks.

In the fall, I went to the Pumpkin Fair with Casey. We met Sharon and Matt, Jeremiah, Judy and Tony, and Cheri and Alan, to see a concert. It was one great show.

Thanksgiving of that year, Casey went with me to Joe's. It wasn't much of a Thanksgiving, since Dad and Mom couldn't be there. We did take them out for their anniversary dinner a few weeks early, since Dad can't be out in the cold.

Dad's going downhill fast. I did visit with Mom and Dad and he got up from his bed to give Casey some money, like he always did. Casey told him, "I don't want any money. I just want you to get better, Grandpa." Then Dad sat back down. Hearing Casey say this, I was proud of him, but sad, since I know Dad won't be getting any better.

For Christmas, I went back to see Dad. He was in good spirits.

On New Year's, I just got back from Sharon's, where we had a good time setting off the fireworks. Well, it's two-thirty in the morning, and I better get to bed.

Dad is back in the hospital, and isn't doing very well. Tim wanted me to let the girls know. Cheri, Sharon, Casey and I went back to see Dad. Cheri drove us in her van. Dad says he's feeling much better. Dad is out of the hospital, but, he's not doing too well.

Us guys at the office got the girls a gift, and gave each of them a rose. Daphne cried and Tina didn't know what to do. She said that no one had ever done anything like that for her.

This really did remind me of how lonely I am, and how lonely I feel, and, it hurts a lot. Also, all of my friends are either married or have girlfriends, and they have someone that they can hold, or be held by.

They can say, "I love you" to them, or be told, "I love you." All I have is silence, a deafening roar of silence.

There isn't a day that goes by that I don't think of Lynn. There's an email I received two days ago from Joe that explained from his lieutenant how Lynn died. He stepped on a land mine, and immediately went down. He was even concerned about the other guys till the end.

I can't bring Lynn back, but I felt a little better, knowing what he did and said.

Dad isn't doing well and he is talking to his mother, and wants to go home.

I went to see him, and I brought Casey. He was out of it, mainly due to his painkillers. When I left, I kissed him on his forehead and gave him a hug.

Sharon, Matt and Jeremiah went to see Dad. He's very weak. A few days later, Joe called and told me that the doctor put Dad on morphine today. I sort of knew in my heart that Dad wasn't going to live much longer, even though they said he had six months to live. I figured that I better get home this weekend to see him.

Sally called at work in the afternoon, to tell me that Dad died.

I called my girls, one at a time. Only Matt answered the phone.

I decided to keep working, and I went back to finishing a cabinet I was working on. I was waiting on Tim to call, knowing that the boys wouldn't know what to do about the paint. I had to keep my mind off my problems.

After Tim called, I went into the office, and started to work on my paperwork.

I was telling Daphne things that needed done for Friday, and she was looking at me, with a question mark on her face. I was sitting down, she was at her desk, and then I told her Dad had died.

She stood up, started to cry, and came over to me. We held each other, and I cried. She said, "Curt, you need to go home."

I hit the desk, with my fist, and said something that revealed how upset I was.

She told me to go home again.

I said, "I can do this, just like Dad." You see, when my grandfather died, Dad stayed, and finished his shift.

I finished the sanding, and some other things. I later talked to my girls; they asked me if I was ok—I wasn't, but said I was. Sharon came to help me pack.

I couldn't sleep much that night, even with pills. The next day, I got up, gassed the car, and I headed out to the funeral home.

I got there at nine fifty-five a.m., meeting Joe, Candy and Mom. Barry decided not to come. Tim came after me; I realized I passed him on the 'pike.

We three boys picked out the casket, and I gave Mom the money to get her hair done. I went to the graveyard to talk to Lynn, and back to Mom's. Tim, Joe and I went to the graveyard to make sure that they marked where Dad was to be laid. They had the wrong plot, and Tim walked around and asked questions. Joe talked, too. They both cried. Tim cried again when Joe said that Dad said, "I love all you boys." Tim didn't know that.

It was a great moment in my life, when Dad first kissed me and said, "I love you." I've been after my two youngest brothers, to tell Mom and Dad, before it's too late. I don't know if Barry did, but at least Joe did. We decided to be pallbearers, with Johnny.

I stayed in a motel there. I needed to be by myself, to talk to myself and to go, and to ask Him to keep me strong, in all of this pain. I knew he was in a better place, but it was hard to see him there.

Daphne and Tina came to see me, just to support me. Daphne is the best friend I have. Cheri and Sharon came, and Cheri didn't tell Casey till Friday since, like Mom says, "Casey and Dad had a special thing going."

Judy and Tony came in; she told Sharon, "What do people think about me being there?" I wanted her there. I was in turmoil, but I needed her there for me.

I knew it was going to be hard on all of us. After the service, Mom went up to Dad, hugged him, and said, "Oh, Carl!" and started crying. That was hard. Candy cried. After we helped Mom with her coat, I helped Candy. We all then got in the cars to go to the cemetery. We pallbearers did the last thing we could for Dad. I held up Candy to steady her. At the end of the service, she said, "I'll miss him." We all will.

After the dinner, Cheri and Sharon hugged me, gave me a kiss, and asked if I was ok. Then Judy hugged me and asked me if I was ok. I really didn't want to let go, as I was holding her. I was in such turmoil. I was hurting over Dad, but I enjoyed her arms around me once again. I didn't want to let go. I know in some way, I love her and always will.

It was snowing and I decided to go back home. We went to the funeral home and picked up planters. Then we all headed back home.

I called Mom when I got back, and told her I'd be back to see her.

I'm glad I had to take care of Candy. She needed someone to lean on, and I had to be strong for her. If I didn't have her, I don't know what I would have done.

I went back home today to help Mom with some papers, like Dad wanted me to, and since he entrusted me to.

We found papers that proved he was a WWII vet, but I didn't find his discharge papers. Mom called to see if I'd be coming home for Easter. She said that Joe and Barry had a big argument, and Joe is mad at Mom for not sticking up for him. Joe just wanted to see what he could get and take some things, and that made Barry mad. Mom isn't ready to clean out Dad's things yet.

She told me that Lilly wants Mom and me to come to Easter dinner.

Lilly's birthday. We got to Joe's on time, but they had already eaten.

Joe's been treating Mom rotten and I feel sad, since he's been my best and closest brother since Lynn died. It's been a real tough Easter since Dad died. Mom started to talk to me from the heart about how she feels. She even cried a few times. I know she needed me, and she wanted to talk to someone who understood what she was going thru, and how everyone is pushing her, and she isn't ready yet.

I know that going thru a divorce is harder than what she's going thru. She knows that, too. I told her things, about how hard it was for me, things I never told her before. I think I made her feel better.

'She told me that she needed to get a head stone for Dad. I told her to call Joe or me, Tim or Candy, or Barry. I let her know that I understand and was on her side. If she needed something, just call.

I got a letter from back home that we're having our fortieth-class reunion. I am excited as always. This is our first one in twenty years. I do plan to go.

Mother's Day. I went back home to see Mom, and we were going to take her out to dinner. As she was getting dressed, she asked to be taken to the emergency room, and she had a pain in her back. Her blood pressure was high, and her sugar level was greater than 300. The doctor said she could go home after she ate.

Sharon said that there was a message from Millie, a lady who helps with Mom. She had to go to the hospital. I found out from Tim that Mom had a small heart attack and was having tests in the morning. Mom has blockages and they might want to do a bypass.

Meanwhile, Joe said Barry blames him for Dad's passing away. Joe is wrong. I can't believe this is happening! We don't need this now, especially just after Dad's death! None of us are over him dying, and the family will be so upset if she does. And neither of the boys is to blame for Dad's demise.

Mom has decided to go get the surgery. Candy feels that Joe is envious of her, but she is not mad at them. Neither brother is to blame for Dad being gone.

I did go see Mom. Lilly was glad that I talked to Joe. I told her, I accept all of my family for their faults. Lilly got on Joe for how he treated me.

Barry called to say that they're going to operate on Mom. I couldn't sleep much that night and left to see Mom at five a.m. I got there at 8:10 a.m.

Barry, Millie and I stayed, and they had me sign some papers.

The doctor came into see us at 4:30 p.m. Mom is ok! Thank God. They had to do a double-bypass. Thank God.

I went back home for a graduation party. I stopped at Dad's and Lynn's graves, to lay flowers on them. Too much family history is lying in the cemetery.

Joe was still a bit stiff with me at the party, probably because of his embarrassment with how he treated me at Easter.

We went to visit Mom. She is weak, but she is going to be better in a few days. I'm so glad. She is staying with Barry.

We went back to Dad's grave, and then met for dinner at a diner. All in all, it wasn't a bad day.

We went to Cheri's for dinner around one o'clock. Sharon came over, and so did Judy and Tony. For Father's Day, my girls, their hubbies and Justin went together and got me an automatic garage door opener. Wow. I was just telling Casey last night that I needed one.

Judy called me, to tell me Samuel died yesterday from a blood clot to his heart. He was just a few months younger than me. It hits home. He was Judy's neighbor, and we became friends. He was the one that got me my job.

I haven't seen him in seven to eight years. He and his wife Judy were close friends of ours, but we drifted apart after Judy and I divorced.

I took a few hours off work to go see Samuel. He looked good. Judy called Sunday night and we talked for two hours. She thanked me for talking to her on Sunday.

Sharon and Casey and I went to see the Vietnam Memorial Moving Wall. We found Lynn's name, and when I first touched it, my hand started to shake a little, and my eyes were tearing up and my lips quivered, but I held together. Sharon made a rubbing of his name, so she can make something for each of the boys. I wasn't expecting this wall to be as huge as it was. It really does overwhelm you.

I got ready and got packed for the class reunion. There were people there that I hadn't seen in forty years. We took a tour of our old high school. A lot has changed: carpeting, a new gym, and a print shop.

Surprisingly, while I was standing in line, an old classmate walked up to me and put her arms around me, and planted a big kiss right on my lips. I went right along with it! I haven't been kissed like that in years. God, it was nice. Funny thing, she hardly talked to me in high school, but she was one of the popular girls and nice to everyone.

At the dinner I spent most of my time with some of the guys and girls that I knew. I had a great time!

My New Year's thoughts for this year: Dad's death was something on me. I was able to keep myself together until lately—I find myself crying when I think of him and my voice quivers.

Then Mom had her double-bypass.

In light of the good things, I still feel lonely. I guess God isn't ready to answer my prayers or maybe he doesn't hear me. Maybe he does have an answer for it. I have my answer—to be lonely for the rest of my life, and to have the love of my present family. Maybe I'm supposed to be glad of what I have and not to expect more—I really don't know.

What I do know is that I've been waiting for a long, long time and time is running out.

I fell at work; I tripped on a loose floor grate. I was carrying two boxes, and I couldn't get rid of them fast enough to check myself.

Incidentally, I broke my nose, cracked my cheekbones, four ribs and three vertebrae—ouch! I spent ten days in the hospital recouping.

I haven't smoked heavy in a while, and was only smoking two to three cigarettes a day. Cheri and Sharon said, "You haven't smoked since then, so why don't you quit?" so I did. I went back to work two weeks later.

Mom called me to tell me that an uncle died, and then two days later, Cheri called me around nine a.m. at work, and she was a little upset. I asked her what was wrong. She said, "Grandma Sally died. The lady that checks in on her found her lying on the bathroom floor around eight a.m."

I was busy at work, and couldn't get out until five. I had to get back for my uncle's funeral. He looked good. My aunt did well.

I got home around ten; I unpacked and went to bed. Then a few days later, I went to Sally's funeral. She looked real nice. I was wondering about Judy, but she did well.

This New Year's came in fairly quiet for me. Some of my grandkids stayed with me.

My girls picked up their kids the next day. As usual, I was <u>alone again</u>.

Casey and Mom had birthdays soon after. I called her up; she was happy that I did.

We took Casey out for his birthday dinner. He wanted to go to this restaurant where they make dinner right for you at your table. It was really nice, but different.

Valentine's Day—it is a Friday this year. I sit here again, alone as usual, without someone to hold and really love. Life sucks, and it hurts to still be this way. It really pains me that I could live another twenty to twenty-five years lonely. It's the pits when you once had the world in your hands. I did what I thought was the right thing to keep my greatest love with me. Maybe I'll be lucky and wake up in the morning and read my name in the obits.

For my birthday, it was a Sunday. I woke up around a quarter till nine, and lay in bed for a little while. Mom called me to wish me a "Happy Birthday." She forgets some things, but not everything.

I got up at nine-thirty a.m.; I took my pills, and emptied the dryer. I cleaned up and got dressed for church. Then, I looked out my picture window and boy what a shock. Two signs in my front yard. I put my shoes on, and I went outside to check them out. One said, "Simply Sixty." Another sign said, "Curt, you're over the hill," and there were signs attached to the tree in the front yard, with black crepe paper attached to the railing on the front porch. After taking a few pictures, I went to church.

After the pastor's sermon he said, "Our daughter called this week, and she thinks we're really, really special." He brought it to everyone's attention that I was "Fifty-nine yesterday." He added, "Our birthday today. A birthday!" and he looked at me and said, "Isn't that right, Curt!" in addition he stated, "It looks like you're getting a little bit red-faced, Curt." I answered, "I probably am!" Then the congregation sang to me.

Later, I met Sharon and Judy and Casey for dinner.

The next day, Cheri came over. We had apple pie and ice cream, and she got me a new phone.

After reading the paper, when I got to the obits, a name just jumped out at me—Landon James. I just sank in my chair, and felt a great sense of loss. He was one of the first people at work that befriended me. Ken was a great guy. I lost track of him the last four to five years.

I knew he was sick and going blind. He hadn't anyone here to take care of him. I found out this summer that he was in a nursing home, but I couldn't find out where. I have to take some time off work to pay my respects.

I paid my respects to Ken. There was a short service, forty-five minutes long. So long, old friend. We didn't always see "I" to "I", but you were a good friend, and I thank you for that. You were upstanding, honest and caring. I'll always remember your family. May God grant you peace.

I ended up in the hospital again in January, with shortness of breath. They couldn't find a reason. I had a stress test mid-February. I had some other tests, but all I know right now is that my blood level is low.

I also had to go see Dr. Chambers if he could operate on my left rotator cuff. He decided not to operate, because a shoulder replacement is all they can do, and it is a very painful surgery, and things won't be much better than they currently are.

I guess I've lived a few years like this, and a few more years won't hurt.

Casey graduated from vocational school. I'm so proud of him. There was a commencement program at The Music House. I consider Casey my son, but he got himself into some things. I wish I could've raised him myself. Maybe he will be better for it, from the things he had to go thru.

He might be moving this fall, close to his job. It's hard for me to let go, but we'll just have to wait and see.

Mom's been in-and-out of the hospital. She's been living in an assisted-living place.

I went to the fortieth annual reunion. I talked to a few fellows that I haven't seen since I left there forty years ago.

I got my anemia under control in mid-September. However, I am having a breathing problem. I ended up in the hospital. I couldn't sleep much, and I'd get lightheaded. At times, I felt my chest getting tight like having a chest cold, when I would bend over. At one point, I felt like I was going to black out. They rechecked my heart, but it was no different.

They figured that my breathing problems were from my job, and my joy of smoking is my number two problem. Also, I have a moderate case of emphysema. The doctor is optimistic, and believes he can make it better.

I knew Mom wasn't going to be around much longer, the way she was talking to me the last few times I seen her. I got a phone call around eleven at night that she died.

I called Cheri and Sharon. I said a prayer for Mom, but didn't sleep well. Mom had made all the arrangements, so we just had to wait for when she passed.

I went to work, but didn't feel well before lunch. I left after lunch, cleaned up, talked to Sharon and went to bed.

I was woken up by Sharon. She couldn't understand anything I said. She told me to stay in bed. Cheri and Justin came over to see what was wrong. They took me to the hospital after Justin dressed me. Cheri stayed with me as I was getting admitted.

She filled out most of the paperwork, but for the life of me, I couldn't even make a "C". I had to ask Cheri for help. It was like learning how to write again.

In the room, they gave me aspirin, a few shots, an IV, O_2 and a heart monitor. They told me I had a heart attack. A few days later, my speech was back to normal, and it took me a week to get my hand writing back.

I told Cheri to call Judy and Tim and Daphne. Judy called me the following day, and I was floored with what she told me—she didn't know why she divorced me, because she stated that I am the most honest and honorable man she had even known.

At that point, I didn't *want* to hear it. Of course, it was great to hear, but I spent the next three days crying over what she said. It further broke an already broken heart.

It still hurts to think that after all those years, that you can't remember why you divorced someone. It hurts me that every time I think about it—I got divorced for *nothing*.

I know she never meant to hurt me. She just wanted me to know how she feels about me; that's nice. But, I'm still in love with her, even after all these years.

I had to wait about a week to be transferred to another hospital. I had transfusions in the hospital I was at, because of my low blood count.

Once in the other hospital, I had a stroke. I lost my peripheral vision in my left eye. For a few days after that, I had an orange line running down the center of my right eye. Scary!

Also, I lost my sense of taste because of all the meds I had. I also got an infection.

'I spent over a month in the two hospitals. I lost over thirty-five pounds, down to ninety-eight and one-half pounds. I had a walker for two weeks.

I came home to stay with Cheri. I had Thanksgiving in the hospital and I was sent home for Christmas.

I had trouble breathing and was put on O_2 and sent back to the hospital for ten days. They found out that my lungs were filling up with water, and they had to drain my right lung. It really didn't hurt. It was great to be able to breathe right again. I went back to Cheri's after. Then, somewhere in the middle of this, the doctor said I could drive again. Freedom!

On the weekends, I came home, with either Casey or Jeremiah staying with me. At the end of May, I came to stay here by myself.

At the local hospital, Cheri came every day. Daphne called a few times a week; then a friend called from Florida. He found out that I had a heart attack. That picked me up that he phoned me!

The girls called Joseph, and he came up. Judy called; the pastor came every other day. Sharon would come or call.

One of my girls came every day. Joe called; he, Lilly and Tim and his wife came to see me. That was great! Now, my "Joe troubles" are gone.

I was weak. When I sat down, I needed help to stand up. It was like that for two weeks. After I got out of the hospital at the beginning, I was told I had two bad valves and two clogged arteries: one forty percent, one ninety percent, and the other seventy percent. I asked about getting operated on. They had a meeting with me, Sharon and Cheri, and told us that I wasn't strong enough at that time. They gave me a fifteen percent chance to get off the table. I was really disappointed, because I just wanted to get it done.

On one of my weekend stays, Johnny, Julie, Aunt Jeannie and Barb came out. Another time, Tom Johnson and Rob came to see me. Daphne came to see me at Cheri's, and Barry and Jan came out, so did Uncle John, Stephanie, Joe and Lilly. I guess when someone is as sick as me, you just don't know what tomorrow will bring.

The doctors say that I need to weigh at least one hundred and thirty pounds before they can operate.

I got to go back in about six to eight weeks. Not good enough yet.

Judy hadn't seen me in a while. I drove over to Sharon's. Judy was in the dining room. I walked into the kitchen, by the way of the garage.

Judy was glad to see me. I was glad that I was much better than the last time she had seen me, because I could hardly walk then, let alone drive.

She came across the kitchen with her arms open wide, and gave me a big hug and kiss, and asked how I was.

I held her longer and tighter than I should have. I loved every second of it. Imagine that, her arms around me, and I didn't want to let go. I remember saying to myself, "Curt, let go. You *have* to let go. She isn't *yours*, Curt, let go Curt, let *go!*"

I really didn't want to, but I did. To me, it felt like I was holding her for an hour, but it was only a moment. I held onto her, as I felt she also wanted. God, I was in *heaven*.

I spent the evening with her at home, so she could place a photo of Lynn and the poem/letter I wrote to him on the anniversary of his death on the web for me. She then wrote an email to a young woman that placed a remembrance of Lynn on the web.

The young woman replied and Judy gave it to me when we were over at Sharon's for a picnic. (Thanks, Judy.)

I spent Father's Day with Judy and Tony, and met his kids. Weird, isn't it?

Like I said, I take advantage of anything when I can, to spend time with her or around her. I know it sounds sick. I am not sick, just in love. Always have and probably always will be.

CHAPTER 21

Now

Every once in a while, the thought of killing myself still comes along. I'm still hurting. Sadie's not here anymore to save my life, but then I think about my kids, my grandkids, and especially Casey, my oldest grandson, and now, knowing someone who lost their loved one *really* puts things in perspective. I can stack the deck again, to me, to play Russian roulette. I could put all seven shells into the .22 and spin the cylinder and come out a winner. But I don't take it that far, because I think of *all* of them. And Tim, no matter how much we may disagree, he would be crushed since we lost Lynn together. I can't do this to my family; we lost *too* much already.

I didn't do this because the damage I would have done to others would have been devastating: my mother, my father, Tim, living in the town next to me.

The diary helped me make it through. At the end of the day, I would write and read it. I could see how I felt, and *feel* how I felt. I would look for misspelled words or bad language.

Stuff that was down came up. Putting pen to paper allowed me to express myself to myself. It was my own private journal, to see how well I would be getting as the months went by. The devil would wave at me as I would pass him by, as I was going down, and laugh at me. My girls were never to touch it, or to tell their mother.

Getting my thoughts down were like therapy to me, so I could face my demons. It was like talking to a psychiatrist. Someone told me to do this, to sit down and write and express myself, and make myself feel better, even how little it was.

Slowly I would go down, but not as before. This would be a process of up/down, up/down.

I wrote mostly every day for a couple of years. I had to do it. I then went down to once or twice a year. It got to the point where I began to start settling myself emotionally and living with status quo. I got to the point where I didn't have to write anymore. I wasn't going to change anything, and I was going to sit back and wait for someone to find *me*. If someone wants me, I will be secure, and I won't have to go thru *that* again.

I also wrote lots of poems, because my heart ached so much, and it was better to express it this way than to blow my head off.

For a long time, I've been praying for Judy, praying for her to come back, or someone else to come to me.

I did like a lady at work, but I vowed that I would raise the girls myself.

There are discrepancies with what she expected of me, versus what she did. She really didn't want me to date or get married. Then, like she said, she'd be out if something happened; she always thought I'd be there. But that wasn't really fair to me.

I'm ready to get past it now. After all these years, I want to move on. I'm not going to spend the next twenty years of my life alone, without a great woman to spend it with. I'm getting myself healed through getting my story out. I've got a lot to offer someone.

I'm a great guy. I'm a worker; I'm a poet; I'm a writer; I'm a family man. I care about people. I want to live my life and do things. I want a woman I can take out, catch a movie with, go out with and get a bite to eat. I want a woman who can love me, not judge me on the money I don't make or *don't* have.

I've always given the best to my family, the best for Sharon and for Cheri. I'm a great listener. I'm also a great friend. I listen, I learn, and I offer gentle, good advice. I care. I'm also a man who loves God, the most important thing of all.

I don't feel that He was punishing me. I know He wasn't trying to hurt me. As a person of faith, we have to understand that people have free will and have to choose how they're going to live their lives. It's a tough concept to acknowledge and understand. Personally, I feel that the idea of free will is daunting, of course, if it's directly affecting me.

Sometimes, God takes us through things, and boy *am* I trying to understand this. I know that everything that happened to me did for a reason, as it did to all of us.

My story is here to save lives, not to hurt or hinder them. I want to let people know that they're not alone. They don't have to choose to die; they can choose to live. I honestly mean that after five suicide attempts.

This story is not meant to hurt or harm those mentioned. My story is to talk about my feelings and my handling of the situation that, by no fault of my own, I found myself in, swimming helplessly in a sea of lost emotion, not being able to find my bearings for a long time. I have tried to rebuild my life, through faith and love, and any encouraging souls that came across my path.

I wonder now how things would have been, if we would have stayed together. There would be me and Judy, spending time together, and also with Cheri and Sharon and the kids.

I would have taken her places, stopping along the way to eat out and visiting other parts of Indiana. I wanted to do other things with her too, like go to a country concert, or out on a date.

Casey is my oldest grandson, and would I love it if he could come over to see the two of us, not just me. And all the other kids. My girls and their kids: my family, but missing a key element!

It would have been nice to go to a Christmas party, to Beth's, the neighbors, or with the grandchildren somewhere. Those feelings are still there. I feel *great* when I'm with her.

Today, there's still that underlying thing with the girls and Judy. They are still upset at her. We will all be that way; that will always be that way. We won't forget what happened here, and they won't forget what happened here. A girl needs a mother in her teenage years, not a father who's trying to be a mother. A father cannot give a girl the emotional support she needs, even though they say a son clings to his mother, and a girl to her father; at about sixteen the man part comes out of a boy, and a woman comes out of a girl.

An exception to me was Lynn, who would write to Mom. They had a special bond. When Tim and I worked with Dad, we started to cling to Dad, but Lynn clung to Mom. They had something special. He would write her things that I couldn't at that time.

I could always talk to my Mom, but after Dad died, we talked more. I'd spend hours talking to her, about how lonely she and I were. I finally had enough nerve over time to tell her that I tried to commit suicide more than once. She looked at me in tears, and said, "No, Curt, no you didn't." I said, "Yes, I did," and then it was dropped. It was nearly five years after Dad died. If you think about it, it took me over twenty years to tell her that. I felt that she could at last handle it.

First it was Joseph, then Beth, then Kathy. I told Mom, then a good friend, and a few others I could trust with my secret. I just didn't feel I should tell *anybody*. My brother's going to flip out, my daughters, and Judy. They're going to be upset. I look at my friend Allison and think about what could have been. Daughters running around making bad choices, having their mother to guide them, but they would have hated me. It would have been that antagonistic sense between Cheri and Judy. Since they would have lived with their mother, the roof would have almost fallen off of the house.

I won for several years, but boy did I lose after that. Why didn't I listen to some of my friends, and date someone else? I would be going against my morals. They would always slap me in the face. My parents wouldn't allow me to do that. My grandparents wouldn't allow it.

It's a snowball effect, the people who would have lost out.

I still need somebody as a substitute for her, but not to replace her. I was telling Joseph the other day what Judy said to me, and he said, "Did she tell you what she told you because she meant it, or was it to give her a piece of mind?" I'm still not sure. I'm a special person to her, a *brother*. I'll always be 'special' to her. Tony is only older than me, and holds grudges. These are the only differences.

I still get irritated, but I don't give up on life anymore. I don't try to avoid the pain of it all. I know it's there. It hurts a lot. It always comes up. I try not to bury it. But, some of the things I have to bury, and when it comes out, it comes out.

It's been coming out as I'm putting my thoughts together about my life. As I've been reading my diaries, I can't believe I did that. I can't believe I put up with that. All the love, and then more. To touch her, a hug, a smile, a phone call. All for what? I look back now, and wonder what it was all for.

Between Sadie, Joseph and Matt Madden, they were my angels. I *do* believe in angels. I used to think that angels could only come in the form of people, but who would have thought it would come in the form of black and white and four little legs? Matt was such a good person to talk to. Talking to Joseph was like talking to my own son.

What I think cuts down on divorce is communication. Years later, she tells me that she doesn't know why she left me. Everything else was excuses, like money, no attention, etc. If she only would've told me that there was a problem before it got out of hand.

I want someone for me that deserves me. I'm a hopeless romantic. It's kind of like an old movie that you watch. The guy likes the girl, she thinks they're friends, and then he goes out with someone else. She then stands there, saying, "I blew it." That's what happens a lot.

And then that guy that came in and said, "You loved a woman that didn't deserve you." Someday you're going to want me to want you, when I'm in love with someone new.

Like I said before, I'd feel secure because I wasn't the one to make the first move. Then they are the one to come after me. I'd feel secure because they wanted *me*.

I can't go thru it again, chasing after someone, pouring out my heart and soul, committing myself, and then getting my heart broken all over again.

And I don't have that much of my heart left. It's been broken in so many pieces. I *am* shattered glass. I *am* in a million pieces. How many more times can you break a broken heart?

For twenty-five years I prayed for Judy to come back. I was even telling my pastor about it. He was shocked that I wanted to kill myself so many times. He said he's coming to the house to talk to me, but I'm still waiting. In the beginning, I wanted her to come back, but years later, it was over when she married Tony. Since then, I've been praying for someone else to come to me. However, there's still that glimmer of hope that she would come back to me, even if it's just a small chance.

We have seen the progression here. It's what happens when you decide to kill yourself.

You get in that mood, you're so self-centered, and you don't consider the reactions of others. Nothing counts but *you.*

Telling my story has helped me get it out, to release it. When I hear someone talk about loss, I say, "Oh, no, another one!" You get in the trap. The trap is love. You just can't get out of the *trap* and not that easily. One-sided love never works.

Some people can handle it better; some people can just go about their business. They get divorced; they and their ex-spouses get remarried, have boyfriends/girlfriends, and even have kids with these people. That's not me; that's *not* Curtis Statten. I'm a man of my word.

I wasn't the kind of man to bring the outside world in. Life was already disruptive enough to us; I wasn't going to bring another woman for whatever reason; I wasn't going to have someone stay here and bring their kids over, or have a kid with somebody.

I didn't want to mix things up. I'm not trying to cut other people down, it just wasn't for me. I'm not going to have my kids get lost in the middle. It's like when someone passes away, you're still respecting that original family unit.

It's just how some of us are.

I was brought up and taught to find one person, and get married. Today, it's date everyone, and then maybe one will work out. I don't believe in that.

I was raised in a strict way. I don't go for this modern-day lifestyle of whoever comes along you sleep with, and then that's it. I think it's a mess. I like the old standards. I'm not into the new standards today, even with the TV shows.

Today, since my girls are grown, I don't have a problem meeting someone. I wouldn't mind meeting a lady whose husband didn't appreciate her. I would like to care for her the way that I care for Judy.

I would like to find someone with a sense of humor, who I can joke around with, and when I pick on them, they take it in stride. It would be nice to find someone that can laugh at themselves. I want that understanding from that person, where that sense of loss can be shared. I want someone that feels like I did, and possibly still does. It's almost like a death that's still living, because they're still there and you can't touch them.

Like I've written, "The want is there, but you do not dare."

A holiday dinner this year went well. I got used to the holiday setup by now. At first it was awkward, but after many years, you just do what you have to do. I got to hug her, but I wanted to kiss her. I *never* kiss her.

Ok, I'm here now. I don't think that she's with another guy. She's close to me, sitting next to me. I'm glad she's there. I think it's done by design, the seating arrangement. Sometimes I think she likes it, too.

I often have thought about what would happen if I bring a lady friend, how that would shake things up? I wonder what her expression on her face would be, although years ago she told me how she moved on, and how I should have moved on, too.

I'm sure she knows something about me since I haven't gotten married or met someone for a reason.

It bothers them that she's remarried and I'm not. I feel I may never find anybody.

A friend believes I will.

I have an item that she gave me while we were dating. I treasured it; I wore it for years, until she married Charlie. I didn't wear it again until she married Tony.

There was no particular reason why I started wearing it again.

I had another link chain I wore, but the clasp broke.

I bought myself a bracelet a year ago, for something different.

I do keep her item on my dresser, with two of my watches, one of which is from my parents when I graduated high school; the other watch is from Cheri.

The item from her means something to me. It's the first thing she ever gave me.

I don't buy her or her husband any gifts. They do buy me something small at Christmas. We do send each other a card. We ironically entered the same contest. She won something and gave it to me.

I visited her and Tony the other day, and that intense feeling wasn't there. When she calls in the morning, I do get that old feeling again.

If she came back, I don't think I'd bring our/her old issues back up.

It's like, you always have questions that you want answered, but you don't want to ask.

It would always bother me, and I don't think I could completely bury it, but I would try to go on with it. It would cause pain on both ends, and some things should stay there.

I'd still give Judy her own room if she came back. We wouldn't sleep together. Jumping into bed won't solve your problems.

I recently asked Cheri for permission if I could date. She thought it was great. She said, "Dad, I told you a long time ago that you needed to start dating again." I was pleased that she said that, and I said, "Let's go find a redhead." I would never date again unless the girls would approve it. I'm ready now, but I'm going to wait until after the heart operation. I don't want to do this until after that time.

You can have many loves, but only one great love, and she was mine. I really think that.

Working on my feelings is really helping me to let it all go. All those memories that are deeply imbedded are starting to free themselves. The pain and anger that were deeply-seeded and rooted is starting to subside and get freed up.

I don't dwell on it as much. It doesn't hurt as much. The stress of it is subsiding. Finally, this weight is being lifted off of me. It helps to talk about it.

I'm finally putting closure to how I reacted to this situation. I'm putting this behind me, and I want to move on. I'd like to meet someone special and enjoy my remaining years. I'm feeling less stressed. However, I will die alone if I have to; I've always dreamed of Judy holding my hand when I die. I don't want to be alone when I die.

It's like I said before, there has to be something that pulls you out of it, my angels: my girls, Will, Beth, Lou, Joseph and Sadie, and Kathy. When we were down, we'd call each other. Joseph carried me like no other, though. I could talk to him man-to-man.

Kathy and the group broke up a couple of years later. I don't know what happened to her. She might still work in the area.

Beth, after the divorce, lived in the area, raised the kids, then met another Lou, and moved. Stacey left; Justin went with Lou. Beth got sick and passed away.

What would I say to someone who is thinking of suicide or who would consider doing it? Don't do it. It's not an easy road. Look at all the things I would have missed: my daughters' weddings, my daughters graduating, and my grandkids. How devastated my parents would have been, my brothers, younger siblings, and all my friends and co-workers. You're not the only one to consider. My daughters, how they would have handled it? What devastation their lives would be, like Allison's? Why did *my* dad or mom chicken out and take their life, and leave me like this? That would be their thought.

The idea is, don't be like me; don't fall in love whole body and soul. I can't go thru this another time. A part of my soul will *always* love her. I'll always have her with me.

I wouldn't go into something body and soul. I probably won't go into it with a full heart, because I don't have an entire heart this time; it's incomplete. I won't go into it the same way. I'd be cautious. I can't afford to do this again; it would wipe me out completely. I'd be guarded again. I don't want to hurt once more.

Judy, with her several marriages, never went into it with a total heart. She was always protected.

At this time, I feel that I am getting to a point again of coming to the sense of living in the status quo. When she sent me my birthday card recently, it reopened those wounds.

Today, I feel you need health and love to survive. Without love, you can't survive. My health issues added to my stress. I was in Cornerstone Hospital for ten weeks in a period of fifteen months. It was tough. Judy did call me, to see how I'm doing. I was happy that she did. She's the best medicine I could ask for. She'd never let me get into a fix like this, if she were mine.

I feel that I let things go, since I have this need in me to self-destruct.

I wait too long to go to the doctor's, and I'm really stubborn.

But in relation to my 'heart' issues, a good friend has asked me, "Do you really think it takes two to get divorced?" "No," I said, "I don't think so." I would have tried to do anything. Often, people just get bored and want out. They see other people doing other things, and they want to try it.

I once heard someone say, "When you get around divorced people, it becomes like an epidemic." It does happen that way, doesn't it?

It took me until this day to just about bury my pain again, and then she had to send me *that* birthday card.

It said on the front of the card, "Happy Birthday." And, "That it would be your best so far, sincerely sent by someone who knows how ~~nice~~ wonderful you are." She doesn't know how much that bothers me. She always says how special I am to her, but I wonder if she even sits down to think *why* I am so good to her.

That was <u>real</u> <u>nice</u> of her, and would have been ok, but she crossed the word "nice" off, and put "wonderful" in its place.

That knocked my legs out from under me! I couldn't believe it. Wonderful. It rang thru my head. What's wonderful? Wonderful is getting your girl back. But me, *wonderful*?

I fell to my knees. Tears ran down my face. I remember yelling. I wondered why the doors of pain were opening again.

I knew that she meant it in a different way that my heart took it, but I just kept thinking, and still do. I am a wonderful guy, just not good enough to be married to. I just *can't* and *don't* understand it.

But, she's probably just thinking of us in terms of our family situation. Because of me it is nice, because we get along and have holiday and birthday get-togethers as a family. She's often commented about our family situation, the way that it is. It's different than most divorces. It's nice compared to most people. Recently, we spent a holiday together.

She thinks we get along because we are friends. I don't think she realizes that I'm *still* in love with her. Although, I've been praying for years that God sends me *someone* to love. Like that old country song by Connie Francis, "My Heart Has a Mind of Its Own."

It took me years to get to a point that I could live with the idea that Judy wasn't coming back, ever. I would just have to take every treasured moment I could get, and live with that, and I wasn't doing well.

Then, she had to say she didn't know why she divorced me. That threw me for a loop. Because, she said I am the most honest and honorable man she has ever known.

After that, the doors of pain opened up again. I cried for three days.

And now, I'm having a hard time closing the gate this time, probably because I'm reading my diaries again.

It's been such a long time, and after this if she doesn't know what happened to our marriage, then I don't know what to say.

Love is something that needs nurtured; it needs taken care of. Some people have to have it more than others.

I just think about what I went thru, for what reason? And not only me, but what my kids went thru. I didn't need this at the time.

I endured this for so many years, and there seems to be no memorable reason for it. I knew she never meant to hurt me when she told me that, and to this day she doesn't know that it did.

So it really doesn't matter, the lineup of the guys. I'm mad at Bob because he wasn't the man that I thought he should be. He should have called me and told me that there was a problem. It just could have easily been one of the other guys.

As far as Bob is concerned, I still dislike him, but not to a great extent. People who run around, they don't want someone else who's like that—they want someone they can trust, even if they themselves can't be trusted.

Bob had a good job, and Charlie gave her a false sense of security. Remember, Judy said that one of the biggest problems we had was money. Tony was older, and all three of these guys could offer her the financial stability that I couldn't. It was just a thought of mine that she was looking for something; I just never put it together what it was. My love for her was still at my doorstep, as apparently two of her exes told her so.

Lately, I've been thinking, that maybe Judy and I won't get back together. It doesn't bother me, though. I'd like to get back together with her, but maybe it won't happen. I've gotten used to living alone. I don't like it, but that's just how it is.

I don't smoke as much, and my drinking is up-and-down. My eating is a little better; I'm trying to get to bed earlier. At this time, I feel that I am getting to a point again of coming to the sense of living in the status quo.

Treasured moments, to me, are being in the same place as her: be it in a car, a room, or at our daughters' patios. They are seeing her smiles, hearing her voice or her laughter, or the touch of my fingers touching hers when she gives me a cup of coffee. I cherish the hugs I receive from her, or when she lets me open a door for her. I relish the times when she calls me on the phone asking if I want to go along with her and Tony someplace. Every occasion I can be around her is heaven to me.

Until God sends me someone, I will be that way. No one will *ever* replace her. But, maybe someone will stand-in for her. God only knows the answer to that.

I only know that I would like to be happy once more before I die. I haven't really truly been happy since that night, the one that tore my heart in two forever, so many years ago. I just wish, truly, that none of this had *ever* happened.

They say everything happens for a reason, but, I can't see <u>why</u>. There is no good reason for what I've lived thru; what I've had to endure, let alone what my daughters have gone thru.

Although Tony is a nice guy, he's got what I want, *her*. And, my kids and grandkids like him. After I got to know him, like I've always said, he's like me, just a few years down the road. He's the kind of guy I would probably choose for her.

Until a substitute love is sent to me, then I can forget the love I have for her, and I can finally put my love for Judy on a shelf.

Jennifer

CHAPTER 1

That fateful day

It was just a few short weeks before *her* birthday, and only six days before mine.

It was six-thirty a.m. in the morning. I told *her* I was going to school as usual. I was walking down the street to get the bus, and *something* told me to stay home.

I went out to the bus stop. Then I went back to the house; she was sleeping. It was around seven a.m. I went downstairs and watched TV for a couple of hours. Around eleven a.m., I came upstairs and she was awake.

She wasn't herself, and she was staring off into the distance. I remember her saying that she was no good for us, and we were better off without her. I could look into her eyes, and I could see that it wasn't *my* mother that day. There was a gloss in her eyes. She said that we should go live with Don and Nancy. I remember saying to her, "But Mom, we're your kids. How could you not want us?"

How could she say something so cold, so mean? That's when I got concerned, at twelve p.m. We talked again about my dad, how he died in a helicopter crash.

I didn't ask any more questions about it since he had passed. She was distant and just lying in bed, with a white robe on. No makeup; her usual blonde made-up hair was now in a white terry wrap. She had grayish-blue eyes that didn't even notice I was in the room at all. She tried not to look at me when she talked.

I went into my room and got down on my knees and prayed. It was around one p.m. I asked God to forgive her, watch over her, and *please* take care of her.

My brother was in the house with his friend Logan. Greg was sixteen; I was thirteen. They asked me to go to the park around two o'clock. I went to the room to talk to Mom and to let her know that I wanted to leave for a while. I gave her a kiss, and told her that everything would be ok, and that I would be home soon. She was still lying in bed.

Who knew what she was up to that day, but I did have an uncomfortable feeling. I went to the park since I was upset with the things that she said to me. I thought that she would be ok. The guilty part of me was laughing and having a good time, while she was at home doing *that*.

'At this time we were living in a house. We rented-to-own, and Omi, my grandmother, was helping us like she always did.

We were coming home around four-thirty p.m., and there was an ambulance at the house, as well as police cars and other cars. My neighbors came running down the street, to Logan's white car, maybe a Dodge. Logan stopped the car, and Greg rolled down the window. The three of us were up front, with me in the window, and one of the neighbors yelled to us, "Where have you been? Your mother just hung herself!"

A shock just went right through me. What would I have done differently? How could I have changed that day? What if I was there, would she have done it while I was downstairs?

I hated myself for leaving her when I felt something tell me not to. I took care of her when I was eleven; I would have never left her that day. I had prayed for God to watch over her.

I was in shock. I didn't know what to say. Tears rolled down my face. Logan said, "Oh, my God," and proceeded to pull up to the house. It was a two-story house, and painted light green. Greg had a lot of anger on his face and didn't say a word. We then got out of the car. Logan stayed in his car. When I got to the steps, I noticed four big black trash bags; I didn't know what was in them.

We walked into the house. Greg ran upstairs and punched the large mirror in the upstairs hall way. It shattered everywhere. I found Omi downstairs in the entranceway on the floor, up against a wall. Her knees were bent up, crying endlessly from the strain of it all. Her elbows were on her knees, and her hands were on her head. She was buried in despair. Paul was there, with his arm around her.

Greg didn't want to talk to anybody. The cops were there, going over what happened. I ran outside, crying, and they were trying to comfort me. Neighbors came over from across the street to console us, too.

That day she broke down completely—she had given up. I found out that in those bags were broken statues, crosses, and anything religious.

She would always talk about God, and always wrote poems about Him. The three of us attended church regularly. We were Lutheran, and we attended a church on nearby. She loved God, but why would she kill herself over a relationship that was wrong for her? She lost her faith, and we lost our mother. It was just too much to bear; I couldn't believe this was happening.

The day Mom died, Omi had talked to her. She told Omi, "No, I better die." Shortly before she passed away, she had a complete hysterectomy; she didn't want any more kids. She didn't tell Omi why she had to get this done. Omi didn't recommend the surgery. She wanted to go to the doctor, and Carole, my mom's friend, came to visit her. They were supposed to go to the doctor. Instead, Paul found her; they found her together.

I remember she drew a picture of the house six days before she died of where we were living, and I still have it.

My grandmother took care of all the funeral arrangements.

For days after, I would go up to the attic and I would try to feel her presence. I remember that it was warm in the attic, as opposed to being really cold. She had a bunch of clothes that she stored up there on racks.

I really try not to think about the day of my mom's funeral. There were calling hours the day before. She had an open casket. It was surreal, like it wasn't really happening.

The day of the funeral, we went to the cemetery where my mother was to be placed after she was cremated. I put silk flowers there. It was hard.

Stephanie was there, so supportive as she usually was. My other stepsister was there as well. I just tried to get thru it all. Greg, Omi and I couldn't believe it was for real, that we lost Mom.

CHAPTER 2

When I was younger

When I was little, we lived with my Grandma.

Then, my mom met David. She wasn't in love with David; she married him for security. He had a good job and we lived in a nice house. It was a beautiful house, behind the woods with five bedrooms. It had a huge living room, with a big bay window. It was gorgeous. There was a sunken family room, with a nice fireplace and nice kitchen, dining room, and beautiful piano. He had money, which is why she could dress up. She would come to my school with her hair and makeup just perfect.

My room was blue with two beds and lots of dolls. My mom was always buying me German dolls. I was collecting them, and they were all dressed up. We had a beautiful white tree for the holidays which was decorated in front of the bay window. It had lights all over it, with an angel on top. There were also gifts galore. I wasn't spoiled, but I had a great Christmas. We even had white furniture in the living room. Everybody had their own room in the bigger house. There was a tree house in the back for Greg and me, and a lot of yard to run and play in.

She called me "pumpkin," and also "baby girl." She was always nice to me.

She always cooked me delicious food, and she would have snacks for me when I would come home. Mom even packed my lunch every day. She cooked dinner regularly, and it was really good.

On the other hand, there were outbursts at the dinner table. David would instigate something. He did have his moments. He would scold me and correct me.

Life at home was scary. They would start screaming at each other, and get into an awful fight and be slamming doors. One Christmas day, Stephanie, my stepsister, got us out of the house since they were fighting so much. David yelled at Greg all the time, and I heard it.

After four years when I was nine, everything went downhill and downsized. We moved into a smaller house. We switched houses with another family; we stayed there until they got divorced.

I had my own room there, with yellow, fluffy carpet. When we moved into the smaller house, however, it was a big adjustment, and it was small. It was clean and fine.

Appearance-wise, she was changing. It started at the second house. She didn't dress up as much; she didn't cook as much. Everything was lame and falling apart. We never really had a Christmas again. At the big house, I had big birthday parties, even so for Greg. Then things changed. No more birthday parties. No more big holidays at home. She still cooked; there were just no more family meals.

My mother divorced my stepfather when I was around eleven. She had been with him since I was a baby, and my brother would've been around four at the time.

I remember I didn't want my stepfather to leave. He didn't want to leave either; she wanted the divorce. I remember I screamed to my mother, "I hate you!" It wasn't much of a family, but it was the only one I knew. I was very angry at my mother for the divorce. I felt like the only and whole family that I knew was falling apart.

I never remembered sitting down and having dinner again at the small house. One time at the big house, I told Greg, "Let's go and get out of here." We grabbed a small bag of stuff and left. When we ran away, it was my idea. I was unhappy. I was mad at her for getting the divorce. They were arguing all the time. We got three blocks away, and she rode up in the white car. Mom was upset at me because it was my idea. She was really scared, and didn't want to lose me. I was very little when this happened, and in a small bag I took some socks and clothes and my little doll.

I first had seen her depressed when she moved into the smaller house. She would lie in bed all day, not wanting to get out. She got worse at the apartment.

David lost money, and even used money that Omi gave my mom for

Greg and me. At the new house, they began to fight a lot more. At one point she said, "Your dad and I are getting a divorce." She added, "You're coming to live with me."

From there we moved to a townhouse apartment. After she was divorced from David, she tried to kill herself. She cut her wrists. I was upstairs when she cut them. I heard a muffled cry, and I went to check on her.

Why, my mother, did you do this to me? Did you not care how your actions affected me, how your decisions have affected me my whole entire life?

She was alone, as far as not having a man, and she cried a lot. This was such a confusing time for me, growing up with a mother who was in good spirits one day and was depressed the next.

David was the only father I had ever known. I was angry that she divorced David, because I never saw him again. I also was angry that she lied to me, and told me that my real father had died. I didn't even know at that time that David wasn't my real dad; I was too young. It wasn't until after the divorce that I learned that he wasn't my real dad. I wanted to live part-time with my dad and part-time with my mom, and that wasn't going to happen, since my mom said that I wasn't going to live with him at all.

I didn't want either one to feel bad, so I decided to split it up like that. She wasn't going to give me that option. That's why I got mad—she didn't give me a choice. I didn't want to be out of his life completely. "You're coming to live with me; it's not going to happen," she said.

I didn't see him for birthdays, holidays, visitation, nothing. My dad was just taken away from me. She was just controlling everything in my life.

Then we moved to a two-story house for three years. While we were living on there, she took a lot of antidepressants and other pills. She took pain pills as well.

She often hung around the house in her bathrobe if she wasn't out shopping or working. Off-and-on she would be depressed through the time I knew her.

She again talked about my real dad dying in a helicopter crash. This was very puzzling for a thirteen-year-old girl to find out that I had a real father, and that David was a substitute.

There was a guy who she periodically went out with. When she met him, he would come out to the house and hang out with us; he even told us he was going to marry our mother. One day, he was over and left. She thought he left for good. I heard them screaming; I heard him leave, and she was crying in her room. Mom loved this guy, and she thought he could change her life and make it better. I remember her saying the next day that he left her and told her that they were done for good. She thought he went back to his wife. His wife supposedly called my mom; he was in the process of getting a divorce.

She would often say to me, "Don't ever settle," because she did. She didn't want me to make the same mistakes. "Make sure he treats you good. Don't ever settle; make sure you truly love each other."

At the time I really didn't hear it, and I hear it now. I followed her in her footsteps. When I grew up and I had seen the choices she made and related them to the ones I made now, I can't believe I made those same decisions. I had to learn *somehow*.

I flunked the seventh grade because of all the stress that my mom and stepdad put me under.

I wasn't real close to my stepfather, yet I still called him "Dad," because he was the only dad that I had ever known at that time. I *missed* our family.

Then, after she died, everything changed *again*.

I had three choices of living arrangements after my mom died: one was to live with my grandma; another was to live with a foster family; a third option was to live with my stepfather. I remember that both Greg and I wanted to live with the foster family; it was a joint decision. I remember I hurt David really bad, choosing a stranger over a man who was my dad since I was young. At that time I remembered all the arguing.

My mind wasn't thinking at all. My grandmother was very hurt. All I remember is that I wanted to be around a family, that's why I went with them. They had kids of their own, and I thought that I would just fit right in with them. It didn't turn out that way.

I didn't go with Omi, because I didn't see her that much. I would've been better off with my grandmother, because of her love and affection that I always wanted. As a foster child, you always come last. I didn't think they thought that they did this, but I know how it affected me. It's kind of hard to open your heart and soul to another woman who's not your mom. She wasn't the warmest person to me. Indirectly, she favored her own over my brother and me. I was rebellious. With my foster mom, I thought I could yell at her; she wasn't my mother.

After my mom died, I wasn't hanging around a good crowd. Same with my brother, just to cover the pain.

I was very defiant, and liked to start fights. Someone would look at me, and I would say, "Want to fight?" I would smoke, too.

Some kids at school were mean, and would tell me that my mother went to hell. I always had it in the back of my mind that she went to heaven.

Unfortunately, I never got to stay in any place too long. I was always making new friends. That was hard. Ironically, my name is Adams, and I attended Adams Elementary when I was in the seventh grade. I never really had any mean friends when I was younger; they just fell apart because we moved a lot. They were nice to me at the time, though. Through high school, it was the same.

CHAPTER 3

Meeting my 'real' Dad

When I was sixteen, three years after my mom's death, my grandmother told me that my real father was alive. Perplexed and distraught (since my mother told me that my real father had passed away in a helicopter crash in Vietnam), I remember I asked my grandmother, "Why did my mother lie?" Her response was, "She remarried, thinking we would have a better life with your stepfather."

My grandmother knew my dad was alive the whole time, but she had made a promise to my mother not to contact him. She felt that it was time to meet my father. She didn't want to hide it anymore. And, I always wanted a father-daughter relationship.

Could you imagine how I felt? I was devastated when I found out I thought I lost my dad, and now I was finding out that he was alive. Wow! My mom did it to me again. She lied *twice*. My grandmother said that my dad met another girl.

I felt my childhood was stripped. *She* hid this from me. She took her life, and then lied to *me*. I never knew the truth until later. I felt <u>betrayed</u> from my mother.

My grandmother contacted my dad not too long after that. I was shocked when I found out about my dad, whose name is "John." I couldn't believe he was alive, but I was very excited to meet him.

He came to my foster parents' home. We met; I hugged him. I looked just like him. It was very hard and strange, but he was very nice. He was very handsome, tall, has a smile of gold, but I didn't feel that closeness or connection with him.

Greg was angry at my father. He, on the other hand, didn't want to see him. He felt he left us.

He invited me to come visit him, and I felt uncomfortable, because I also met his wife. It was odd, because I was seeing my father with another woman.

I told him, "Mom told me that you died." He didn't understand why she would do that, and didn't understand why she didn't contact him. He answered, "No," when I asked him if he had a girlfriend, like Omi said. He stayed in town a couple of days. We went out to eat; it was awkward. He was glad I had a good foster family.

I was surprised that he didn't want me to come live with him. My dad never said, "Come down and live with me!" At that point, if he would've asked me, I would've gone. I would've left Greg, Omi, everybody. I told my foster parents I wanted to go. They said to go. They wanted me to be happy. My foster mom even said it would be a good idea.

He wanted me to come to his home, to try to get to know him. Each time I got a paid ticket. He wanted me to visit him, and I did.

He had his wife, horses, and a dog. I felt then and still feel now that there's no need for me. It's the truth. I feel like I'm by myself, and no one's daughter. My friends are my family, and they each in their own way are nurturing and caring to me, and it fulfills the emptiness.

We really didn't talk much, call or keep in touch. It isn't that different today. He did come down for my wedding. My husband at the time and I did go visit him together for a week.

CHAPTER 4

Getting married and after

In my younger years, I was friendly, but not giving. I was selfish then; I would make plans and cancel them if something else would come along, like a man. I would *always* break plans for my boyfriend.

I did live with my foster family until I was twenty-three. Then I got married to my high school sweetheart, a man I had known for eight years. I met him through my foster brother who was friends with him. The marriage lasted for over two years.

When we got married, I thought things were going to change. I was the perfect wife. I cooked, cleaned, and did the typical things a housewife would do. We lived in an apartment. What I didn't know was that even though I was changing my life for the better, my husband was the opposite. He was always going out with his friends, and coming home at four in the morning.

My friends were also married at the time. I was wrapped up with my husband. I felt he tried to control me, and he would get upset every time I wanted to go out with my friends.

That second year our relationship fell apart. There was name calling and screaming continued. I felt bad about myself. For six months it seemed every day I was hit with some things that I couldn't control. I got blasted daily, but I always fought back.

Never did I ever let him think that he could walk all over me. I was a fighter, which made him even angrier. I still continued to work at the bakery, do my daily chores, cry to my friends; each day I just did the best I could. Some days I'd wake up, tune everything out, but night would come; he would come home.

For a time, it would be quiet, until he'd get upset. I tried to sit there, and say to myself maybe this time won't be so bad. He always found something to fight about. Every day he always told me he loved me, and that he was so happy. I couldn't understand this, because deep inside of me I couldn't feel the same. My feelings towards him faded every day. I started hanging out with my friends more, acting like I wasn't married.

I was going to Al-Anon meetings, and he wasn't going to his AA meetings. I was trying to work this out with him. I sat up a lot of nights talking to him, and I wanted to work this out. The final day when I left him, I came to my wit's end.

We were supposed to go to dinner and work things out. After work, instead of going home and getting ready, he went out. I waited for an hour and a-half; I was dressed nice. I had on a jean skirt and a nice black and white shirt. But something happened. I had enough—I was tired of trying. That same day, he came home and his eyes were red. He was slurring his words and told me, "Give me a couple of minutes, and we'll go." I was so angry and I didn't love him anymore. So I told him, "I can't do this anymore. I've tried; I've offered to go with you to get help. You refused me; you've humiliated me. I just don't have it in me or the strength to stay here. I need to leave for a while, to think."

I recall I walked away. He was really upset with me.

The inner strength in me said to him, "I am walking out of this apartment and whatever you try, I don't care." As I was moving towards the door, he was screaming. I had no fear whatsoever. He didn't touch me. I went to my Grandma's, moved in with her, had meetings with him, and told him I was not coming back, unless he cleaned his life up. I would be there for him, but not live with him. He said, "No," and he moved in with his mother.

I remember the day I had to go to court. He was sitting across from me, sad and lonely. I was smiling, saying to myself, *I can't wait till this is over.* I walked out of there. The sun was shining, the birds were chirping, and he was standing outside. I felt that a weight was lifted off my shoulders. For no more name calling, no more cutting me down. I looked at him, and I wished him well. He didn't say anything back and just walked away. I celebrated that day, but the next few days I went through a depression that was so deep. Here I was alone, and I was living with my grandma for two weeks, then I moved into a duplex. I didn't want to live alone, and I thought my grandma was going to come live with me. She said, "No," because she didn't want to live there. I wanted to be a family with her.

From the people I lived with I got comfort, and the feeling of someone being around. That's when I got really depressed by myself in this big huge apartment. I didn't have any mother or father contact.

I ran all the thoughts over and over of the things my ex said to me. I think in my mind that after being around somebody who did this to me continuously, it was tearing my self-esteem down. For a while I started to believe it. I thought I was fat and worthless. I would go out with my friends; not too many people would approach me. I was very quiet and kept to myself. Some guys would come up to me and say, "Put a smile on your face," and this happened often. I started to think that I didn't care; I started eating a great deal, and picking on myself every day.

The days were short and the nights were long. The loneliness, anger, and feelings of rejection surrounded me every day. I thought, "Well, gee, my mom left me, she didn't love me, and this man that I loved was criticizing me." I was twenty-six at the time, my father wasn't in my life (remember, I met him when I was sixteen), and I wasn't talking to my brother since he was in the Marines for three years. I literally didn't like myself. My husband cut me down for over two years. My father wasn't there, my stepfather wasn't there, my mom left me, my brother wasn't there, and I had a few friends. I would see my foster parents, but I was alone.

Anxiety came, sleeplessness came, and the days couldn't go fast enough. I would come home, eat, take a shower, go straight to bed, and cry. Thoughts of suicide would arise. I would be in the tub, planning and thinking, looking at my razor how to slice my wrists. I knew my mother didn't do it the right way, so could I succeed in my way? I grabbed the razor, took the blade out, and held it up to my wrist. I sat there and I just trembled and cried. I set the razor down, got out of the tub, put a robe on, and got dressed. I was so suicidal. *What would be the best way?* I thought to myself. I went to the cupboard, looked for some pills; I trembled, threw them down, ran into the living room, grabbed my mother's picture, got on my knees, looked up and asked God to help me, to come into my life, begging, "*Please* let me not be like her." I begged Him for help and I wept for hours.

When you're like this, there is a dark cave with no light. What wakes you up, gets you out of it, is God's intervention. It is the darkest, deepest cave you can get to.

While you're in this position, you need to think of how this would make other people you know feel. You need to actually see how this would affect those in your mind. You need something or someone to pull you out when you're in this state. I would think how this would affect my grandmother—my Omi, so strong and supportive. She's lost so much, and I wasn't going to put her through that again.

The next day came, and I found myself tired from being up all night, but I also had a better feeling inside. It wasn't much, but just enough to get up and start another day.

After that night, I still was depressed, and I didn't have good thoughts about myself, but the thoughts of ending my life were gone. I decided to join the gym and lose the weight. In my mind, I thought I was fat, but people told me I always looked good. However, the compliments that I would get wouldn't even break the ice. So I joined a gym. I worked out four times a week, and went to work. Slowly, I started feeling better.

I knew in time that my life would change. I felt in my heart when I asked God for help that night that things would get better, but I also knew it wouldn't be overnight; it would take a long process. I worked out, I still had my job, and I hung out with my friends, but I still felt lonely.

I remember my foster sister telling me that her friend was looking for a roommate, so I called the number. Her name was Jackie, she lived in a house, and I moved in with her. We were like sisters, got along great, never fought and always laughed, and had fun. She was always there for me.

After three years of living with Jackie, I met Tony. I dated him, and she left and moved. Even with Tony, there were verbal comments giving me low self-esteem, although at the time I knew deep inside that his remarks weren't true.

Unexpectedly his daughter's mother died. She was only eleven. I wanted to take her in, because she needed a mother and I remembered what I went through. She was a sweet, loving girl, and I loved her to death, and I still do. But she and her father were always arguing, and she was always screaming, slamming doors, and I would come home from work tired and stressed from the both of them arguing.

He took it out on me; I tried to work it out, because of her. But the stress, the anxiety and yelling was more than I could take. I didn't want to hurt his daughter by leaving, but I had to. My hair was falling out, my weight was terrible, I couldn't eat, and it was affecting my health. So then I went to the apartment where I still live. I stayed single. I was with Tony for seven years.

I took Cameron, my cat, who I found while dating Tony. He's as white as an angel, with two different colored eyes, and he was my companion for two years.

I had continuously jumped into relationship after relationship that wasn't good for me. That's how you make choices sometimes, and you go with what you're used to. I want people to think about that.

I took my cat and got my apartment. It was a Sunday, and I thought it was strange that someone answered the phone. The lady told me to come down, since I asked if there were any apartments available in that complex. I chose that complex since my grandmother lived there. I went down at five-thirty in the evening, and she let me see the apartments. I told her that I didn't have the whole deposit, but I could do half. She said that it was fine, and she would hold it for three months, which the supervisor doesn't normally do. I knew it was a sign to get the apartment; that was the right move for me.

Two weeks later, I went over to see my grandmother to get her mail for her, and my name was on the mailbox. It didn't say "lease" or anything. She didn't even make me sign anything until I gave her the other half.

As aforementioned, I had previously lived with Jackie, and I was a dental assistant for five years. I got his pamphlet in the mail for joining a massage therapy school. I looked at this and set it aside. Then one night, Tony and I were at a restaurant, and I ran into a friend of mine who just mentioned that she signed up to go to massotherapy school, and they just opened one up in the area.

She told me about it and it sparked my interest and I called the place.

The class itself was $7800. I didn't have the money; it was a new school. It wasn't accredited yet, and I remember calling my grandmother telling her that I wanted to go there. She told me to call my father. There wasn't a grant or anything available, and when I told him about it he was very negative, and said, "It doesn't sound like a good idea." I told him the name of the school.

He then hung up the phone with me. I remember crying, because he had told me that if I wanted to go to school he would pay for me. I felt in my heart that I really wanted to do this. I sat on the couch and stopped crying, and said to myself, "Ok, God, if this is a gift from you, and you feel it in my heart as much as I do, then it will all work out. If not, another door will open."

Twenty minutes later, the phone rang. It was my father. He had called the school and he told me if this was really something I wanted to do, then he would pay for it. I went to school for two years, and I knew that this was what God wanted me to do. It was hard and I struggled with a lot of classes, but it went smooth. I studied hard, and the day of the state board I felt nervous because I thought maybe I wouldn't pass.

I knew in my heart and I said to myself, speaking as God was speaking to me, "I would have never have taken you this far, If I didn't believe in you." A month later, my anatomy and physiology teacher and called me herself to tell me I passed and my grades were great. She was so proud of me and even spoke about me at my graduation.

I've been a massage therapist for years, and I've helped and healed so many people. My gift continues and gets better as I age.

Then Bob came into my life. Nicest, charming man that I ever met. He was so giving, that I never had a man like him. It scared me, for I've never experienced love of that magnitude. This man was always there for me, rain or shine. Then I started to get sick. I couldn't eat, keep anything down, and I had body aches like crazy. I finally went to the hospital. Doctors did tests on my gall bladder, blood tests, etc. They said I had hepatitis; I looked at them, because I told them I got all my shots, being in the health field.

He told me it was either "A" or "C". My skin was yellow, and so were my eyes, my liver was so inflamed, and it didn't look good for me. I had a severe case of it; I'm lucky I even survived. I was so sick, I lived on

IV's. I was in the hospital for seven days. I couldn't go to work for eight weeks after that.

This guy took care of me, and came to the hospital every day, and brought me food and water when I was at home sick and in bed. He took care of my grandma, and made sure she was ok.

Unfortunately, it didn't last. He was tired of trying with me. I couldn't give him the love he wanted; I was afraid. Then, two weeks after we broke up (after six months), I realized I *did* love him. I fought to get him back, but he said it was too late. "My God, what have I done?" I thought. To this day, I still regret it. He had met this other girl, fell in love, and is now married to her. I wish nothing but happiness for the both of them. He was the first guy that turned my heart around.

As stubborn as I was, I was depressed for a very long time. We broke up right before Valentine's Day. It hurt for a very long time. Everywhere I would go, I would see her in the car with him. I never thought it could hurt so much. I thought to myself, I should have told him I loved him, because, he would say to me, "I love YOU!" I would tell him not to tell me that, then he would just say, "Don't forget."

I was very down after that. I've never experienced anything like that in my life before. This guy was there for me, stood by my side, and gave me so much love and attention. I cried with Grandma for many years. I don't think he realized how much I did care.

From then on, I was pretty cold towards other men. I would go out but never get real close. I felt that my heart turned to stone. It was a very bad heartbreak. I didn't think I was going to get over it.

After him, I again got into relationships with the wrong men. I got involved with men that did not want a connection. That way, I could keep myself safe from the heartache that I once felt before and the guilt that it was my fault that I lost him. Bob was a strong foot in my life. My grandmother liked him; my brother liked him, too.

I closed myself off, which a lot of us do in life. When you're hurt a part of you shuts down. I was never happy in any of the relationships since.

You have to spiritually build yourself up, inside then out. Eventually you do.

I dated a few guys and then I met Mike, who I dated for a year. He was very kind and nice, but very controlling. I wouldn't have that, so I ended it with him.

After Mike, I met Kyle.

We dated off-and-on for three years. He was a great guy, but couldn't offer me his heart. We broke up because of that. He's everything I wanted in a guy and prayed for, but since he was hurt he had a hard time opening up himself.

I choose men that leave, that won't get too close. I don't think they'll leave me, but if I don't get the affection I need, I disappear. I've already done this. Bob left me; he was sick of trying. I go for distant guys who don't really want to commit to me or anyone. Sometimes I don't want a relationship. I say I do, but then I don't. It's just a dichotomy.

I don't know why I do this. I partially can contribute this to a mother that died and an emotionally distant father. I hope to marry someday, but only if it's meant to be. I'm ok if it doesn't happen.

If I meet a guy who's straight and honest, I wouldn't know what to do with him. I've never had that, except for Bob. On the other hand, if a guy who's too forward asks me out, but then he backs off, I don't get it. Why did you bother at that point? A friend doesn't get it either, and knows how I feel.

I've gotten into things quickly, and then it doesn't work out. In the beginning, I back off. Then when I really start giving, they back off. I get confused. When you're really attracted to someone, for three months it's intense, everything is going great, and then it just falls apart.

I'm trying to make better choices now in my life. Through each relationship, I've learned something about myself, and what I'm willing to put up with. The counseling for three years has helped me open doors that I have kept shut or refuse to see for many years. Each time I was fitting the puzzle of my life together. I know what I want and what I don't want.

CHAPTER 5

Letting it go

My thirtieth birthday was really hard. I felt like breaking down and crying. My emotions were all over the place. I was out eating with my friends. Everyone said I should be smiling. I was with a boyfriend at the time, and he leaned over and gave me a big kiss, and I remember that something was bothering me. I couldn't figure out why I was so upset. Six days earlier I was crying about my mother and I stopped myself that day. *It's time to grow up and let it go,* I said to myself.

A few years later, I remember my thirty-third birthday. Six days before that I broke down again, and I continued crying. *Stop crying; it's in the past; let it go,* were the words I kept repeating. When I was thirty-five, before I was dating this really nice guy, I was again emotional. I was crying, but I was angry, very angry. The dichotomy of the situation was that I was very spiritual, believed in God, but then I started having these thoughts toward the Almighty. I was swearing. It broke my heart. I did not know why I was having these feelings, since I believed in God since I was a little girl. These thoughts have haunted me for the last five years. I would go to church, but still the thoughts were there.

No matter what I did, the thoughts would not go away. I would talk to friends, asking them, "Do I hate God? Why do you think I have these thoughts?" I talked to the pastor, and asked the same questions. The pastor said, "You've been through a lot in your life; I think you're angry at God, and you're still grieving."

I did go for counseling, and started to open the doors from the past. I began to remember things that I shut the doors to in my life. The memories I felt were not happy memories. I would sit for many days trying to remember anything good from my childhood. All that I remember was my mother in bed, sad.

I didn't get to do much, and I remember when I found my mom's diary I started to read what I believed in my mind. I remember I read a verse that my mother was taking me to the movies, and she had written, "Poor Jenny, she never gets to do anything." I remember my stepfather drinking, yelling, and screaming. The only times I could remember having fun and laughing were very few. My mother and stepfather were always arguing. I remember one Christmas Day my stepsister got my brother and me out of the house, because she was afraid of the argument that they were having.

I've been divorced for a while and haven't remarried yet. My reason was that the relationships I've picked in the past made me feel rejected, like I felt after my mother died.

A lot of relationships were a learning experience, but painful ones. I've discovered through therapy that I was choosing what I was used to. Growing up with my stepfather, I married a man like him. And from there, I would choose men that could never get close. Although, that was my comfort level. When you're growing up in a family the child will learn what it sees. If it sees love and affection and joy between two parents, the child will grow up the same way. If it sees pain, rejection, fear and resentment all its childhood, then it will seek out what it's used to.

I am finally starting to realize this at age forty, and the closer I get to my mom's age of forty-two when she died. Through counseling, I was learning that I was making wrong choices in the past like decision-making, and I needed to allow myself the opportunity to get close to someone and open up my heart to love, and get my anger out, which I never did when my mom died. Instead, the angry feelings at God came because I felt I couldn't be angry at her. I did forgive her, over and over again, but the thoughts were always there. I finally let go of the guilt of leaving her that day.

I have gotten angry, put her picture out, yelled and screamed. I have cried each time I told her, "How could you have left me?" I've learned now that when we're stricken with grief, the feelings are sometimes uncontrollable until you get angry, cry, and forgive the person for the pain they've caused you, what it's done to your life, and how selfish they've been. And, how thoughtless they were in their decisions, since they didn't think of what it would do to their loved ones left behind.

Through talking about how I lost my mom, I was able to get out emotions that were deeply buried. I was able to express my grief and sadness over her leaving me. Now, my thoughts aren't as bad and intense as they used to be.

CHAPTER 6

Greg

Greg was really affected from everything that happened to us. He had some issues after my mom died. He quit school and dropped out of the tenth grade. He had to leave our foster parents' home. He went to a halfway house and lived there until he went to the Marines when he was eighteen. He served for three years and got an honorable discharge.

He came back a year or two later. I stayed away from him because I was looking down at him. He was asking my dad all the time for money, and Omi. Her bills weren't getting paid. He lived with Omi.

She would always believe his stories. I think she was just being nice but she wanted to believe him, too. She didn't want to look down at her grandson.

I did keep my distance from him for a couple of years. I was around twenty-four and this went on for a while. There was minimal contact during this period. We never saw him during holidays, either.

When I was dating Tony, he told me to get in contact with my brother and he brought us together. He said, "That's your brother, and you need to be with him, no matter what he's done." Then shortly after, I may have called him and set something up. We met at my grandma's house. I believe we talked and just started to converse more and more.

He had lived about 45 min away since he came back from the military and stayed there. Only for a short time he lived with Grandma. One day, he passed out and went into a coma. This was six to seven months after our talk. He went into the hospital and they said they didn't think he was going to make it. I called my foster parents and they went up to see him; Tony was with me.

I remember going to the chapel and asking God and praying for him for one more chance at life, and that he was a good person, but a person with a problem.

A few days later he did come out of the coma, and I remember telling him that God gave him another chance at life.

A year later he started bleeding from his esophagus. They had to do the surgery with the rubber bands to stop the bleeding.

Then he met this guy who was in the room with him. He put his hands on him and prayed. In his prayer, Greg said this man knew that he had a problem with his liver and about his other troubles. Greg was amazed that this man knew about his difficulties. He drank a lot of juice, and a lot of pop. He then started drinking a twelve-pack of Coke instead of alcohol.

He gave it up completely, and that's when we started talking. I would still speak to him and keep in contact with him. He would come and stay with Grandma for three days every month. I would go over and visit while he was there.

This went on for years. We didn't see much of each other at holidays, but that didn't mean we didn't talk. His friend Sam would come bring him and drop him off. I would gladly bring him back. We had some great conversations driving back to where he lived. We spoke about guys that I was dating and other things. This went on for a long time.

During the last four years of his life, something changed. We were driving back to his home and he was speaking about a verse in the Bible. I said, "Since when do you know the Bible?" He said, "I read the Bible all the time." I asked, "How did you get your faith back?" He said one word, "YOU! I listened to you, and everything you always talked about." Greg was curious, and wanted to check it out. His heart changed. He still didn't have the best job, but he was working and he was trying. Greg was sick with his liver and his back, and was limited physically. Someone once asked me, "Did he have any dreams?" When he was younger he was good a basketball player and that's what he wanted to be.

Greg didn't want to be married or to have kids. He was happy to be by himself, so he says.

Those last four years, things changed. He would call me for an hour and he would just talk. My brother would tell me he loved me and open himself more and his heart, too.

Those last four years if it was snowing badly, he'd call me in the morning and let me know about the weather. I remember him saying, "Hey sis, it's time to get up." I'd talk to him and he'd talk to me about guys and know if I was having a problem. He'd say it'd last six months, and it did.

But we grew close and he would make fabulous dinners. He loved to cook and he would prepare gourmet meals for his friends all the time; I told him he should be a chef.

He and I would hang out at our apartment and watch a movie or just talk. I felt like I had a brother. We always told each other we loved each other.

In both of our lives, it took a long time for each of us to tell the other that we cared that deeply. This was a long time before we could tell other people, or Omi.

I remember about a year before Greg died, we were sitting at Omi's house. I spent time with Grandma every Christmas Eve. Greg would often come, too. I did this when I lived with my foster family, when I was married, and after.

He just said out of the blue sky, "You know I'm not going to make it to forty-one, and I'm going to die when I'm forty." He looked at Omi, and said, "You're going to die when you're ninety-two." I was like, "No!" She laughed. How true it all was, though. I can remember it to this day.

That year before Christmas he went on a big spending spree. He said it was in his heart and that's what he wanted to do. He bought us all these wonderful presents. My brother bought me a jacket, a DVD player, and a nativity set. It was a great Christmas. Somehow, he knew what was to come. He was so excited when we opened up our gifts, like the eyes of a child.

He didn't even want to open his presents. He worked a lot of hours at the video store to have this extra-special Christmas for us.

He would say as we would talk on the phone, that he couldn't wait to give us our presents, and that he bought lots of stuff. I'd say, "You don't have to," but he said he wanted to.

He bought Omi clothes, silverware, and other things.

That Christmas was very close, since it was just the three of us. He cooked Christmas Eve dinner. On Christmas day, I went to see Omi and Greg in the apartment underneath, and then went to my foster family.

That following year, I noticed he would cough a lot and sometimes he would cough up blood. He was always in pain; his back always hurt him and he never felt good. Greg thought this was from an old basketball injury. He would never go to the doctor because he didn't want to go.

That year in September, he was having problems with his right eye and he said he couldn't see too well. It felt like he scratched it, it hurt, and it watered a lot.

On one of his trips he was over at my apartment. He was staying over with a heating pack on his back all the time. I slept on the couch. I got out my medical book and we started reading the section on the eye. He got to a point about cancer and freaked out. I thought nothing of it at the time. Greg gave me the book back and said he wanted nothing to do with it.

After he settled down, he decided to make an appointment. He called me the following week and said he had some bad news. Greg had a tumor in his eye and they were going to do some radiation treatments at the clinic soon.

Those six days before he was scheduled to go, he said his legs were giving out and he couldn't walk. I told him to go to the hospital and I'd meet him there. I went to the emergency room, to find him, and they gave him a shot in the back for the pain. We were joking and the doctor came in and wanted to do some x-rays. They came back in an hour and the doctor said he had some bad news for him.

"You have cancer in your spine," they said. I remember just sitting there, shocked from having had read the book and I cried. Greg cried and he looked up at that doctor and said, "What can we do?" The doctor said, "Let me call the other doctor at the clinic, but we do need to do more tests." The next day they did.

They found two ten-centimeter growths in his lungs; the cancer was all over.

I couldn't believe that my only living brother was diagnosed with lung cancer. I thought that he was healed, but I was wrong. The anger came back when my brother was lying in the hospital bed, with doctors around him, telling him he was going to die. I remember my brother's face turn red as a tomato, tears filled his bed as he wept, and I ran out into the hall. My real father was there at the time. I was so mad I wanted to punch something. I lost my mother, my stepfather, my younger brother and now my only living brother. I thought, "Why God, *why* is this happening?"

He never had what he deserved in life. He never got married, or had children. Greg had just met this girl five months before this and he loved her, and she loved him. It just wasn't fair.

The anger that I had for my mother and pain had now doubled-up, inside for the loss I was going to receive again. The thoughts came back worse towards God. I tried to verbalize it out, saying, "Okay, I'm angry at God." I'm an auditory person. I punched my bed, that my hands were so red; I could've punched the wall. I threw stuff in my room, and said, "Why was I ever born?" I basically asked God to take me. I told him, "Let my brother live, because I know I can't handle it."

September and October were very difficult. Friends came by a lot of times; I just wanted to be alone and not talk to anybody and not associate with anyone. I would sleep for hours, get up, eat, take a shower, and go back to bed. For a short time while I was sleeping, I didn't feel any pain. I really just wanted to die. I didn't know how to be there for my brother; I couldn't bring myself alive, but I knew I had to.

It was a period of anger, then resolving, then the anger would come back.

The growths were as large as oranges. He was willing to fight it, and go to the clinic. Greg wanted to save his eye at this time; his other eye started bothering him and he was really scared. The doctors wanted to do chemo and radiation on his back and on his eyes.

We wanted him to go where he would also get radiation in his eyes. He was in there for quite a while. My brother had close to twelve treatments for two weeks straight.

There were times there that he was very angry; he wanted me to take him to smoke because he didn't care. There was this girl up there, Stephanie, who was really sick. I was trying to talk to him about God. He didn't want to hear it. He was mad and angry and he started to bring up things about Mom. He stared out the window and cried. "Why did

God let this happen to me?" he asked. This girl tried to talk to him too, but he didn't want to hear it. I did try to keep in touch with her for a while, but then we lost touch. She was very sick.

My brother was mad and went thru angry spurts and he was mean. He was so upset. Of course, he would take it out on us.

"You've Got Another Thing Comin'"—this song's about Greg. He was disgusted at the world, at his life. He lost his mom, and then he got cancer. At first he was so strong and had such faith in God. Then he got angry; then he got strong again.

I remember once at the clinic, he wanted to get a cigarette and said, "I'm so mad at God! Why did he let this happen to me?" Then he cried.

It was too much for Omi to go up with us. A couple days after, I knew he was going to go and I told her she had to go and see him.

After a few days he went back home, and the following Monday he was supposed to start chemo. He was finished with the radiation. My brother wanted to be home for the chemo, since he lived right up the street from the hospital.

I remember I was there with him and he looked great and he said, "I'm on my way to recovery." Then we went to the hospital, and they wouldn't give him the treatments because he was too weak. At that time, I felt very hopeful and I was actually thanking God for him coming thru. I really thought he was going to live.

He wanted this book called *The Purpose Driven Life*; twice he had told me about it. He couldn't see very well, but Sam (his roommate) or his girlfriend could read it to him. I felt really good about it. I was so happy that day.

Two days later when I was at home, Sam called me and said Greg wasn't doing too well. Sam said he was on the bed, crying in pain. He was using medicine patches for the cancer. He thought everything was turning around for him. Then Sam took him to the hospital.

A doctor looked him over (I was there by then), and said to me that there was nothing more that they could do. We still didn't want to believe that he was going to die. His girlfriend was sitting there (she took care of him), and said, "Every time I meet someone, they die." She really loved him.

I went outside and called my father and told him, "Dad, you need to come here," and he did. He flew in the next day. Remember, he hasn't seen Greg for years. Greg always called Dad for money. He wasn't there for Dad. My father came in and talked with his son and the doctors to see if there was any treatment for him. Of course, they ran more tests.

At that time, I was trying to get close with my Dad. John and I were going to go to dinner, and Greg was angry and jealous. He was angry because he couldn't be there; he was hurt. I felt so much guilt because I was able to enjoy a dinner with my father, and there was my brother dying in the hospital. My dad and I would laugh and I would stop to remind myself that I shouldn't be having such a good time.

We ate at a restaurant on the way home. We would eat there and at a couple of other places. Driving back, I asked him, "Why did you leave us? Was there another woman? She (Mom) told us that you died."

He said, "I couldn't believe that." That's when he told me, "She wanted a divorce and she wanted it very quickly, and wanted it on extreme cruelty. Your mother said she was going to marry David, and he had a good job."

He was back from Vietnam and he wanted to buy a house. We were living with my Grandma at the time, when I was little.

Here I was, listening for the first time to his side of it. I basically said, "How could you give us kids up?" He said it was very difficult for him.

He was driving and telling me all of this. I asked, "How could you just sign us over?" He said that it was hard for him. He lost his family and had to start over, and he felt this guy was going to take care of us. My dad didn't realize what kind of life I lived.

He thought we lived a happy life; that's why he didn't contact us. John said, "Why didn't your mother call me?" I said, "I don't know; she said you were dead." So now, I don't know who's telling the truth.

My dad and I spent those days getting closer, and I felt like a little girl getting to know my father. I saw him when I was sixteen, at twenty-three to twenty-four, and when Greg was dying. We've kept in contact, but I don't hear from him every day. He was here for four days.

He'd spend time with Greg, and then we'd spend time together. We stayed at a hotel together; we ate together. I felt Dad was getting back in my life. We went to the hospital one day, and there were six doctors with Greg. They said the cancer had spread. This was the day after the tests.

That is a memory that just kills me. There was nothing more they could do for him. When Greg was sick, I was over Mom, but it hurt with Greg.

He was in tears. I went out into the hallway. I could barely hold myself up; I just cried. I lost all my hope. My dad came out and tried to talk to me. My friends came up to the hospital, and spent time with me. After that, we spent some time with Greg, but he didn't want to be around anybody. We then came back to the hotel.

The next day, we went back to the hospital. He was slipping away and getting worse. He couldn't talk much. We called hospice in. I remember telling my dad as I was standing in the hallway, "You need some time with him." What was said I didn't know, because he closed the door. It was basically the last time my dad saw him, because he was flying out the next day.

Hospice came out and said he had maybe one to two weeks left. My dad was holding me; I was a mess. During that whole night, he dropped badly. My dad flew out the next day to go home to his wife and horses. I didn't want him to go; he said he had to.

I said, "Goodbye," to my father and went back to my hotel room. He slipped a note underneath the door saying, "It was really nice getting to know you." I woke up early the next morning and went over to his room, because I wanted to see him before he left. I gave him a hug, I was crying and I told him I loved him. And he said, "Ok." He didn't say it back. I felt really empty because when I put myself out there, usually someone responds. At that time, it was so empty because my brother was dying and my father was leaving. And, he couldn't tell me that he loved me.

I went home and I was going thru a very bad time. I was angry and that night I punched the bed; I don't know how many times. I was angry at God and I prayed for a miracle. I even got prayer cloths that a friend gave me and I put them underneath his pillow. I prayed and believed that my brother was going to be ok. I was so weak; my nerves were shot and I was so tired; I was crying.

I was just *angry*. I felt and thought "My God, I had to go thru this with my mother, now my brother, and my father doesn't even love me." I sobbed all night long, and cried myself to sleep.

After that incident with my dad, I was *really* mad at God. I really wanted him to be in my life. It was frustrating time for me. I was angry, because I wanted and needed my dad to be there for me. I thought God wasn't there for me. I needed my dad's affection and love. He then had to leave.

I was so upset about everything. One of my friends even gave prayer cloths to me. I really believed that Greg was going to be healed.

The next day, I was so depressed and laid there. *I'm not going; I'm not going to see my brother*, I thought to myself. I couldn't do it. I hadn't eaten; I was beside myself. My friend called me that day and I answered the phone—she knew I was down and depressed. It was in the afternoon. She said, "Hon, you have to get out of bed." Cindy asked, "Are you going to see Greg?" I answered, "No, I can't." That's when she said, "I understand how you feel, and I know you're hurting, but he needs you." She added, "You need to be there for him."

So, thank God she said that to me. Things always happen for a reason. She then said, "You need to get out of bed for him, and get dressed." I did. I went to the hospital; I sat there with him. He couldn't talk and he was breathing very heavy. I remember just holding his hand, and saying, "How am I going to make it without you?"

His hand moved like he didn't want to let go. He was trying to tell me something. That afternoon I told him that I loved him and how I felt about him. We were both scared. Then Hospice came in.

They said, "If there's anybody that needs to say goodbye, get them in here." I called Sam, and my brother's girlfriend who was sick. She wasn't going to come but then she did. Sam said he'd be right there. I called my foster father and told him if there was anything he wanted to tell Greg and I heard him say, "Greg, let go. It's time to be with God."

His girlfriend said, "Baby, I'm here." She grabbed some water and said, "Here honey, drink." He took a couple of sips of water and towards the evening he just sat there. He was getting worse. I said, "It's ok, you can let go." He didn't want to. He was breathing heavy and his hands were turning blue. He wouldn't let go. The three of us were there and that's when she said, "Maybe we should get a priest." The nurse couldn't find one. The nurse said, "I don't think one's here."

Even though they knew there was nothing they could do, he still didn't want to give up. Even when he was lying there on his dying day, just breathing heavy with his hands so blue, he was holding on and he didn't want to let go.

He was breathing heavy, and fighting with everything to stay on. I was holding his hand, and Sam and I told him, "It's ok. You can let go."

Then a Catholic priest came in and said, "Did someone need a priest?" I was surprised. He was a nice man. He prayed with him and blessed him, and he said to me, "Boy, he's such a young man." He gave him Last Rites. Then after he walked out, Greg let go.

I watched his eyes go back in his head. I started to cry; I put my head on his chest, and he took his last breath. When Greg died, it was awful.

He died very peacefully. I remember that he tilted his head to the side, like Christ. I cried and felt sad, but I felt peace that he wasn't suffering anymore. He didn't want a funeral; he just wanted to be cremated.

After I left the hospital and was on my way home, I called my friend. If she didn't push me out of bed, I wouldn't have gone. I went because she called me that day; she had said, "He needs you, Jen, go to him, do it for him." He would have died alone. I called her and I told her, "If it wasn't for you, I wouldn't have been there for him."

I went home and I got my next-door neighbor Mary Jane and went to tell Omi the news. I opened the door. Omi was sitting at the kitchen table. I cried and told her, "He's gone." We just cried together.

I felt bad for Omi. She's been through a lot. She lost her only daughter to suicide, her first husband left and her second husband died (my grandfather) in 1976. Then Paul died from cirrhosis in the 90's.

This is what I was thinking, that now she just lost her grandson. It was so hard for me to tell her. After Greg died, John was there for the cremation, and he was there for me to help pick things out. Stephanie was there, too. The cremation container is in my house. Dad put his arm around me when we were talking about getting him cremated. My dad came in for a few days, and so did Stephanie. Dad stayed with me, and brought back his computer for me. He was here for two days. Then he went back home.

I never really got the chance to ask him about suicide, if he even thought about it. He never talked about Mom since she died.

I didn't know if he did because when he had cancer, he wanted to live. If someone was suicidal or had suicidal thoughts and was stricken with an aggressive cancer, most people would say, "I'm done! Take me out!" My brother wasn't like that.

He stopped going to church when she died. He never wanted to go to church again. He didn't have any faith until two years before he died.

It helped him through the cancer. He made peace with God and everyone else before he passed away. I was talking to him on the phone when he had first told me that they found the tumor in his eye. He wanted this book and he said the author's name was Rick Warren. He believed it was called *The Purpose*, and he said, "It's not about you."

I said, "Ok, I'll get the book for you." A week before he died, when he was back home for a short period, he mentioned it again. Even if he could not see it, he said, "My girlfriend or my friend Sam can read it for me." I never got it to him.

It just happened so quick that he got sick and went back to the hospital; my mind was more or less focused on him.

The day after he died, I was sitting and got on the computer. I was thinking of the book, this *Purpose*, and then I thought, "What did the it mean?"

I looked it up online and found it was called *The Purpose- Driven Life*, by Rick Warren. I said, "I have to get this." I ordered it online. A week, ten days went by, and I still hadn't received it. It was on a Tuesday in the mid-afternoon that I was going to see my hairdresser. I went in and sat down. I looked over and I saw a little book on the counter. It was *the* book. I said, "Oh my God, this is the one my brother was talking about!"

Then she pulled it out of her purse and she said, "Oh my God, didn't I tell you about this?" We got chills and at the same time we said, "It's *not* about you!"

Since I didn't have it yet I said, "I'm going to go buy it." I went to four stores: to a Christian store, Barnes and Nobles, Borders, and then to Walmart at her suggestion. It was all sold out.

In my mindset, I wanted it. She would have given it to me, but she was letting someone else borrow it. I gave up, thinking it got lost in the mail.

I drove back after that, since I got my hair done early that day, and she was nice enough to squeeze me in. I was on a mission to get a copy. I could just hear my brother saying, "I *want* this book."

It was so intense. It was so late and I didn't get it. I thought that I'm not going to get it, since everywhere I went it was sold out. And people were telling me about how good the book is.

I was feeling bad and finally gave up and decided to go home. As I was pulling in, I went right up the side walk and passed the UPS guy. I *knew* it had been delivered!

I went up the stairs and it was there right in front of my door, right before Christmas. I smiled, picked it up and opened it.

The first page that you see is a dedication. I put my brother's name on it. After I opened it, it said you need to read it for forty days. Each day I read a chapter.

When I went to the first chapter, it said, "It's not about *you*." I knew in my heart that I was supposed to get this book. After I read it, I was talking to a friend of mine, Mark. I told him that he had to get a copy, too. I also told him about the circumstances that happened at the hair place, and that I was on a mission to get it.

While he was on the phone with me, he looked down at his coffee table and he said, "Oh my God, my daughter just got this, and she was telling me about it." Then she told him, "Dad, when I'm done with this book, you need to read it."

I got chills again; here it was right in front of him. He did read it, and he passed it on.

There was so much that we heard about it. Remember that lady that was kidnapped for about a day? She brought up the book to her kidnapper, and he let her go.

I would see it everywhere. Basically, I kept passing on the info about it on to all of my friends.

On the covenant page, I wrote my name and then my brother's name and I read it till the end of January, 2004.

Chapters 24, 25, 26 stood out in my mind. On page 202 of Chapter 26, it states, "God develops real *peace* within us, not by making things go the way we planned, but by allowing times of chaos and confusion.

We learn real peace by choosing to trust God in circumstances in which we are tempted to worry or be afraid."

When I read that, it showed me what he was going thru. Even though my brother was angry, worried and confused, he still had strength from God because he was still fighting, and he couldn't give up. He trusted Him.

On page 194 of Chapter 25, it reads, "Your most profound and intimate experiences of worship will likely be in your darkest days—when your heart is broken, when you feel abandoned, when you're out of options, when the pain is great—and you turn to God alone. It is during suffering that we learn to pray and our most authentic, heartfelt, honest-to-God prayers."

I began to realize that my brother had so much strength to live. He wanted to keep moving forward. Even though he was angry, he believed that he could get better. He never gave up. It's true, when you are at your darkest hour, and everything is going haywire, you do turn toward God.

And that's what I would say to my mom if I could, "Why, why did you do this?" When people are flustered and are at a dark moment, they need to look towards God for help.

At her darkest hour, why didn't she recognize God and call on Him for help? She was a spiritual person, and that's why I don't understand why she didn't do this. She always talked to me about having faith.

I recently asked Omi what she would say to Mom and Greg if she could. She said she would say to them that she loved them. And I have said, "Are you angry at Mom?" She answered, "No." She added, "No, I'm not angry, I'm just hurt." For Greg, she would give him a hug.

She wouldn't ask her, "Why?"

I would say to Greg, "I learned how to forgive more, not to sweat the small stuff, and I learned from your strength because you were my rock."

It's hard being without him. I miss laughing. No matter what, when I was down or depressed, he always made me laugh. I look at it and say he died when he was forty, and I'm forty now.

What sticks in my mind is what he had said to me one day that he would never make it past forty. He told me that a year before he died. The Christmas gifts he gave us were something that he felt in his heart to do.

His favorite team was the Eagles. The other day I watched *The*

Invincible, and I felt him. I said, "My God, my brother would have liked this movie."

Other things also remind me of Greg-my dad bought him a Marine's jacket when he was sick; I still have that jacket

Greg's anniversary is coming up, Thursday, Dec. 13th. It's been four years. It just flies by—he'd be forty-four. I miss him and our talks. We'd talk a couple of times a week.

The one time he called at five forty-five a.m.; he wanted to let me know about the snow.

I'd often drive to see Greg. I'd pick him up and he'd stay for three days. I miss him making me laugh.

Every guy I'd tell him about, he'd say, "Red flag!"

He knew how much I loved one of my boyfriends. He liked him, too. As I was thinking about my brother a couple of days later, I looked in my phonebook, and there was this guy's number. I recently got to reconnect with this person, and it was great at first. Then it fizzled out, not by my choice. I got a second chance to rectify some things with this person that in the past I couldn't. I'm sad when things end, but it's always not meant to be.

This day will be a quiet day, like his anniversaries in the past. I'll have a calm day before I go to work, and I will just try to get thru.

CHAPTER 7

Telling my story

I am telling my story because I want people to know what I've experienced.

When I tell someone that I lost my mom when I was young, they usually ask, "Did your mom die from cancer?" I reply, "No, she killed herself." I add that she hung herself. Someone will say, "Oh, my God!"

When someone tells me that they lost a family member suddenly and also other people that they loved, it makes me feel better that they understood. It bothers me when people say, "There are other people that have lost more than you." It's your pain, and it's your loss. Any loss is a pain, and it is driven deep inside. You're not human if you don't feel that anguish. Yes, there are people who are suffering more, like those with handicaps and cancer. Nevertheless, we all have our burdens to bear. This is *my* individual sorrow.

I like people I can connect with, because they understood what it's like to lose a loved one, no matter what the loss is or how they died.

People who've also suffered the passing of family members, you can communicate with them. They are on the same page. They are more understanding. I deal better with people who have lost. I do, too. Most of my closest friends have dealt with loss, and I've picked most of them up in the last five years.

About my story, there's so much to write about. It's complex.

I know I am meant to tell you my story at this point in time. This is how God works. He takes his time healing up people, and it can't be measured in human terms. It might take years. This story is to be told and shared, in order to heal others. It might stop someone from taking a gun and putting it to their head, or using a rope, taking pills, or driving into a wall. It might make them stop and think, for once, of all the people that they could be hurting, and the effects on others, and especially all of the people they're leaving behind.

I understand when someone like that breaks your heart, it breaks your spirit; it tears your soul down. The negative thoughts come around yourself and take down everything around you. You have to build yourself a stepping stone. You have to have positive thoughts.

Personally, I can relate to someone losing their brother it. I know what it's like to lose a brother before his time. I looked up to him. He was my rock; he was there to protect me.

Also, I can relate to the heartache, and I know what it's like when people say they don't want you; you feel unwanted.

I went to tour the area where my Mom lived, and where she cut herself when I was eleven.

I took a friend, and we then went to where mom is buried. The mausoleum was closed.

We stopped by Grandma's old house, where she used to live. We also went out to the final house we lived at.

Then we went out to the cemetery to see where Michael is buried. We looked in the areas I thought he would be, but no luck that night. My friend knew it was in a different location.

We then went over to the house I lived in, and we also passed the park and the school I went to.

I was surprised to see the house was in good shape, but I wish we could just go in there, and I wanted to show the crew the attic.

I was sad that we just couldn't. It was hard going to all these places. You're reliving it all.

When we were at the mausoleum, I was upset that we couldn't get in. I never went back to visit her for nearly twenty years. On that day, I forgave her and a pink, silk rose fell from the original bunch of flowers that were there. I picked it up. I believed it was a sign from her, and I have since kept and treasured it. I felt that she heard me and she dropped it for me to have.

I thought about how my mom and brother both wanted to be

cremated. I just remembered hanging out at Grandma's when we passed that house.

I was desperate to find Michael's grave. Even though my friend had a feeling to check another spot, I kept looking elsewhere.

It was sad that I never got to meet him, to get to know him. It's another hurt. I guess that's what happens when someone dies young.

It pains me that she had to go thru all of that. It's not reasonable to me that he didn't get a chance at life.

It's not fair. I have a brother out there named Michael, and he could be here with me right now, and holding my hand when I went thru what I went thru with Greg.

When we went by my old neighborhood, I had flashbacks. Some were good; some were bad. I loved going to the woods, but then unfortunately other memories weren't good.

At the closing of our trip, I was glad to have gone.

My friend called the cemetery the next day, and called me. I was glad she did, and when I have a chance out there, I'll try again.

I was driving down the road, and something told me to put in the CD, one of several that my friend gave me, and the first song that I heard was "Let's Get the Show on the Road," by the Michael Stanley Band. I thought, my story needs to get out there! (Easier said than done, though.)

When you hear a song, the lyrics relate to something going on in your life. That's how it is. When I heard "Lover," another really good song by the Michael Stanley Band, it reminded me of how many of my relationships didn't work out.

CHAPTER 8

Mom again

Around the time I was turning forty-one, the thoughts I had of her on the day she died and after were different for me. I didn't cry as much. My eyes started to tear up and I thought about her, but I didn't break down. While I was at work that day, my eyes watered up, but I wasn't really distraught about things.

The only thing I thought about was that in six days I was going to be forty-one, and she died when she was forty-two. My grandmother was fine when I talked to her around that time, and she didn't say anything about it.

I'm currently reading *Motherless Daughters* by Hope Edelman, and boy, can I really relate: the mom dying, the distanced father. I felt a connection to this book, and with several of the examples given.

When my mom was alive, she was very caring to me, so I do have to say that it was great during the years I knew her. We were close. I'm lucky to have had my mother longer than someone who, say, lost their mom when they were five or younger; but it doesn't make up for the loss.

I've had several dreams about her since she has passed; some I remember and some aren't clear. I usually remember my dreams specifically; that always makes me feel connected to her. Sometimes it's like a big fog.

Recently, I dreamt we went shopping in a big store. It had a little of everything: clothes, antiques, books and movies. I went over to a section of the store, and I saw her stacking up several books. One of them in particular was shiny and white, with a black photograph on the front of it. It was a medium-sized book, and she placed it on top. I really didn't see her face. She talked to me; I seen her hands, but I didn't clearly see her. She was in a cream-colored and white, dressy pants outfit. I knew it was her, and I heard her say something to me, but I don't know what it was.

I was looking at a gold shirt, and then she left me and went shopping. She put the items in the cart and we went to the cash register. She wanted to buy her books, and we wanted to go to another store. Then I woke up; I don't know what she said to me.

My dreams of her are sometimes foggy; I get bits and pieces of her.

I also dreamt that there were three silver chains: a bracelet, a necklace, and another chain. Something told me that I was getting these three chains when she passes on. I had them in my hand and I looked at them and said, "These are going to be mine." I know she was there; I just didn't see her. I just kept thinking that I like silver. They were real pretty, silvery, sparkly and brand-new.

What's more, I had seen *The Good Shepherd* with Matt Damon. In the beginning of the movie his father kills himself, and the father leaves a letter. The son reads it later in his life. It really hit me: why didn't my mom leave me a letter? I also don't have any videos of my mother. I can't go back and watch her, because I don't have any. I can't "see" those memories. A lot of people have that and I don't. I can't "see" her moving. I've often wished I could sit down and watch it. I don't have any videos of my brother, either.

I have lots of pictures, but nothing else. I already took some of my grandmother, because that wasn't going to happen to me. I have tapes from my stepfather talking to my mom, but I'm pretty sure it's just him on the tapes. It says, "Tapes to Ingrid," with his nickname on it.

I am envious and jealous when I see a mother and daughter or a father and a daughter out together. Not that I wish them bad, but I missed out on those years. Most people get the chance to have their mom and dad, although the grass is not always greener on the other side. You don't know what's behind closed doors. I see relationships working out and I see families living together, and I don't have that.

I ask God, "Why not?" We all have to go through something, but some people go thru other things, or less. And there's that saying, "God will only give you so much that you can handle." Well, I'm tired of handling so much. I've told God I can't handle any more. My shoulders aren't that strong.

I feel it's unfair. I want people to know that even though I went through all that and all the heartache, pain and rejection, and every time I talk to someone they don't see it all happening to me, and don't believe it how I came out. It was *my* journey.

A few years back, it was another anniversary day of her death. I started lighting a candle, and it was dark. I was talking to her and I told her again that I forgave her. I told her I loved her and that I missed her, and that I wished we would've had more time together. It was dark and I had lit a white candle. I wasn't afraid when the flame started immediately to flicker high, sideways and around. It was almost as if you had a fan in your room; it was moving as if there was air but there wasn't. I felt her presence strongly that night. After I blew the candle out, I felt someone at the foot of my bed, sitting there.

I was alone in the room for about an hour with the candle being lit, and it almost felt as if she was there. That comforted me; it was a reassuring night.

When I was lying on my side, I felt like someone brushed over one side of my hair off my face, and I pretended like it was really her. I pictured that it was her stroking my hair.

Last year, I was leaving to go home and I got in my car as usual. I turned the car on, and the dials were flashing in front of me. I didn't know what to do, and it never happened before. I was in the car, and I thought, "Mom, is that you?" Then the lights flashed again. I was so taken aback by it, I called a friend. When I was talking to her, it kept happening. It never happened since then.

Shortly after that, the light stopped. I feel that when our loved ones pass on, whether a light comes on or something kicks on, we want to believe it was them. It's always to hold on to them. Holding on to memories keeps us closer to them, whether it was good or bad. I think that if I didn't have any memories I would be worse off, because I would have nothing to hold on to.

For my forty-first birthday, I went with a few other people to visit my old home in with my stepsister and her husband. As we were walking down a path, she mentioned how she put me on an inner tube and sent me down the creek. My mom was so upset, since I came back so dirty. Mom used to dress me like a Barbie doll.

Boy, did she get it that day, she mentioned. Stephanie said that she liked my mom a lot, but she remembers how they fought often. We walked a little further and went to the old green bridge. The porch is a little different now.

I was fine. I looked right at my mother's room; it was an addition to the house. I was looking around at the old trees. They looked thin and fragile now that my sister's husband was pulling down some branches. They remodeled the back porch. We had a nice tree fort and campouts there. The yard still looked the same.

"Fly to the Angels," by Slaughter, is a song that reminds me of my mom.

CHAPTER 9

Dad, a 'mom' and others

Recently, I tried to get back with my dad. We were talking around Christmas, and I asked him to come to see me for a couple of days, and he said, "Yeah, let me check my schedule." I called him, and he said, "I can't come, because there's no one to take care of the horses."

I felt sad, because it seems like he has all these responsibilities to take care of at the farm, and he can't come out and take care of me when I need him. I told him just a few weeks after Greg died that I needed him in my life, he had just lost a son, and wouldn't he want to get to know his daughter more? I said, "I always call you; I make the effort." He said, "You are the better person than me." I felt really down about it.

I wish I didn't have to try so hard; I wish I didn't have to get my dad to love me. I am not trying to bother him, but I just try to get his affection.

I've told him that I love him. He never says it back. I'd like a dad to be there. I'd like a dad to call me, to spend time with me; a dad to come over for the holidays.

After I talk to him, I realize what I don't have. It'd be nice to have a 'dad' again.

On Father's Day a few years ago, I didn't call him. I decided not to because I'm tired of calling him and he never calls me. I wanted him to feel like, "Wow, she didn't call me today." I knew in my heart that it didn't even dawn on him that I didn't call. It was just another day passing on.

I think I'm at that point where I don't want to put myself out there anymore, be it him or anybody else. I can forgive but I can't accept being treated like I don't exist.

A few weeks later after Father's Day, before the 4th of July, I decided to call him. He answered the phone and I was just asking about my car. I needed advice on an extended warranty, if I should get one or not. He said, "No, you've got a good car."

He then began to tell me about the flooding near his home. I felt bad for him.

My dad had to have surgery, and the night before I told him that I loved him. He said, "I love you, too." He's never said that before, or since then. I believe it was because he was having surgery. It was inevitable that he might not make it. He's been ok, and survived the surgery. Although now he has Alzheimer's and he is starting to forget things.

I'm hurt that he never told me that again even. I've only asked on many occasions why he never tells me he loves me. He said he doesn't even tell his brothers and sisters that, and I felt he was skirting the issue. He said it makes me a better person than him.

I did meet some aunts in Florida years ago, when I was seventeen. I met cousins, too. Too bad we didn't keep in touch. We were going to go to the family reunion in the summer in 2008, but by then he was sick and couldn't go.

I still care, but I can't talk to him since he's forgetting.

He put a deposit in the "memory bank" for me to have. It's there when I need it.

I called my Dad the other day. He seems happy to hear from me. He was glad that I called, and asked me about his trip. Unfortunately, his mother-in-law died; I felt bad. He said he and his wife were concerned about me, and he told me to call back.

I feel things are getting better between us, and growing. Things are changing for the better. He was worried about me. That shows something.

This past Easter I called my dad and left a message in the early afternoon, so he had plenty of time to call me back. But he never called, and he never does call me.

Just like on my birthday. It's pretty sad. He wasn't there the day I was born; he was in Vietnam.

If I was a mother and I had a child, how could anyone not remember their child on their birthday?

He's retired; he takes care of his animals. I'm sure he remembers his wife's birthday. I called him on his, near the end of January.

He said, "Thank you for calling!" We laughed about his age—he's in his early seventies. How much time do we have left? I can't see there being a lot there.

Last phone conversation with Dad—we ended with, "Ok, I've got to go."

If he won't come live near me, then why doesn't he come and visit me? I am his only daughter; he's lost his son. Doesn't any of this matter? How would he feel if something happened to me?

I even called him eight days before my birthday to remind him. He didn't even remember the date. He said, "When?" He was getting ready to go to Vegas for a week to watch a horse show.

Was it that important that he couldn't call me from the show on my birthday, or on Easter? It made me feel the same way it always does. It never changes. I am disappointed. You would think during a holiday that he would want to talk to me. That showed me he doesn't remember. Even on the answering machine I said, "I hope you and your wife have a Happy Easter, and I hope things are going well." I let him know that Omi said, "Hi." I ended with, "I love you." He's never told me that he loves me. He always says, "Ok."

So, the question is, does he love me? *Does* my father love me? If you love somebody, don't you show it more?

I don't know if I'll ever get what I want, but I do pray about it. I hope that one day he realizes that he wants to be in my life. Say if he got cancer and was going to die. Would it change things? Would he start to care? Would he suddenly show up on my doorstep, and want to make up for lost time?

I think things are going so good in his life, he's always happy, healthy, and has never been sick. He had some high cholesterol, but that's it. I don't think he realizes that time is running out.

Sometimes I wish he would have a dream that he would see me telling him that I want him in my life and telling him to be a father to his daughter.

I think this would heal the broken bond between us.

He did call me on Sweetest Day. Hearing my voice doesn't do much so I pray about his, and I am waiting for God to answer my prayers.

I did tell my dad that we need to get together and establish a relationship, since I've been thinking about that. I also was feeling low because I lost a good friend of mine, Mary Jane, who was like a mother to me. "We really don't know how much time we have left on earth," is what I said to him. I would like some kind of father/daughter connection with him. I told him, "I know it hasn't been easy, but I've told you a few times that I love you, and I want a relationship with you. And to be quite honest, I don't know how you feel about me."

He didn't have an answer and all he said was, "Well, we'll just have to work on that."

I wanted him to know how I felt about him, and I was surprised that he didn't just jump on it. "It would be nice if you would call more," I mentioned. He said, "Ok." For a while now, I've told him in the past, "I love you and I want you in my life." I also told him that, "I've said that, and are we going anywhere with this?" He doesn't say anything.

Our phone conversations last about two minutes, if that; maybe once a month. I probably have not spent more than thirty days with this man. It's sad. I shouldn't have to beg him for a little bit of attention. What do you do? What can you really do?

After this conversation, I felt I shouldn't have to try so hard.

This past week, I was watching a talk show about fathers and daughters who haven't been on the best terms, and were now getting back together. Boy was I mad. There was a father who told his daughter that he knew he hasn't been the best father, but he wanted her in his life. She was on drugs and had problems, but she accepted him in her life. It made me feel, well, if he could try to get into her life, then why wouldn't my dad *want* to get into mine?

That's what I don't get. Doesn't he want to be in my life? Doesn't he want me to help take care of him when he's older? I don't even think I'm in his will. He does help with my car payment, but that's about it. I'd rather have him in my life as a dad.

What if two people were to show up as adoptive parents, would I take them in? No. I don't want to be hurt again by any more parents. I am too disappointed at my own and my foster parents.

I never call my dad "father," and he never calls me "daughter." He never says, "I love you."

He calls me "Jenny." I hate it. My foster parents call me "Jenny." I want to be called Jen or Jennifer. I'm an adult now. Please take notice and call me by me proper name.

I look back now, and I realize I didn't have good parents or even parents when I needed them. I'm too old now to get them.

I want my real father to step up to the plate.

My foster father was a good man and was always easy to talk to. We always didn't have the best relationship, but that connection has begun to heal, as well as a lot of other situations in my life. I recently had dinner with my foster family, and I'm finally starting to feel more like their own.

I'm thankful that they took care of me all those years. I could've been in an orphanage. They did the best that they could for me.

And as for David, I really was hurt that I never saw him again. We did write a letter to each other years later. In the letter, we asked how each other was. He said everything was fine. He didn't remarry. He died shortly after writing the letter from throat cancer years after my mother died.

So that's the story of all of my "dads".

At one time, I did meet someone who was like a mother. She seemed like a good woman at the time; she was very caring and always made me laugh and smile. I hadn't felt like that in a long time and I felt like I was born again.

We became very close. I saw her often; we talked on the phone every night. This went on for a couple of years. Even though she had children of her own, she considered me a daughter.

I went to her house to see her often and we talked, ate and hung out together. There were cookies at Christmas, and the comforts of home: coffee, tea, whatever I wanted. Omi even knew her.

I did bring Omi one time. It went well. I looked up to her, as she was like a mother.

One day it crashed. She got mad at me; we had a disagreement, and she ended it. She even sent back a necklace that I bought her. It was a silver locket and it had my picture in it.

She told me before that she would cherish that forever.

I was mad; I was hurt; I was angry. I was upset because everyone has disagreements; everyone has arguments. Just to drop me because she was annoyed at me? This was *unfair*.

I tried to call her. I left messages; I waited. Weeks went by and months went by. I just gave up.

After that, that's when the angry thoughts came.

I lost a boyfriend, and then I lost her. It was a double whammy.

She opened herself up to me quickly; I did the same with her. I went to see her more than my foster family.

Wherever she is, I wish her well. It's nice that I got to meet this person, but I trusted her and she betrayed my trust. It was a learning experience.

I shared too much with this woman. "Mom," I affectionately called her. She made me feel special; she was caring. At times she would be hugging me, just laughing with me.

I could show her things that I bought. She'd tell me that I looked good, and complimented me all the time.

Even though it was for a short time, it felt good.

When it ended, it felt worse. I felt like I lost my mother all over again.

Someone who was like my mother was gone. I had my foster mother, but this special bond I had with this other woman had vanished.

It's always going to hurt. It's a part of my life I went thru that I wish I didn't. It felt like rejection, like so many times over. That's why I got so angry, and had so many angry thoughts at God. I said, "You put this woman in my life, and she was like a mother to me." She was very spiritual, very uplifting, and prayed. She even knew Bible quotes.

She just walked away from me. Anybody who could walk away from somebody for something stupid or minor, made me question, is she really that spiritual?

That's when the thoughts started. I was angry at God. I swore; I cussed. It threw me over the edge. Not that I wanted to kill myself, but it made me really upset. It was from the entire trauma I've been through. My mom took her own life and left; this woman just walked out of my life. I haven't really been able to get past it. I never had thoughts like this before.

This was the culmination of a relationship that endured for three years. We exchanged birthday and Christmas gifts; I even seen her on Mother's Day.

Years later, I had run into her at a friend's funeral; I did get to talk to her. I said, "Hello," to her, and she said it back, but that's all there was with that.

Mary Jane, who I lost recently, was also like a mother to me. She lived nearby. I was crushed when I found out she died. I didn't get a chance to say goodbye to her. I wish I did. It was like losing a mother all over again. She did remind me of my mom: her features, how she carried herself, and the personality. I felt good again about myself. I will never forget her.

When she passed away, it was another awful experience, because she reminded me of a mom. The first time I met her, I felt very close to her. She told me things about her life, and I told her things about my life.

She always told me she loved me. What was really freaky was, two years ago she was having a birthday party for her grandson. It was outside; it was a nice day. He looked up at her, and said, "Grandma, two more birthdays, and you're going to be in the sky."

"The Flame," by Cheap Trick, reminds me of Mary Jane.

It was really hard to say goodbye to her. She always told me she'd be there, to get me thru my Grandma's passing.

It's another loss that was close to my heart. That's how I feel—just add it to the list.

Now I look at my grandma as my mom. When I'm around my grandma, I have so much peace and so much love. Sometimes I wish she was younger so we could go do things together. For years we would go out to eat, go have a beer together, even hang out locally.

If she was younger, we would be going to the mall, to the spas or go out to dinner and having a glass of wine. We'd just be hanging out. I know that would be cool.

It's going to be really hard when I lose her. I'm going to need a lot of support when I do; I'm real close to her.

Looking back, I regret the time I wouldn't spend with Grandma. For over fifteen years I would visit her here and there, but we weren't close as we are now.

She had dreams about me having a baby, and I have, too. She and I have also had dreams about Mom.

I wish I had a different mindset. I just wasn't thinking. I wish that my priorities were more on what they should have been. I wish I would have scheduled more time with her. My friends and boyfriends took priority then, and I don't really even talk or hang out with any of them now.

It's always later in life when we're maturing that you sit yourself down and look at yourself. You look at how you are with others, and you start to realize who's really important and who's not.

It's not that I didn't see her, I just really didn't spend enough time doing things with her that she could've done when she was younger.

She did have Paul but I should've been there more. I wasn't grownup enough.

CHAPTER 10

How I feel

Losing my mom early in life, I don't think I grew up at the times that I should have.

I feel left out because my mother left me. I feel rejection and loneliness.

When I read my mom's diary, sometimes it feels comforting; sometimes it feels sad because that's all I have left of her. When I hear how she talks about me, about her "sweet, little Jenny," that makes me feel good. I'm happy.

When I read the parts about her depression, it makes me sad.

When she's unhappy in her marriage, it makes me sad.

When she says she wishes she would die, it makes me sad.

I can't believe she fought these feelings for so many years.

She obviously didn't have a good relationship with David; it was up-and-down. One day he wouldn't talk to her much, or not take interest in her personal life like her surgery, and the next time she would write how they took a walk in the woods near our home, and he carved their initials in a tree. A loving gesture, at times, coupled with angst in other matters.

There were days when my mom would write how she felt no one cared about her, how she would feel we were all selfish, but we were young and just didn't know any better. I don't think anybody meant to harm her or be disinterested in her, but she took it that way.

I feel she was very unhappy and didn't enjoy her life. It seemed like she hated her life.

She wrote, "Me, awful me," and "Jump in the lake, Ingrid, best thing for your loving family!" I was devastated and angry; I was disappointed. I read it a few years ago. My grandmother gave it to me when I was in my twenties after my divorce. I was just looking thru her drawers one day and I said, "Here's Mom's diary." I couldn't believe it that it was there. I was surprised. She let me take it with me, and told me that I could have it.

I brought it home and put it in my drawer. It was very sacred and spiritual to me. I couldn't believe I that that I had such an important piece of my mom's history. I never really read it much; I only took some occasional glances at it.

A few years ago, I read it and I then started to reread it before telling my story. I wanted to portray mom in a fair light, but being honest.

Mom and Dad were married, and then they were separated within ten years, and then divorced. I was eleven months old; Greg was three-and-a-half. They divorced on grounds of cruelty.

My mom would write a lot of poems. I was reading them recently. They were poems to her dad and her mom. She must have loved her dad. However, were they about her real dad, or Opi? I don't know.

She didn't have any brothers or sisters. Her relationship with her parents was good, and her life growing up was fine. She worked here and there, maybe at a store in the mall for some extra money. What I thought really did it to her was losing Michael, who was stillborn. I was around five or six when Michael died. Mom was traumatized. She had carried the baby to nine months. She was at a routine visit, and found out that Michael was dead. I would go to the graveyard with my mom. I remember my mom holding flowers and changing his flowers on the grave.

I don't think she ever got over it. She wasn't happy with David. Then she chose a man who belonged to someone else, and couldn't have him, either. I wish that she could've met a good man, who could've cared for her and our family.

She really was never happy. In her diary the beginning says, "Hello, whoever chooses to read this, be my guest."

She had a major surgery, and wrote in her diary how David wasn't there for her: "I feel lost and lonely, like a little girl." She built a wall around her to protect herself. David wasn't there for her operation and later in life. It also felt that way for me when I had thyroid surgery later in my life.

My mother wrote on October 21, 1973, that she knew I found out about her surgery and I cried. She was scared. She had a lot of procedures; I can't remember what for.

Mom writes, "I'm so blue and depressed, not bubbly," on November 10, 1973. And, "I'll never go back to being happy." She was out of the hospital at this time. She added, "I'm so deprived of my life."

Same date, with an exception of "How to live life: watch a snowflake, love and enjoy life. The snow, football games, marshmallows..." She obviously had found joy in some things.

She also wrote about how a family member knew Dick Clark. My mom was really excited to meet him, and I remember meeting him. That was a highlight of my mom's life.

A woman called and told her to give David up. On March 19, 1973, she wrote "I am good and ready to jump in a lake." This lady must have said something to her.

I never really got settled down with myself. As aforementioned, my relationships hadn't panned out. After that first marriage, I didn't want to get married again. For many years, I would choose people that didn't want to get married. That's why they didn't work out.

Probably because of what I grew up in, I chose to be alone, live alone, and be independent. In my thirties, I thought about having a family. Now in my forties, I don't know. Sometimes as odd as it seems, I don't know if I want that now.

I didn't get that from my parents what I needed: you learn things from them; you look up to them. You learn about self-esteem, growing, caring, nurturing, discipline, guidance, and making decisions. When I think about it, they teach you not to do drugs, and not to get into certain levels of relationships before you're ready. If you have no one to teach you this, then how do you know what is right from wrong?

These are things that you talk to your parents about. You might go off and do your own thing, but you still need that guidance.

Now, I see and feel myself changing. I know I'm finally getting to a point in life where I could settle down. My ideal partner would be someone who gives me so much love and affection that would open me up and open my mind up to new possibilities.

I've never really had this much affection, and it would make me feel so special.

When he hugs and kisses me, and cuddles me constantly, I would feel like a new woman. I could see myself settling down.

When I meet him, I will tell him I'm tired of going for the bad boys, the players. I'd like to give him a chance. I never gave a nice guy a chance because when I was growing up, I went with what I was used to—rejection, not much affection, and half-heartedness.

My ideal guy: he wants to spend time with me as much as he can. He likes doing things with me; he's so comfortable with me.

I haven't really thought much about kids, because I don't know what kind of mom I'd be—overprotective, not wanting any harm to come to the baby—not that any parent would want harm to come, but maybe I would take it a little too seriously.

For many years, I didn't think I was "mother material." Maybe because I lost my mother young; I don't know.

Lately, I've been thinking about how life would be if I had children. I'm not sure why I'm feeling this way, but maybe it's because I'm getting older. I have spent some time with friends who have little ones, and we took them out for the day. I really enjoyed it.

I've thought about adopting, but it may cost a lot of money, and I don't want to be a single parent. It would make me happy if I could meet someone with kids, and be a parent to them.

If my mom was here, I would have a child. Because she's been absent for a lot of years, I didn't have that mother/daughter time. If she was here right now, I wouldn't be so scared to make that decision. Since she left me young, I feel vulnerable. If she was here, she could help coax me into making me feel that I could make that decision.

I don't want to get married, have a kid and end up a single mother. I give a lot of credit to people who work, have kids, and do it on their own. If I'm going to have it, I want it right. I want it to stay together.

If the child grew up, and thru normal adolescent phases didn't want to hang with me, and would want to go away to college or move, it would make me feel bad. I would want to have a continuous relationship with that child.

It's not that I wouldn't put the time into my child; I just am concerned about myself right now. Hanging out with my grandmother, my friends, finding someone, and just getting myself together is important at this time.

I'd like to have a brother, someone to hang out with, laugh with, get a bite to eat with, share stories, and sing "Happy Birthday" to him.

I'd like a mom to go shopping with, go to spas with, make cookies with, and watch movies together.

I'd like to be married to a good husband—someone faithful, and a good communicator. Someone affectionate and someone to come home to and have dinner with: my best friend.

I'd like a child, if it's meant to be. I would want that child to laugh, to be a child, and for the opportunity to grow as a parent.

I need to get my life together. I need to get myself in order to take care of someone else. Let's see what happens.

When I was younger, I took care of my mom, and then my childhood was swiped from me. It's not fair for an eleven-year-old to have to take care of her mom. She was supposed to take care of me; it's true.

As I've previously stated, I was with Mark from fifteen to twenty-three. After the divorce and thru my late thirties, I went out here and there, but not like I do now.

I feel popular. I've met most of the people in my life except for Jackie in the last couple of years. I love spending time with them. My friends care about me a lot and are like my family. I've learned now that people may come and go, but my friends are still there.

That makes me feel good, because I know I could trust them and they look out for me. They call me for advice, and they look up to me. It makes me feel important.

I love all of them; they are all there; if I'm down they all cheer me up. They all make me laugh. Some have cooked for me, some have taken me special places for my birthday; they care for me. They haven't forgotten my birthday. I go out with them, and I can count on them.

My stepsisters are truly sisters to me; just because we aren't blood relatives doesn't make it any less important to me. They *are* my family.

I did get a chance to run into Tony. We are still good friends today, and we made peace with each other before Omi went into the nursing home. I talked to him the other day, and I talked to his daughter and I met his fiancée.

With all these significant people that I've lost, life is lonely. I still don't understand people who've got everyone together. Their holidays are just great, especially if they're close. Their mom and dad are together. They take it all for granted. I don't deny them that, it's just I'm feeling left out.

I spent a quiet holiday with my foster family, but I missed my family. I tried to call my dad, who I still call "John." Not much has changed there.

A small surprise, though, my stepmom sent me a nice turtleneck for Christmas. I thought that was a kind gesture. I didn't have much to get them this holiday season.

My stepmom did have to call and ask me what day my mom died on. She was real gentle about it. It was necessary to find out, since Dad needs to get medical help from a VA clinic where he lives. I did let Donna know the information. Of course, it's going to bring up memories, but what can you do?

I did meet a guy recently, but as usual, he just wants to be friends. It's the same old situation. However, I'm going to keep on trying. I'm not going to give up just yet.

For my birthday, I went to French Lick Resort, in Indiana, where there is a casino and horse race tracks. I relaxed, shopped, and did something different for myself. I forgot her that day, and I didn't cry; I didn't let it bring me down.

On Mom's birthday, it was a quiet day.

On Greg's birthday, I worked, and thought about him. I was down, and missed him. He came to my mind.

The last couple of days, it's hit me strong that I'm going to meet someone. I just know it's going to happen. He's going to be special, and caring. I've got a lot of love to give, and that person will, too.

On a good note, work is going well; I'm very busy. People are becoming regulars and new people are saying I come highly recommended. That makes me feel good.

I wore both Mom's and Mary Jane's rings on Greg's birthday. The ring from mom is a long-shaped turquoise gem with silver. It is a beautiful light blue. The ring from Mary Jane is gold with several light blue stones. Mary Jane's ring was a gift for my birthday a few years back, and my mom's ring was on her hand when she died. She wore that ring often. It's the one I remember her wearing the most.

On Memorial Day, I spent the day at a park but I remembered him. I talked to him about how much I missed him, and I asked him to help me. I know he's always looking down on me. I wonder what he thinks of my story. I know he's proud of me for trying to work things out with everybody, and trying to make amends with the past.

CHAPTER 11

A letter

Two days after my brother's birthday, for some reason I found all this stuff—the separation/divorce papers of my parents, the marriage license of Mom and David, my birth certificate with my stepdad's name on it, a military I.D. of me (my dad's), and a picture in the newspaper of my Dad and Mom, as he was receiving silver bars signifying his promotion to first Lieutenant. My dad looks so handsome, and my mom just gorgeous.

Also, I found some poems, a book of Mom's, *Lord, Hear My Prayer*, her cards from the funeral home, tucked in a sympathy response card in an envelope, and also an interesting letter from Omi, dated August 22, 1982, written over two years after she died.

In it, she recounts the story of the last day she talked to Mom and the night before. Mom told her she said she had to have a talk with us kids about the house, and how she couldn't live off Omi all her life. Omi mentioned that she didn't understand that, and made a joke and tried to laugh it off. The next morning around ten forty-five she called my mom.

Later that day, there they were making her tea, thinking she was upstairs in bed. When she went up there, she saw the attic door open.

I could only imagine what it was like for her. This is her letter.

Here it is:

I finally got myself together and picked up the coroner's report. By reading it, I found some differences in timing. This is what really happened.

The day before Ingrid's death, we had a talk that night. She was very

344

upset and nervous and told me, "Mother, I will have a talk with the kids tonight about the house. I cannot live off you all my life. You paid all the money you had left for the down payment and pay the mortgage every month with me having no money." I answered her, "Leave that up to me, once you are well we will see what we will do; I may take you on a trip or go to Hawaii." She laughed and I finally calmed her down. The next morning around ten forty-five she called me and the conversation went like this: "Mother, I talked to the kids last night about moving in an apartment. I told them it is too hard on Omi to give all her money to us; she should enjoy her retirement and we should not lean on her all the time." She said the answer they gave her was, "We don't want to move; we like it here." We talked about her doctor's appointment. I asked her if Paul should take her like the week before; Ingrid said, "No, Mother." Carole told her she would pick her up about three-thirty and she would go with her. I told Ingrid we would talk about all the things when we come over.

I had a funny feeling about her being upset and called about two forty-five (the time I know exactly because I sent Paul to mail a letter for me and the mailbox time is three o'clock). The conversation was like this: "Hi Ingrid, I just want to know what time you think you will be back from the doctor's so that we are not so late." Answer from her: "I am not going." Me: "Why not?" Ingrid: "I might as well be dead," and she hung up. Immediately I told Paul, who had returned from the mailbox, and I said, "There is something funny with Ingrid; we better go right now." And I told him the short conversation which was the last words I ever heard from my daughter. We packed everything. Paul and I arrived about 3:25 and put all the stuff down on the table. I changed my boots, calling up to her, "I will be right up now. Paul is making you some tea." No answer. I went upstairs and there was nobody, only the door to the attic was open.

I called down to Paul in the kitchen: "Come up here fast, Ingrid is not here and the attic door is open." He came running up going right in the attic; I was halfway down the steps when he screamed, "Ruth come up here, Ingrid hung herself!" I was in shock and at the same time Carole came I told her to run up and help him which she did. Paul tried with Carole to get her down and they both did. I still could not believe

345

it and while Paul gave her mouth-to-mouth resuscitation we both tried frantically to get the police and ambulance. During the time of their arrival, Carole helped with Paul. After the police came (they came first after 10 minutes), Paul asked them to help him to resuscitate with him.

They answered him, "We don't know anything about this; we are not trained for this." Finally, the ambulance, as a matter of fact two ambulances arrived and they tried for what seemed to me half an hour and finally took her out. I only saw her when they carried her out on the porch. Between my complete numbness and being stunned I saw that she was blue and not a sign of life. Carole went with her to the hospital; I was unable to go. We waited at home until the call came from the hospital that she had died. By that time Jennifer and Greg both had arrived, and so had some helpful neighbors. I went to the hospital and made all the arrangements. I am only writing this to establish that we did not arrive at 4:25, but at 3:25. I often think if we would have been ten minutes earlier, maybe she still would have had a chance, but think if I would not have called at 2:45 I would have walked in the house finding her the same way. There is nothing I can say any more about this; I was only trying in this case to establish that the timing in the report was wrong.

Signed,

Her forever deeply sad Mother.

Just ten minutes late. Can you believe that? Maybe there could have been a chance, as Omi said.

I never really got a letter. I don't know what I would've done if I got one. I don't know how I would've handled it. She never said goodbye.

I swear that there was a letter that my mom left, but no one says they have it. I did check into this a couple of years ago. I tried to find Carole, my mother's friend, but I couldn't remember her last name. When I called her phone number, it was disconnected.

On the day of her death, I swear I heard a cop say to me, "There's a letter, but it's too graphic to read." Five years ago, I looked into this and didn't find any new information about the case.

On the other hand, I was watching this movie on TV—this lady ended up in jail, because of killing her husband. Years later, she hangs herself.

The daughter comes in, and they tell her what happens, and they give her a letter that the mom wrote.

She asks to see her mother, uncovers her and reads the letter. The mother told her that she loved her. She wanted her to be strong, and not to make the mistakes she made in life, and to be proud of who she is.

In that movie, she wrote beautiful things about her daughter. It was closure. It was no coincidence.

It made me feel that I wish I had gotten a letter. I wish she would've written something, so I could've gotten some closure. I wouldn't feel so rejected now, because the words would have been on paper. It would've helped if she had, because then I could've had the chance to say goodbye.

I would've had something to look at, and I wouldn't have so many emotional problems now, over such a length of time. Perhaps some of the years could've been knocked off of that, and maybe I would've suffered less.

I always had Omi, but, nothing can replace not having a mom.

CHAPTER 12

Omi's life

Omi was never close with her mom but she was very close with her father. She said her father told her constantly that he loved her; her mother didn't.

One day in the nursing home, I decided to ask her about her life. She recounts her story:

My father died when I was ten years old. He died in his sleep. He coughed a lot, but he didn't drink or smoke.

He died at home. I was very upset and I cried. "Mowsel" was my nickname. My real name is Ruth. My mom's name was Elizabeth.

My parents were always working at the beauty shop; my dad owned it and my mom worked there and took it over when he died.

I was the seventh baby; the only one of them that had lived. All her brothers and sisters had died.

My parents fought all the time. When he died she was sad, but she was not devastated. Dad had given me love and attention. Life was very gloomy for me after he died. After high school I learned to be a beautician. I worked with my mother for a year-and-a-half, and then I met my husband. We saw each other on the weekend. I married him within a year. He was a man whose ideas I didn't agree with. We were close to my mom, about an hour away. He worked as a window cleaner. He had five brothers; they all worked together.

A year later, I moved nearer to my mom to be by her. I wasn't pregnant until two years later. I was married for ten years to Zepple. I met Opi before the war was over. I was divorced by the next year. My first husband left to go to the war. He met a girl, and later got married to her.

Opi died in his sleep. Paul died from cirrhosis; he had a bad liver. He died in my apartment. At his funeral, there was only you, Sam, Greg and me.

What was mom's life like growing up?

She grew up as a happy child. When she was in Germany, she met another guy when she was eighteen. He got transferred to the States. Then she met John, and he gave her a ring. She didn't date him very long.

How old was she when she first got married?

She was eighteen; he was twenty. Greg was born. They went back to Germany because he was stationed there.

Was mom happy being married to John?

I'm not sure if she was happy with John. They were married for about five years.

Are you from East or West Germany? What town?

I am from north Germany, from Hamburg.

Did you do other work in Germany?

I worked for the British as a secretary in Germany.

What was it like during the war?

We went through a lot of stress during the war. I had to move. I was devastated. He was in the war. We had an apartment.

When did you come over here?

In the 1950's, by boat. She was eighteen.

Why did you come over here?

It was a bad place to be, in Germany at the time.

What was your first husband like?

He only had seen Ingrid once. She didn't ask much about her father. I was her mom and dad and everything.

Tell me about her marriages.

She and John were married first, and then she and David were married later. It didn't work out. You were three or four when David adopted you and Greg. They got married too quickly. She would say to me, "Mom, why did I get married?" She made a mistake. On a Christmas Day in the sixties, John told me and Opi that he had a girlfriend. She got a divorce, then she started to go out, and she met David who wanted to marry her right away. She drank very little.

When she was pregnant with Michael, she was married to David. She carried him nine months, and he died right away. It carried in her mind. She went *kaputt*, and everything fell apart—she got depressed. Ingrid forgot about David and John. She wasn't happy being pregnant with David; she only married him for you and Greg. She was happy being married to John.

When we left David, we moved to a town nearby. She worked, but not very much.

Did you know about mom slitting her wrists?

No, not until today. I am in shock, and I didn't realize it. I had no idea. You tell me that no one knew but you and Greg.

How was your relationship with mom?

Our relationship was great and we talked often.

How about any other relationships?

Ingrid was very depressed. She dated a guy named Bob. She loved Jack; they were together for a while.

When did David and her divorce?

You were four when David and Ingrid married. Then they got divorced later.

What was it like when Ingrid died?

I went thru such commotion. It was *so* emotional for me. You cannot understand it.

•

How did you feel about me and Greg going to live with other people?

I had a terrible time. The foster family took you in; I wanted you to stay with me.

Why did you wait till I was sixteen before telling me about my real dad?

I didn't think he was really happy with his second wife. I had his address. I wrote him after three years. He couldn't understand why she died. I told him that she was unhappy in her marriage and got divorced. She always liked John but he didn't want her. I knew you didn't have a dad anymore, and I knew where he was, so I decided to give it a try.

What was that day like for you?

When she killed herself, I couldn't believe it. When she called that day, I still couldn't believe it. I don't know why she ever did that; she was such a nice girl.

Did she believe in God?

She often went to a Lutheran church. We prayed before dinner, and went to church on Sundays. Ingrid would often talk about God.

What were her younger years like?

She was happy as a child, but became continuously unhappy as a young adult. She loved another guy, but he had a girlfriend. He would come on a few days to see her. Ingrid was naïve. John said, "Marry me," and she did.

She was happy with John, but he left her at home to go to work. She couldn't go out because she didn't speak much English; she learned on her own.

Did you ever sense that mom was going to kill herself?

I didn't know. I was just upset. She had a hysterectomy and was forty-two. She always had problems female-wise, and stomach problems, too. I don't know if this had an effect on her.

Did the hysterectomy change her?

I'm sure of it. She had problems with her uterus. I don't think she had cancer.

.

What happened that day?

We were worried. There was some snow on the ground. "Good heavens, we got to get over there right away, Paul. We must drive fast," I told him that day. That was a terrible day; my boyfriend Paul had found her. There was no note.

Her friend was there because she was going to take her to the doctor. I'm not mad at her. I couldn't even think about anything at the time.

Did you ever forgive her?

Yes. Did I ever get over it? No. It's not pretty what's in my head. I have a lot of sadness. She was a very pretty girl, but like I mentioned, she went totally *kaputt* after losing Michael.

Why did you do this?

I couldn't say. I was just hurt, but I forgave her right away.

What was it like after?

I had to go thru the furniture. I sold all of it; I gave away the clothes. I couldn't think; I was so upset. Then I sold the house. It was a bad time.

What was it like when Greg died?

That was terrible for me. I can't even say how I felt. took me to see Greg. You told me after he passed. He died from the smoking, I feel. He even smoked in the clinic.

CHAPTER 13

Losing Omi

Over the summer, I knew I was going to lose Grandma. A friend and I were sitting at a place for lunch, and I said I knew she was going to die. I had a feeling; my friend was sad.

Then she got worse. Seeing her in the nursing home, I knew my days with her were numbered. She would ask for Greg, "When is he coming?" She was beginning to go thru this a month before she died. Omi also had a lot of nightmares one month before she died, and would also dream about Greg.

A couple of weeks before she passed away, my friend came in to the nursing home. We were going to go have lunch again, but we sensed that we shouldn't go. Then more of my friends came in. Later, my friend Trish had one of the priests that she knows come into bless her, a few days before she died.

"I don't think I can stay awake anymore—I'll always be around you," she said one time.

One day, Omi reached out to me. She touched my cheek, and it was hard for me. I cried. I knew she was trying to tell me that she loved me.

As time was passing by, I was very sad about losing her. I would tell friends, "I'm trying to prepare myself, but I don't know how."

Since I knew she was going to die, I was sad and down. I was losing my mother's mother, the last link to my own mother. That was hard. She was the last part of my mom that I could touch. When Grandma would speak to me, it was like I was talking to a part of my mom.

She would always call me "sweetheart," like my own mom would, and tell me she loved me very, very much. All the time she would say that. I'm going to miss hearing those words. Who else can you say that to?

I wish I had her voice on tape. I have a few videos and pictures, and that's about it. I miss her accent and her voice and her words she said the most, "Oh man, oh man."

I was at work when she died; I didn't know until later. Somewhere between two-thirty and three p.m., I looked at the clock and I knew I had to go see her. After work, four out of five calls were from the nursing home. They had said her status has changed, and I needed to get there.

I flew there and when I arrived they said they were sorry. "She had passed away this afternoon after two o'clock," someone said.

They kept her there for me. A nurse said she died in her sleep. No one was with her at the time. Her breathing was getting shallow.

In some way, I wish I could've been there when she died. I wanted to hold her hand, to comfort her. I wondered if she thought of me before she died. She was worried about me being by myself.

I stayed with her a while. I took her rings off. A friend came in. Then I called other people. I said my goodbyes to her. I told each of my friends, "What am I going to do without her?"

I called the funeral home. They came and got her; I left. My friend went home. Another friend came down for the weekend to stay with me. I called my sisters and other friends. They flew out as soon as they could. I'm thankful for my stepsister. She has truly been there.

That whole weekend I was just trying to get thru it, since I was still in shock from the whole thing. It was tough going thru the arrangements.

The calling hours were good, but the day of the funeral was difficult.

There was a service at the funeral home, and we played two songs that meant a lot to me, "There You Are," and "Anyway", both by Martina McBride. My grandmother is like an angel watching over me. When I hear this song, I cry all the time, and I can picture her in white. With the other song, no matter what people do, Grandma still cared about them, and I admired that quality about her.

She is buried near her husband and mother. I knew that my great-grandmother Elizabeth came here, but I didn't know she was buried here.

The dinner turned out nice. So many cared and came to both that day and the evening before.

That day, I went and got a massage, and I bought Stephanie a facial. Another friend came, too. It was nice to get away from it for a while.

The next day, Stephanie had to go home. It was hard because I was by myself. I cried so much. It hit me hard that day.

It was hard all that week. A mother/daughter combo came in. Another client survived lung cancer. I'm happy for these people, but sad for myself.

She started going downhill from the spring.

She knew about me sharing our story.

After the death of a loved one, there's that emptiness and you grieve; you have to. I'm still grieving over here, but I'm doing much better. When I'm alone at night and it's quiet, I hear her little voice. I miss her.

It's been six weeks since we've last written. I was on vacation, and I got really sick. Now we're back.

My friend Trish asked that since I've lost Mom, Grandma, Mary Jane, and Greg, which was the hardest passing for me? I answered, "My mom, because I was young and tried hard to be strong. I didn't cry enough at the time for myself."

When Greg died, I cried and cried. The pillowcase was soaked, so were the sheets. When Mary Jane died, I was very sad. When Grandma died it was hard, but it didn't make any difference that she was older. She was all I had.

When Grandma and Greg passed, my friends were very supportive, because more people were there. I didn't have too many people and friends at thirteen, compared to what I've got now. I have lots of support, the older that I've become.

I've changed since Omi died; I've transitioned into a new person. I'm not putting up with anybody's stuff anymore. If I'm upset, I'll tell you. I'm not going to let you walk all over me.

This holiday is going to be tough. Thanksgiving was difficult, but Christmas Eve is going to be worse. It was her favorite holiday. We were together for so many Christmas Eves. She would bring out the wine, crackers and cheese, German pastries, ham, rye bread, and German chocolates. The table was set well with all of these treats.

She would wrap all the gifts herself. Omi always bought me jewelry, perfume and lotions. She'd order thru the mail, since she didn't drive.

On Christmas Eve of 2003, she gave me Greg's watch. She wrapped it up and wanted me to have it.

We spent several Christmas Eves together. Sometimes Greg would come, like the last one in 2002.

Christmas Eve was special, just for me and her. It was a way for her and me to bond, and she loved watching me open up the gifts.

I would buy her slippers, clothes and pajamas. One year I bought her a big TV. This year, I'm spending it alone at home. I don't mind, because I just want it to be this way. I'll light a candle in remembrance of her.

For Christmas, I'll probably go to my foster family. I went there for Thanksgiving, and it worked out well. I'm glad I went. We're even getting along better now.

CHAPTER 14

Hannah

Trish asked if Greg wanted to get married or have any kids. I brought it up about Annette, an ex-girlfriend of Greg's, who was also a friend of mine. Annette had called my foster parents a few years before he died.

I was lying on the couch; the phone rang, and I answered it and Annette said, "I have to ask you something." Her son was hanging out with Hannah, a girl who supposedly is Greg's daughter. Hannah's mom, Ellie, also dated Greg. She was living with him when she was pregnant. Annette asked me, "Did Greg ever say he had a daughter? Because, Ellie said he doesn't keep in any kind of contact with her."

Then I told her in my excitement, "Oh my God, I need to call Greg, I need to find out!" I then called Greg, and in a nasty and smug tone he said, "No, I don't feel I'm the father; I am *not* the father." I felt awful; and he didn't want to talk about it.

It was a short conversation, and I called Annette back and said, "My brother said, 'No,'" and she let it go. She said, "Ok," and never called me back.

I let it go because I believed my brother. I didn't want to hurt his feelings by pursuing it.

But Omi was giving him money, and didn't know that Ellie was pregnant.

Grandma told Greg he could stay with her as long as he wanted, but he had to work. He also had girlfriends, but, like me, he didn't make good choices.

Grandma has said, "I couldn't stand or handle the drug problem. I didn't know what to do. I didn't give him money, but Jen says I did."

Her number sat around for a few years on this purple piece of paper until my friend Trish mentioned it. We were talking about the last conversation with my Dad, how he never comes up, and she was sitting on the couch looking at the TV, and beneath that was my brother's ashes. His birthday was close to Memorial Day, and he was in the Marines.

That's when I told her about Annette, and I decided to call her. I said, "Hello." She was very polite, and glad that I called. I asked her about the situation with the girl, and about her being my brother's daughter. She was ecstatic and anxious to get us together. She said that her son was married to Hannah, and they are currently separated. She would call Hannah. I said, "If you talk to her, give her my number."

She called her and left a voicemail, and then she called me. I didn't hear the phone, and I heard the voicemail, and called her right back.

The initial hello was very nice. She was very sweet, and she was kind and generous. She was hurt really bad in her life by other people.

We just talked about my brother, and she told me how she remembers him on his birthday and the day he died. I was touched.

She has pictures of me and Greg and pictures of her as a baby. Hannah told me that in the baby picture, she said she looks like Greg and me. She had baby pictures from Annette, who lived near my foster family. Hannah treasures the pictures. She wants to meet me.

I called my dad about it. He said, "Oh." I don't think that he was too thrilled. I told him she was looking into DNA testing. I didn't even ask him if he wanted to take the test. I knew that I wanted to. He said, "I don't know, I wouldn't pursue it; those tests, you don't know how accurate they are."

I said, "You don't know, you could have more family out there." He said, "You never know; that could be possible." From the sound of his voice, you'd think someone would be so excited that their son has a child. He wasn't. I thought he would've said, "Wow." I guess he looks at it like another obligation. He added, "What does she want?"

My grandmother said, "Why of all this time, did she try to get in touch with you?" Omi didn't understand how this is possible with Greg gone. I explained that we (Hannah and I) were looking into DNA testing. It's around one thousand dollars. Omi stated, "Then we'll never know." She was upset, but I said, "Do you want to meet her? She said, "Yes."

Even if I had told my dad that I wanted to do the testing, he would've said, "I don't know." I don't think he would've bothered. We're not pursuing it at this point.

Hannah and I did talk after my grandma died. She did have a baby. I did talk to Ellie, Hannah's mom, a while back. Hannah is a great girl and looks so much like Greg. But, I haven't heard from her in a long time. I hope to run into her again.

CHAPTER 15

My own feelings

You have to go thru all the emotions of grief: anger, guilt, hurt, and others. So many people, if something tragic happens to them, try to guard their emotions, and they try to put on a strong shield as if nothing ever happened.

They put their feelings in a closet.

Even though I was hurt and cried and missed my mom, the anger and guilt that I did not let out came back to haunt me in my thirties.

I tried to be strong, and thought that I could handle it on my own. I was never really sure if she went to heaven or hell. She was a spiritual, faithful woman.

I blamed myself for a long time. I had nightmares about if for years, with variations of it. I would be finding her over and over hanging in the attic. Also, I would dream that I would go up to the casket, and her eyes would open.

With all these significant people that I've lost, life is lonely. I still don't understand people who've got everyone together. Their holidays are just great, especially if they're close. Their mom and dad are together. They take it all for granted. I don't deny them that, it's just I'm feeling left out.

I feel like my life is a puzzle. You know how you try to put the pieces back together to mend everything? Well, there's always going to be pieces missing.

I like people who are supportive of what happened to me. However, I went out with this psychologist once, and I told him what happened. He took me in the car one night, and we drove by the house. He asked me what I would do to the house. I remember him saying to me, "It could have been a lot worse; you could have found her." I was shocked that he said that. I had him drop me off at home.

It was the worst thing that could happen to me. I was traumatized. One time somebody said to me, "Your mom killed herself. She had a mental illness, and it could run in the family." I was really upset. I don't disagree that this could be true. Depression can run in families, but that doesn't mean that people have to say that. It's always the dumb things that people say, isn't it?!

Interestingly, I met someone that lived in the same house where my mom killed herself. It was strange that we met locally. He lived in the same bedroom that I did, and he remembered the attic. We only hung out for a short time.

Catholic people, young and adults, have in the past told me that my mom went to hell. I was hurt, and I disagreed with them. My mom was a believer, and she wrote many poems and went to church. I was hurt at their dumb comments. How could they be so cruel and say those things? I don't think people realize what they say before they speak it. I think too many people are judgmental, and don't understand. People will say, "Oh my God, that's terrible. I don't know what I would've done if that happened to me." I would like to say to them, "But, you've still got your parents, and your brothers and sisters, and your grandparents." They've never had a loss, and they really can't say anything because they haven't experienced it.

I always said to myself, I would've handled it better if it was an accident. When she took her life she took my life, too. As a child, you bond with your mother. I feel that accidental deaths and heart attacks are hard, but suicide is a *rejection*. It's a selfish act. You're not thinking of anyone else at that time. She did love us, but not enough to stay. Did she ever stop to think, what this would do to us, to her mother, me, Greg, and her friends?

You can think about it, and you get to that point, and the stronger part of you gets in and takes over.

I feel that everyone probably has thought about this, but some people can get over it more than others. If they're hurt, upset, or have an addiction, they're strong enough to get past it.

CHAPTER 16

Suicide

I was recently telling Trish about my friend that died from an apparent suicide. It was tough going to the funeral. He was a friend from high school.

There was no reason given for his death, and there was a closed casket. He was such a nice person in high school, friendly to everybody. I couldn't believe it.

I feel bad for the daughter that is left behind. How can this young girl understand? Who is going to tell her what happened? How is she going to react when she finds out, or learns what he did? I personally know the coming loneliness and stress for the girl and can really relate to the circumstances.

And all the people there are left questioning, "Why?"—a reply that will by no means be answered.

The young lady has to go on with her life without him. This is an unfair situation that could have been avoided.

Trish's friend, who she recently lost, has had quite an impact on her. She says she's angry; at first, she was shocked. I know she's going thru the different stages of grief.

I know she's remembering words that were spoken from him on New Year's Eve. I could see in Trish some guilt. She asks herself, "What could *I* have done? Why couldn't *I* have seen it? Could *I* have talked to him? Could *I* have been there for him? Could *I* have changed his mind?"

These same things I thought about with my mom. Could I have talked to her about it? Could I have stopped her? If she had seen me, could she have looked at me in a different way, and said, "Oh my God, what have I been thinking?" And my guilty part was, why did I leave that day?

I always feel that I left her *alone.*

You're always trying to fill in the space that was emptied. You're always trying to find an answer.

After, your mind goes racing. You're always trying to find someone or something to blame. Was it that guy that she loved—his fault for this?

You have questions, and you don't have answers.

That's what upsets me, is that they don't think about what they're doing when they're doing it, and how it will affect everyone for a lifetime.

Please don't do this. Suicide affects too many people that are left behind, especially if you have kids. Their loved ones will question until their dying days, "Why?"

I've run into a lot of people who've lost someone to suicide. They just pop up. I've met people who've thought about committing it, and people who know people who've done it. It's an unanswered question in their mind. It plays there like a record without the needle coming off. After they talk to me, they feel relieved. It's like they've been carrying around this secret, and they finally let it go.

Loneliness is a terrible thing, and comes a lot around the holidays. It seems a lot of suicides happen around that time. I've been lonely; I've been there.

Especially when you lose your family, you sometimes feel without a friend in the world, as if no one cares. I lost Greg too early.

Because of this, I relate to people that I meet who have lost someone to cancer. I share my story about my brother with them. They just listen. It makes them feel better, because they know someone is there to hear what they're saying.

I speak from experience, about the emotional trauma, and decisions that I've made in my life, insecurities that I have, and nightmares. I have a need for love; I have a desire to have both parents around. When you don't have it, you have no backbone. You grow up strong when you grow up in a good family. If not, you grow up feeling rejected and you don't make good decisions.

My mom didn't make good decisions. I have good people around me and I make good choices with friends, but I don't make good choices in relationships.

I'm making better choices than I used to, and what I want and what I'll put up with. That's why I've been single for a long time. I'm not going to settle, and my standards are much higher.

I ran into this lady at work that I gave a massage to last year. She was so glad to see me. Her fiancé had killed himself not too long after she found out she was pregnant; they have another kid together. It's amazing for me to see pictures of this adorable little baby, and know that his father will never know him.

This is what I don't like: there's people out there who have cancer and they're not killing themselves, but then there's people like this guy and they don't think of the consequences, of who they're leaving behind. I really wish people would stop and think about *what* they're doing.

I think about what it would have done to Omi—me committing suicide. I always thought of her; that's why I never did it. You have to think of someone before you do it.

I don't think it's fair that some people never experience that much loss or pain. Then some of us are dealt different cards. That's why we get so angry. Think about it, when you've suffered a big loss and other losses, and have trouble when you're growing up, it's too heavy to carry it all on your shoulders.

When someone kills themselves, they take their own life; it's hard to take. It wasn't an illness; it wasn't an accident. It wasn't an act of God. It was basically at their own hand.

"Trish, do you think there is a special place that God has set aside for these people?" I asked her once. "Yes Jen, I do," she replied. Suicide is a special place. These people are hurting. They harm themselves, and in the process, they also hurt the people they leave behind.

Have you ever noticed suicidal people? They are the sweetest people. They'd never hurt anybody. They're hurting so bad that they want a way out.

I do believe some of them ask for forgiveness before they do it.

Is there anyone out there that survived this by a second that was on their deathbed, and how do they feel now? If they almost crossed over, were they sent back?

I did have a girlfriend who tried to kill herself—she took a bunch of pills, and went into the garage and turned the car on and shut the door. Luckily, her ex-husband was there to intervene; he seen the smoke coming out of the garage and took her to the hospital. Later, she said how stupid she was, and she never tried it again.

Things happen for a reason. But, why are some saved and others aren't? Why are some spared, and others aren't? Why are some people healed from cancer and others aren't helped?

I really wish that people would seriously think about what they do before they do it.

CHAPTER 17

Now

I called Trish tonight. I am upset since all my friends have someone, and I don't. And, it's been six years since Greg died. Not fair. I miss my mom, but I still read through her diaries. You will read what is in her diaries in the next part of my story. I hope you gain some insights into my mom's life.

I thought about Greg, and about how Mom isn't here. I even had a dream about them. In my dream, Mom is dressed in white and is in this big house. There's a man with her, who I don't know. Mom tells me that I didn't die, and to go find Greg and tell him. I go to get Greg, but then I don't find him and I wake up. I was sad the rest of the day.

I feel at such a loss. I am losing my entire family. I don't even have my soul mate. A lot has passed me by. If I could've had kids and met someone in my thirties, things would have been better.

This Thanksgiving, I'm going to my foster family's house for dinner. I'm glad to go, but sad that my foster dad is sick. We're all closer now, and things are better with my foster mom.

I spent a quiet holiday with my foster family, but I missed my family. I tried to call my dad, who I still call "John." Not much has changed there.

I asked my foster mom if we could go to dinner one night and see a movie; we had dinner in instead. It was good.

When I go to family events, my foster family at times gives me a hard time for not being married or having kids. Like it's my fault. I am bummed about it. It's a double whammy, to not have a family, and not to have a husband or boyfriend. It's worse around the holidays, especially Christmas. What is God waiting for?

I know that God is waiting on me to finish my story. Then, things will open up for me.

A small surprise, though, my stepmom sent me a nice turtleneck for Christmas. I thought that was a kind gesture. I didn't have much to get them this holiday season.

My stepmom did have to call and ask me what day my mom died on. She was real gentle about it. It was necessary to find out, since Dad needs to get medical help from a VA clinic where he lives. I did let his wife know the information. Of course, it's going to bring up memories, but what can you do?

My dad is sick again. He has cancer. He recently had surgery and had to have his ear and a lymph node removed. They reattached the ear. My stepmom didn't let me know about it until a week after; I was *so* mad. She felt I didn't need to know, since she didn't want to worry me and get me all upset. I felt I did have a right to know, since he *is* my dad and he could have died right there and then on the table.

With my dad, we're just friends. We don't have a father-and-daughter relationship. There's no bonding there. That's why I'm trying to get a hold of other family. He's the only link to my family.

I did get to reconnect with one of my dad's stepsisters. They are still close. I got to see her again and her daughter and my cousin.

I took a friend and we had a fantastic time. We went out to dinner and we got lobster. It was nice to reconnect with these folks.

Regarding my dad's family, I wanted to get information from my dad, of where my uncle lives. I'm hoping to get together with my uncle's family.

My dad is sick with Alzheimer's, and recently his wife had to put him in a VA hospital for further treatment. I was hoping to see my dad soon, and I let her know that. I'm sad that he's sick.

I talked to my dad one day; he didn't remember who I was. I felt bad. His wife said to him, "It's Jenny, your daughter." He said to me, "Oh, you're my daughter? Do you live on the south side?" It was sad; he didn't remember who I was.

I called him today after I talked to Trish; he didn't remember me today, either. I am sad. I always just wanted to have a relationship with him, and now that can never happen. I would love to fly down there and visit him, but he wouldn't recognize me.

I am often meeting a new guy who just wants to be friends. I'm tired of waiting for a guy, and I've been waiting for years. It's not fair.

The last couple of days, it's hit me strong that I'm going to meet someone. I just know it's going to happen. He's going to be special, and caring. I've got a lot of love to give, and that person will, too.

On a good note, work is going well; I'm very busy. People are becoming regulars and new people are saying I come highly recommended. That makes me feel good.

I met a woman who feels that sharing my story will help people. This lady was really positive, and said she knows work will continue to pick up, and I'm going to meet someone real nice. I hope so!

Ingrid

CHAPTER 1

What a marriage.

December, 1970

I suppose one starts at the beginning of a diary, but since it's the 2nd of December, I cannot very well start on the first page. I know I was snoopy today.

Man, oh man. What a marriage. A blind man and a used stepmother—this can't go on much longer.

I didn't think I had to continue, but David and I had a big fight. I did not want that at all, and it finally came about. He is accusing me of wanting to fight. The anger in me is so strong it hurts physically. We argue about Tina, what else? She hadn't cooked dinner as I requested, and, of course, as usual he protects her. He said it was his fault; he told her not to. That may be so, but David always tells me I should tell the girl what to do; then when I get angry about things she doesn't do, he gets angry because I nag. I am frustrated, and I feel like running away, doing anything to get peace.

I can't say anything about his daughters, but it's alright for him to scream at my children—especially Greg. He just hollers and punishes. It's supposed to be alright, because they need it. How could they, only being four and seven?

God, I could have had all this with John. Sometimes I feel I jumped from the skillet into the fire. I wonder if I deserve all of this.

Of course, we exchanged nasty words, and I told David he wasn't a man but a coward. It's so true, concerning his daughter. He couldn't take it, and he told me to get out of the room and he wasn't going to argue. I went for a ride, came back later and went for a walk. He didn't come after me as he used to: that says it all. I went to bed, got up, had a lonely sandwich and went back to bed and read. He came later; I gave him the diamond and I feel hypocritical to wear it. No love, it's phony. He tells me he loves me, not then; but he does and he shows it peculiarly.

December 3rd, Thursday

It's early morning; I haven't heard from anyone. Tina is talking to Joe. I cooked and cleaned, and picked the kiddies up. David hasn't called. Oh well, it is better that way. No harsh words brought up. Eventually he'll come home and we'll make up, but the hurt sticks to the heart. We would be so happy if he wouldn't love Tina so much, and excuse everything. That's about all for now. We'll see how the day ends. The stereo works beautifully and I am listening to such lovely music. It makes the hurt of my last love feel strong.

10 p.m. same night

Well, we made up. He came home with perfume. The usual thing, a few kisses. That's about it; how sad. I miss Michael so much.

Perhaps all what happens would not bother me so much, if he would be alive. God punishes hard; I wonder if he punishes John ever. I feel as if I am getting the whole load.

I loved David so much. I so much adored him, I respected him, and I loved him so in the beginning. What all happened to make it go away? I try hard to get the same feelings, but I can't get there because he has let me down. Poor darling, he does not understand. I still love him, but underneath it all are all the small hurts.

Tonight, I stayed home and wrote bills. Greg was really good with me. If they will just leave him alone, he will turn out fine. He has such a good heart. I love him, and I love my Jenny.

Well, another Saturday shot, and why not? I made it clear that two weeks ago, one week ago and practically mentioned every day that Saturday was my day to go shopping. So, what happens? The girls have to go to the mall. It figures. David went and picked up things for Tina's birthday. So why I bother I shall never know. What an atmosphere again. As usual David says I have no one to blame but myself. He is *so* understanding.

The whole Saturday I cleaned, instead of having my day.

Well, so much for a "wonderful" day—one step closer to saying goodbye. I am beginning to feel it's for the best. David does not understand my needs or Jenny and Greg, and Greg was not allowed to go anywhere. He had to stay home and pick up things. David is so blind.

December 16, 1970.

I went to the doctor today for a checkup because of all the pain. I was so worried and scared. First thing he said to me was, "Oh, are you Kathy's sister-in-law?" I almost laughed out loud. I told him "No, I am David's second wife." Oh well, I went thru the lovely exam which hurt so much, and they found out I have an infection of the uterus, ovaries, bladder and membranes. He also suspects tumors in the uterus, but I won't tell how serious it is, till the doctor and I am sure. I see him the sixth of January, 1971, God granted.

I am sitting in the living room, David is lying on the floor, vainly attempting to set up the village beneath the Christmas tree (Kathy's tree, pooh!). Anyway, he is closer to sleeping than decorating. Well so much for today.

Greg got sick with the flu, and I took him to the doctor's. I thought it was his appendix. Thank God, it was not. Christmas—it was nice. On Christmas Eve, David, Mother and I went to church, then to Mother's home.

Stephanie, Tina, Greg and Jenny came over. The presents were all around the tree, and it was so nice and pretty. We sang "Silent Night" and celebrated. It was real nice, and we came home at 12:30. I put the kids to bed and brought the presents up from the basement. It looked so pretty, but I thought the work would never end.

The kids woke up at nine; Tina threw a pillow on my face—typical humor of hers. The children were all happy, and I think David was too, with what he got. I know I was; I got a lot of presents, surely more than I expected. I got two beautiful pantsuits, perfume, towels, and two slacks outfits from Mother and Father.

I had a big turkey dinner; Mother and Father came over. It was a very lovely dinner, but afterwards Jenny got sick. She had the flu, so we broke it up. I unfortunately got sick the next day.

CHAPTER 2

I am pretty lonely.

October 13, 1973

Nothing against Stephanie, I love her, but she always makes me feel as if I take things away from her and she has no outings and no fun.

Jensen came over. The next day, they went to the fair, and afterwards they went to church.

Thursday-it's cold and gray. The house is deathly quiet. No one has called yet or neither have I seen anyone. I am pretty lonely, but it doesn't matter to anyone. Guess I might as well enjoy peace if you call it that. It's good to have a diary in a way; so many things, one forgets.

October 18, 1973

Jensen called. Stephanie is so excited.

We watched a movie in the morning together.

Greg had practice. Jenny is first my most beloved Jenny, mischievous and lovable, temperamental and teasing. Seven must be the age.

I must not understand men. We were at dinner and Stephanie asked about me going back in the hospital and if it's just for a test. As far as the surgery schedule is posted, I told her I guess it's at eight in the morning. David said, "So early?" As if I had not told him before. Oh well, he is so forgetful. Then he said, "Well, that's a problem. How can I be there so early with the kids having to go to school at different hours?" He didn't think he could make it that soon.

It never fails me to surprise me. If I were a man and loved my woman I would've thought of something. He didn't understand that I was hurt. Nothing is lonelier than going up for surgery. He said "Oh, well, your

374

mother will 'be there'." He can be callous and then turns around and wonders why he has hurt you. I just got up and left the table and lay on my bed. He came a little later and had the nerve to ask why I blew up. Couldn't I see his point? I can see his point, sure it isn't easy, but who said it would be?

Why I have to be always sweet, always understanding, especially when I am scared is beyond my comprehension. As I said to him, I'll do it alone and I'll never bring the subject up again. It doesn't matter inside anymore. The hurt that he can't see is there, and I have faced worse things. I am awfully depressed, not blue, but depressed. Here I have everything, well, almost everything, but all inside it feels lost and lonely, like a girl.

David watched the World Series, and then he fell asleep when the news came on. I went to bed and read till 1:30; then I listened to music. I didn't see or hear from anyone. Big house, no money, lonely. I feel myself receding into myself. More and more I become as I was with John, just building a wall around me. This time, I shall build it so high and hard that nothing will penetrate it.

There will be a little door open only for Jenny and Greg. My faith in people in 35 years is shattered and so what does it matter? Not to anyone and I guess that's what you call "life."

The next day, I got Jenny off to school; I dressed her in yellow. She looked real pretty. David asked me for lunch. I don't know how we're going to go, since it takes 25 minutes to get there, and he wants me to meet him at 12:30 and I have to be back at 2:30. Men— blind, blind, blind.

We went out for lunch and I had a nice time, but I had lots of pain and I came home. I went out and seen a few friends. They wished me good luck in the hospital.

Well, I wrapped the gifts for our anniversary, but he ignored it. There was some kind of mistake with getting a babysitter. This place is a nuthouse. My English must be poor, because I am to be blamed for this mistake again. I wonder if they think I am made of marble. Stephanie went to a dance at seven, and came home at twelve-thirty. Five-and-one-half hours for pleasure and I have not been allowed to go shopping that long. Oh, well.

Monday

I got Jenny off to school. It's cold outside, and I'm nauseated. I guess my nerves are beginning to show that I am going into the hospital on Saturday. Jenny found out yesterday and the poor darling cried. She is such a sweet softy, but no one sees her needs of love and attention. I love her deeply. Greg, Stephanie and David either cover their feelings up or are glad it's not them who has to go, or it's not so important as long as they don't get hurt.

Well, once I am in I hope they find out what is wrong. The test is going to be difficult, but I lived thru many difficult times, so what's one more?

I went shopping and came home. Jensen was here.

It's a beautiful golden autumn day; just about perfect. I have sinus trouble, and, when don't I? And I still have that trouble with the bathroom, not going. Well, four more days to the hospital. How lucky can one get? I'll probably have my period then, too. I don't know if they will make a scope or not.

Tuesday, October 23, 1973

David didn't wake me up. My dearest little pumpkin wanted to be a good brownie, so she and Stephanie agreed secretly that Stephanie would wake her up at seven. Jenny made her own bed, dressed herself, combed her hair and fixed her breakfast. She is between sweet, light, mischievous and tomboy—she found a caterpillar during recess. She and her friend took it to class in her pocket, and then she put it in her folder. There it sat and crawled all during class and when David picked her up, she told him about it. He didn't believe her, and he said, "Jenny you're fibbing, I am going to smack my hand on your folder." She cried, "Oh, no, Dad, you'll kill him!" And she opened her folder and there it was. I think David lost his speech, and I was hysterical, so they put it in a glass jar outside with grass and goodies.

That's my Jenny—lollipops, pictures, horses, honey, pretty and all kinds of animals.

CHAPTER 3

My big dream.

Anyway, David woke me up at nine-thirty; I was surprised. In a way, I had the oddest dream. I dreamed I had one stepchild, and we lived in an old mansion; I was like a governess. The girl looked like Jenny. I pleaded with the mother and grandmother to let us go, that I would take care of her. They laughed nastily and said, "No, you can't go anywhere; you're chained to us forever, because you can't carry his child." I said, "Whose?" They said, "You'll meet him this afternoon."

They put food out; I didn't eat it. A man was there. I said, "No, not you. I could have had other ones." They all laughed and I said, "You are old and married; you'll never marry me." He smiled and said, "That's right, you stay here and have our son." But I knew he wasn't the father.

In my dream, I was real young and beautiful. He just wished he could keep me. I turned and walked thru an open, southern glass door, and he followed and grabbed me. "Don't you know no one is ever leaving me ever? You stay and love me." I just shook my head and walked away.

The man said, "Okay, you want me to marry you, then let's walk and talk it over." He never said a word, because his feelings seemed to change from hate to love. We then came to a street; it was first beautiful with lots of trees and wide, then it was all broken up for repair. We stepped on top of sewage pipe which lay in endless rows, all different colors. I could not see the end of them. The child was suddenly with us. Then we heard music and the man said, "Oh, that's some welcome music for a king who is visiting." My heart beat real loud and I started to walk faster because I know, it was my love coming. Then a young man in a splendid uniform walked towards me. He was serious. He saluted, then he went past and I thought, oh, it isn't my love; it was a king.

The man laughed nastily and said, "Don't think you can make me believe you know kings." I walked over the pipes with the child and in the distance another man with the same and splendid uniform appeared and as he came nearer, I laughed and cried and ran towards him. He was so tall.

I stopped and he looked into my eyes and I in his and all else was forgotten. I opened my lips and he smiled so sweet and knowingly and he said, "You are as always, beautiful and young, have you found a husband yet?" But I knew he hoped I hadn't and I said "No, my love is still the same." We looked at each other and we knew we loved each other deeply and always.

I asked him politely but with a terrible pain in my heart, "And how are your children and your wife?" He smiled and said they were fine and to be patient and he made arrangements. It was a hint at divorce before I could say, "You can't do that." He jumped from the sewage and put his hand on my waist and lifted me down as gently as a feather. I looked up; he was so tall it hurt my back to look at him. I wanted to say, "You are a king, you cannot do this," but my lips only opened hungry for a touch or kiss. He seemed to know what I was thinking and he smiled and bent down towards me.

From his great height he said, "My darling, even kings sometimes have to bend a little to be just mere mortals." And we looked and smiled and we loved each other just looking and standing there and then I woke up.

This dream left me very much as I was at first in my dream, lonely and kind of unfulfilled and wishing the last part was true. Silly.

It's a beautiful golden autumn day again. That's not a dream.

I went with my Big Darling to dinner at a friend's house. Then I packed my suitcase for the hospital. Mrs. Johnson called, Jenny's teacher. She is worried about her motor control and math and drifting to dreamland. I know that as vivacious as Jenny is, she has streaks of terrible self-consciousness and shyness, and she is like me, one minute a big mouth and show off and the next, withdrawing and remote and shy, that it hurts like being all alone on an island. She'll outgrow it, but not before she's between twelve and fourteen. Oh well, she has other fine qualities. He had a new rule for Stephanie. I told David not to put rules down for me to tell her. He told her; she got mad.

David surprised me. He took the day off. We got dressed and relaxed. We had breakfast and went for a beautiful, warm, golden walk thru the yellow and rustic forest. It was so pretty; the river spilled out dull, but its scent was sweet. David carved our heart with our initials. He never did that for me. We had a real fine afternoon, one which we so seldom get and need. I need it because I am really nervous about the hospital.

Well, one day of beauty yesterday can be spoiled by one instance this morning. No one woke me, but by instinct I woke up. David was just a few minutes out of the kitchen before me. He was in the bathroom with Greg.

That bathroom is so small. Greg hadn't brushed his teeth and hadn't cleaned the bathroom. (It's Stephanie's job on Wednesday, but I cleaned my little ones', since Stephanie has to be on the phone). Anyway, David got mad at Greg. Greg cried. Man, oh man, that got me mad! David wanted to push me into the kitchen like nothing ever happened. ("It's nothing, don't get involved," he said.) I was mad at him and asked him, "Do you like that?" Of course, he marched away. I asked Greg, "What do you feel when your father does these things?" He gave me such a look of dislike I knew the answer. I said, "Do you love him?" And he wanted to say, "Yes," but he said, "No." David thinks because he dresses him and gives him food and drives him to certain places, all things I do for Stephanie and plenty more with love, that this is love. Boy, will he wake up one day if he keeps it up, the loneliest man in the world.

I came home from the hospital. I got lots of calls and cards but only three flowers. I had seen the first snow fall. I feel weak and lousy and lonely. David is watching TV, and I am tired and in bed.

It was so good to see my beautiful children. They looked so big, so grown up, and so tall. Oh, how I love them. My darling Jenny—how I love my sweet, mischievous, dark bubble of life. Greg is my big love, too, for he held me and put his head on my shoulder and he said, "Oh, I am so glad you're home, Mom, I missed you." Lovely, lovely words.

I love those two so much. Jenny came running all the way thru the house towards me. Oh wow, what a feeling. Nothing like it in this world. Wendy called. Stephanie, I missed her, too. She is a fine, young, wonderful woman. David is trying to make me happy. I talked with Mother. Goodnight world, and thank you God for letting me come this far thru.

Woke up at a quarter after nine. David didn't come to bed before two-thirty. He fell asleep in the chair. Second day home. David called, so did Mother. I cooked today, but no one said, "Thanks." The kids were out tonight. David thinks I should be happy and content, never going anywhere or seeing anyone. If I dare, I might be allowed to go shopping, that's it. I have no friend who comes here anymore.

I might as well live in a glass cage. Why should I complain when all we have is bills, no money, and no friends? I look at myself and I can see I am getting old, lonely and bitter. Why can't I just be myself and just go like Stephanie does?

CHAPTER 4

I must soon give up.

November 1, 1973

Each day when I think it goes bad, it does. I shall not stop. I must be like Ulysses, always watching. When I think it is found, and then it was just my dream. This must be my nature. So long, today, I won't miss you much.

November 8th, 1973

It is cold and dreary outside. Put my makeup on for the first time; I was a little shaky. Mother called and I called her back at noon. The wedding should be on the first of May. This is the truth: I must soon give up. David slept in the black chair again. Last night I went to bed at twelve-thirty. Wendy called. She is very kind. I went to Jenny's Brownie Fly-Up at the Smith's house. It was really nice. They sang songs, said their pledge and got their pin. They lit a candle, too. It was really touching. We took pictures and had punch and cookies. She looked pretty; I washed and curled her hair. She was without a uniform, but I couldn't get it, being sick. Came home, the usual.

It's snowing and cold. Up until now, someone calls for fourteen days around the same time, which must be a record for him. My goodness, today I got a proposal and I am thirty-four. I can't believe it. I wish it was not so unbelievable, but I can hardly suppose that anybody would want somebody with children. It is a fairy tale.

David took me out to lunch. It felt good to get out. I wore my fur jacket; I still get a lot of looks. When I came home, I talked with Jenny and played records and games with her. Greg got his picture taken, and he was in a bad mood because they didn't turn out how he wanted.

I am tired. My sinuses are terrible today. Mother called. She has problems with Paul and has too many boyfriends. Now it's Steve again and Bill, some guy named Anthony and of course, Paul. She either has no one, or too many.

I finally went to bed. David fell asleep after the news. Stephanie went from eight to eleven to a friend's. I guess I won't be able to go with Mother. I spent the 17th picking up coats and going Christmas shopping, but Stephanie can go any day. Me, I am a prisoner. The minute I can move about I have to give account of everything I do, including what I say to Mother on the phone. I am a bird in a glass cage.

Goodnight cold, snowy 9th. I won't miss you, except my Jenny and Greg got a day older and move one step away from me to grow up. As long as they are healthy. Stephanie came home at five after eleven.

Well, it's Saturday and I must say the Saturdays in the hospital were more fun. It's the usual. The kids run off to the game; David went out. This is my first day of driving and I am going nowhere. I feel lousy because I do not feel well and it is cold outside and the car hardly works well. So, I stay put. Oh, how I hate these Saturdays, the loneliest day of the week.

I have anger; naturally, it was not always there. I will talk to him later. I am so tired and worn out. Well nothing else is new and what should be anyway? I am so blue and depressed. Am I ever going to be me again, laughing and happy inside and out, just bubbling with the joy of living? I am so achy blue and all I can do is fight against it, but it never seems to go away. Me and my blue shadow; I am terribly lonely. Everyone has their life to lead, but I feel deprived of mine.

I never was free of spirit. I don't want to be free of people I love, but just be free to live. I want to see the mountain, the sea, Germany, my Father, Oslo, Spain, lakes, boating, walking, hiking and dancing.

I feel my youth has never been lived when I was young. I went thru agony with John, with all those miserable, unbearable and cruel years. If only someone could guess what I went thru, but I will only go over the surface details. All those precious, lovely young years running away from me, and now I shall never recapture them and be young again.

Jenny and Greg, live each day to the fullest, let no one stunt your growth, let no one bend your spirit, even if you love, let it not shackle you, but love and enjoy life, love the snow and football games, marshmallows and snowball fights, watch autumn be golden and beautiful. Enjoy watching squirrels, birds, Thanksgiving, spring blossoms, tiny Kelly green leaves, bees, butterflies, eating ice cream, getting free of boots and coats.

Go barefoot, feel the sweet earth; touch the flowers, the green grass. Dream in a meadow, turn your face towards the golden hot sun, go swimming, walk on the beach, fly with the seagulls, listen to thunder and see the lightning with awe, and have no fear. Time flies. Enjoy picnics, baseball games, laughing with friends. Pray, believe in God and our sweet Savior Jesus. Believe, live, share, and do. That's life. Oh my God, I am dreaming and not able to untie my spirit. It is bound by ties of better memories.

Well, I am still trying one more time, but I believe that there is somebody. He was there, but, I am near the end. It must be the end.

It's ridiculous; it's it.

CHAPTER 5

"...a step closer to death."

I got up to dress the kiddies for church. I made breakfast, started dinner and washed. It's dreary and cold. I called at twelve, but she wasn't there. I didn't feel too bad. Mother came over, and we ate and left shortly after. I have a lot of pain. I don't know if it's from the surgery, but, boy it hurts. When was there a day that I felt good? I felt better than the hospital. I am tired, so I went to bed. So long, November 10th; tomorrow is another day. I couldn't sell my purses, and I counted on it. Well, it never fails, you think you can make a dollar and it's for the birds.

Twelfth. Went to the bank, shopping at the mall, mostly for Stephanie. Poor thing. I never walked and looked for so many things for her. Well, I called home and my friend. She changed her telephone number due to those crank calls I get about David. That other woman loves him. I'll never keep him; she'll get him. I decided for an unlisted number. That woman has been bugging me for a year.

Maybe I'll get peace now.

The 13th

Oops, terrible date. It's grey and cold and Jenny came home earlier and I overslept. Wow, I better hurry.

It really was the 13th for me. I went to Kmart to pick up my ring and got a drink.

Oh my. Stephanie and Jenny and I went to the mall; Stephanie got her hair cut and I did Christmas shopping and then we three had dinner. We came home at eight-thirty. David kissed Stephanie hello. "Honey, how are you?" I walked in after her and all I got was, "Well, you sure took your time." Now it is eleven-thirty and he is sleeping as usual in his stupid black chair.

As long as Stephanie can go out until twelve-thirty on Saturday I also will go with Mother somewhere. Where? What's the difference? Well, goodnight or bye-bye world for the 14th.

David didn't leave until twenty till eleven. It's getting later and later. I wanted to go to the stores, but I am too tired. It's raining and thundering. Wow, I've got a headache. I finally unpacked my suitcase from the hospital. I told Mother and got no sympathy, but she always wants me to understand everything. She changed her mind about going downtown to pick up the coats. It figures. She never is predictable if Paul is with her. The minute he is on the scene she is so changed. But I tell her Paul is wonderful; that's what she wants to hear. However, after what he told me in the hospital my liking and patience has turned to revulsion. Oh well, it's her life; I have my problems. David and I had a quarrel as usual. I finally fixed my Erie picture. Good nite, stupid, stupid, stupid day, and a step closer to death. Must be a relief to be at peace.

CHAPTER 6

I am lost.

The 16th

Today it was cold, rainy and snowy. Another call! If this woman isn't getting off my back, I will clobber David. I didn't tell him, but she gets obnoxious. She told me today since we are adults and I seem to not to take it so hard to give David up and I told her it's up to him. She laughed and said he loves her and made up his mind up already a long time ago, and he never stopped loving her. Everything with me was a put-on, a farce. He married me to prove a point. I was reeling and hurt, so I said, "Well, why doesn't he leave me then?" She laughed and said that he didn't want to lose her and the house. What a tootsie she is. I just don't understand it anymore. I said, "Doesn't he care about the children?" She said, "Which ones?" Boy, she had me in tears and she knew it. She laughed and said, "Why don't you give up, you can't win in the long run, and you already have taken too much time." What did that mean? I asked her that and that stupid, stupid, hately woman says, "Get lost baby." I told her, "I will get lost when I am good and ready to jump in the lake." She said something like, "Wishful thinking," and then she said "I'll bet you want to know how many times he and I were together?" I threw the phone on the hook and then across the room. I was crying and shaking and had a fit, and that was all this morning. At eleven-thirty, I couldn't write about it until tonight. I wanted to tell David like the other times, but he thinks and pretends it's a big joke. I don't know how much fault one can have. I try to believe in David, but someone just knows him well or is playing a dirty trick.

Got a lovely card today. I also went to see Mrs. Johnson. Jenny is not getting along in school. She didn't have a good report card. We went out for lunch and came home. Jenny cleaned her room. She and I had a sweet talk; I love her so much. I bought her chocolate, then to Kmart where, of course, she needed money to make something for Tina for Christmas. We came home, and I made dinner for the kiddies. David took me to Jolene's for the first time since the hospital. All the waiting, but they were nice.

David and I finally brought up the question about now, how to keep the children happy and where to live and how to support them. I must find a decent reasonable job, pretty hard for my age. I am starting all over again with no help. I have the children and that is all I want for them, not to be hurt too much and to be safe and secure. They are my life. If there really is God, please bless them and keep them happy. Amen and thank you.

Well, David and I made up again. I feel better mentally, but oh my aching body. My legs are so sore from that walk. David made brunch. I took my Jenny to the mall; got her a gorgeous doll, all in white and I bought her a Brownie uniform. They didn't have a beanie hat. She was really good. I took her to a movie, *Instinct for Survival*; it was quite good. All about animals and relations we have with, towards and inherited. Jenny felt quite the big lady. I have never taken her alone to a movie for fear to hurt the other children, but they must learn that Stephanie can't fly from and to every date and meeting and party and Greg runs to the "Y" with Rich and Jenny always stays home. We came home at seven p.m. it was good timing, since there was a detour. We ate dinner and I washed and dried and set Jenny's hair and then watched TV. David fell asleep at news time. So, goodnight the 18th of November. It was a good day. Jenny made it go wholesome and clean, which feels good after so many arguments and accusations.

Monday the 19th

I went to see friends. I got kissed under the mistletoe, only one I'll get this year. I made spaghetti, wrote bills, and went to bed. Our telephone number was changed.

The 20th of November

I bought myself the record *Jonathan Livingston Seagull*. I cried and cried, because it's beautiful, because it says all, what I am, all I feel. My terrible loneliness, my unanswered dreams which have faded into the vastness of nothing. My longing which is never and will never be answered. I can never say it better, but I am Jonathan Livingston Seagull. I hope I never realize leaving here for the beauty of God. Then desperately I want God and Jesus. I am lost.

Thanksgiving, November 22nd, 1973

Happy Thanksgiving world, wherever you are. Thank you Lord for all I have and had. I feel as if I had reached the mountain of my life and now it is all the way downhill. It was like any other day except we, Mother, Paul and his kids went to The Mark to eat turkey dinner, which was not so great and we waited two hours to get it. David forgot to call his Mother. Anyway, they all came over and the kids had fun and we played cards. This house must have fainted, with all the people in it.

Let's see, when was the last time we had company? Can't remember, several years at least. Anyway, they left at eleven. A friend of Jenny's didn't want to sleep over, so Jenny cried.

November 23rd, 1973

David is off, kids are home, mood lousy, but of course it's me, me, me.

Arguments, arguments, arguments, arguments, arguments, arguments, arguments. Me, awful, awful me! JUMP IN THE LAKE INGRID BEST THING FOR YOUR LOVING FAMILIE!

November 29th, 1973

It is ten a.m. David calls or smokes his pipe in the kitchen. I feel lonely and depressed. I cannot smile anymore and I wonder when I will feel like laughing? After the disastrous and stupid weekend, I feel absolutely mentally exhausted. I wish David was more romantic. What we had needed, right then and there, would have been if he would have said, "Well, let's go somewhere, just you and I." But, of course, he first had to be the nurturer and I the beggar and David does not forgive inside. I know this now, yet what I did was nothing really. I had hysterics at Mother's and then walked home.

If he would have brought me one flower or just a cup of tea, but now, he never comes for lunch anymore, he seldom does what I ask, he questions me about everything and if I say something he misinterprets it deliberately. Well, that's the end of my life. I don't think I'll write anymore in here. There is nothing left to write. Goodbye.

CHAPTER 7

My thoughts

My mom's pain and loss are clearly reflected in her writings. Even though they only cover a time span of four months, they are not only revealing but powerful. She brings us into her world of personal-felt failure and deep regrets.

The first part finishes on New Year's Eve, 1970, and begins again about three years later, short of three months. She was a prayerful woman. At the same time, she questioned God often, asking Him why she had to endure so many trials.

Her personal life was shaken-up. Not only was she in the midst of another trying divorce, disaster also struck when Michael was still-born.

Physically, having major surgery only added to her stress.

In time, these stresses did not subside. She seemed to have become further depressed, losing a relationship with a man she loved just before the end of her life.

If she had someone to talk to today, if that would that have made a difference. Would it have helped to have someone to help her sort through her feelings? I truly wish that her faith in God could have carried her thru.

I could sit here and just restate how I don't have my mom and my other family members.

What's important is that I am willing to share my story.

I don't feel that any of this was a waste of time.

However, time does take its toll on all of us. I was diagnosed with stage three breast cancer. I have weekly chemo treatments and my hair is falling out. I am physically, mentally and emotionally challenged with making a taxing decision of keeping one breast or not.

I was in the shower early September and found my lump in my breast. It felt like tissue to me. I felt like something was there. It was inflamed, and I was on antibiotics. My doctor said to wait three weeks. On September 28, 2012, I was diagnosed with cancer. Coincidentally, this was the same day that Greg was diagnosed on years ago. I went to get a second opinion. They said, "It doesn't look good." I had a biopsy. They decided to do chemo first. I had surgery, then radiation. I had to wait several months before having my mastectomy. I am taking Herceptin for eight months, then Tamoxifin for five years, every day. The chemo was horrible. My nails are destroyed, I lost my hair, and my eyesight got blurry.

When I learned I had cancer, it was a shock. I was devastated, and the diagnosis took my breath away. *Oh my God, this is the end for me,* I thought. You don't know what's going to happen. I cried all the time—I didn't know who to talk to. It's the worst thing ever. Your mind just goes and goes. And all the tests.

Each time there is a check, you take your breath. Losing my hair was traumatic. I had to cut it. Then it was falling out, until I was bald. These are the steps you have to go thru to try to survive.

I spent most of my time at my foster family's home, and my stepsister came out for a lot of my appointments. All my friends surrounded me when I needed them.

You are just devastated. It's hard to get thru. I couldn't get all those thoughts out of my head, the negativity, and the thoughts of killing myself. *Should I take my own life?* I asked myself. I cried to God, and asked Him, "Why?" I would wake up in a sweat. I would be nervous going to the doctor's, and also when the phone rang.

Losing my breasts took away part of my womanhood.

It has been a long haul. Currently, I got thru my first reconstructive surgery, and then I will have my second one in several months. I always keep up with my appointments, and encourage friends to keep up with theirs.

My sister and I went by the house again where I grew up in. We got to meet the lady who lives there now. She said her husband died, but she was happy to show us the house. I got to see it again. She said I could come by and visit.

I was also talking to some friends and I met someone whose family member had committed suicide. I know I was supposed to meet this person. I hurt for this person, but it made me feel not so alone.

My dad died in the middle of my chemo treatments. That was so difficult that I couldn't fly out to go to the funeral. I was so sad that he was so sick and died. I would call Trish and other friends to talk with them about losing him. My foster family was also very supportive of me. I miss him, knowing I can't talk to him again.

It's not fair that I have lost all of these family members. I have my sisters and friends and my foster family. Thank God they are around me—they keep me going, especially since I am a breast cancer survivor.

My stepsister took me out to see him months ago. He didn't recognize me, but she was a godsend for taking time off of work and flying there with me. We stayed nearby and spent time with him and my stepmom. It was very trying, but I was grateful I got to go. I needed this trip so that I could reconnect with my father, even though he didn't remember me.

Since then, I have heard from my stepmom. She said she is putting my dad's ashes in a mausoleum so he has a place. I still can't go there at this time. I also ran into my ex-husband at my niece's wedding. He was polite to me. He apologized for everything he had done and said he was sorry. I didn't know what to say. I also lost George, an incredible friend of mine who lived in my grandmother's apartment. I feel lost without him.

I hope when someone reads my story that they will consider how my life turned out and how my life is without my mother and other family. I also hope that someone would take the time to think about what they're leaving behind, and how that's affecting their children. This is a final choice; there is no going back.

I can't change what my mom did; I can only continue to tell you my story and what it's been like living without her. There would be things I would give up to have her back. I would tell her I loved her and I would cherish every moment with her. I wouldn't let any time be wasted; I wouldn't let any moments slip away. It's all too precious to be taken for granted.

I hope that you can take something out of this, something that stops you from making a rash decision, a pained one—a choice that will be permanent. I know you're hurting, but confident that you found something that you can relate to, something that will make you stop and think. I am praying for you!

ABOUT THE AUTHOR

Kerri C. van Lanten is an inspirational writer living in the Midwest. This is her first book. Her heart is in helping people. She has other books that she plans to write, with God guiding her path. Her love for family, friends and animals is a big part of her life.